新版 全彩图解

零基础从头开始学音标

主　编　孙　艳　茅倬蕤　徐宗钰
副主编　王文静　万　涛　胡　妮
编　者　王晓召　刘恩华　刘丹燕

图书在版编目（CIP）数据

全彩图解：零基础从头开始学音标 / 孙艳，茅倬蕤，徐宗钰主编. -- 上海：上海社会科学院出版社，2019

ISBN 978-7-5520-2592-7

Ⅰ. ①全… Ⅱ. ①孙… ②茅… ③徐… Ⅲ. ①英语－音标－图解 Ⅳ. ①H311-64

中国版本图书馆CIP数据核字(2019)第017171号

全彩图解：零基础从头开始学音标

主　　编：孙　艳　茅倬蕤　徐宗钰
责任编辑：王　芳
封面设计：京珍文化（北京）有限责任公司
出版发行：上海社会科学院出版社
上海顺昌路622号　邮编200025
电话总机021-63315900　销售热线021-53063735
http://www.sassp.org.cn　E-mail:sassp@sass.org.cn
印　　刷：小森印刷（北京）有限责任公司
开　　本：710毫米×1000毫米　1/16开
印　　张：17.25
字　　数：351千字
版　　次：2019年4月第1版　2019年4月第1次印刷

ISBN 978-7-5520-2592-7/H·046　**定价**：45.00元

前言 Preface

近年来，随着全球化进程的加快，英语作为国际化通用语言的作用日益显著。在这种趋势下，国内掀起一股学英语的热潮。但是，很多人学了多年的英语，说出的英语仍然带有浓重的口音，究其原因，主要是学习方法和学习习惯的问题。中国的教育一贯是以灌输的方式为主，学习材料呆板无趣，无法激发学生的兴趣，而且以往一直以考试分数来衡量英语水平，对口语的重视不够，加之中国学生容易受汉语发音习惯的影响，所以，拥有一口流利地道口语的人凤毛麟角。其实，英语口语的学习也没有那么困难，其中，语音是基础和关键，只要掌握了正确的方法，再加上日复一日地练习，英语口语也就十分流利了。

语言是一种技能，一种习惯，熟“练”才能生“巧”，仅仅是每天背诵几个英语单词或是阅读几篇英语文章是学不好英语的，必须要多听、多练，要把自己尽可能多地融入英语的语言环境，多听、多看一些英语原声杂志、电影，并大声地模仿，保证足够的“输入”，有输入才能有输出。其次，要多大声朗读英语材料，模仿原汁原味的语音、语调。最后，还要将所学的东西运用到实际生活中来，多与他人用英语进行沟通和交流，多开口，不开口就永远提高不了口语水平。但是，所有这一切必须要有坚实的基础——准确的发音，如果发音不准，一切都无从谈起。英语的发音不是一朝一夕就能练就的，必须坚持不懈地练习，因为发音是一种习惯，只有养成了正确的发音习惯，才能读准单词、词组乃至句子。中国人学英语的一大弊端就是容易受到汉语语音的影响，因为汉语与英语的发音存在很大的差异，很多英语的发音在汉语中都没有对应的音。而我们经常会用类似的音去代替，其实发出的音相差甚远。英语中的每一个音都有自己独特的发音方法和发音位置，只有熟悉、掌握这些方法和发音位置，并勤于操练，才能练就一口流利的口语。三天打鱼、两天晒网是永远也学不好英语的。要有不怕丢脸的精神，抓住一切机会，锤炼自己的口语，才能练就一口地道的口语!

本书专为中国学生解决发音不准的难题而编写，首次同时设置了口腔图和真人发音图，为读者提供了一个正确发音的范式；“大话发音”从相近的汉语发音出发，指出两者的区别，让中国学生在汉语发音的基础上自然地过渡到英语发音；精心归纳的“常见发音字母及字母组合”，为读者总结了发音的常见规律，使读者能“以不变应万变”；“发音操练”和“以句识音”通过设置代表性的单词和句子，不断地强化、巩固所学发音；“听音乐学音标”将发音与歌曲相结合，在轻松的歌曲中感受原汁原味的发音。你还可以边学边唱，既放松了心情，又收获了知识。

本书全彩色印刷，让人赏心悦目，爱不释手。它抛弃了传统枯燥的学习方式，带给你无与伦比的学习感受。本书既可以作为成年人和大中小学生矫正发音的辅助用书，也可以作为儿童学习英语的启蒙书。只要你存在着英语发音的问题，我们都可以助你一臂之力，为你的英语学习打下坚实的基础!

学习英语贵在坚持，只要你足够细心、有耐心和恒心，坚持不懈地刻苦训练、模仿和练习，纯正、地道的口语就指日可待了。

因时间仓促、水平有限，错漏之处在所难免，希望广大读者能给我们提出宝贵的意见和建议!

编者

目录 Contents

Chapter 1 元音发音

Unit 1 [ɑː] & [ʌ]

[ɑː]

发音要素

发元音[ɑː]时，嘴巴张大，上下齿分开，且上下齿前端部分露出，舌头位于口腔中央，舌尖不抵下齿，双唇稍稍收圆。

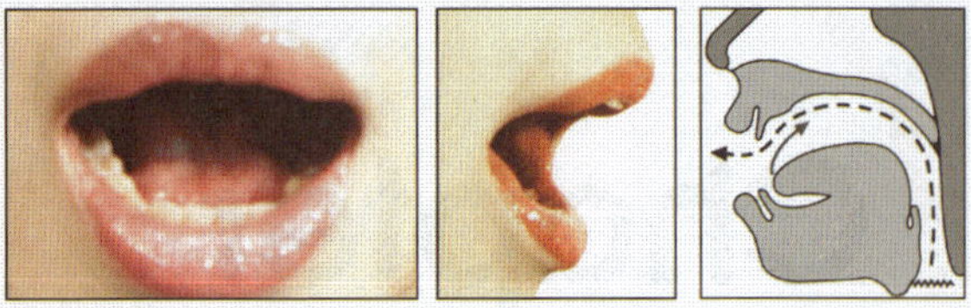

大话发音

检查牙齿时要张大嘴巴，发出“啊”的声音。

感冒了去检查，医生会让你张开嘴说“啊”，拖长些，就是[ɑː]的发音。

啊

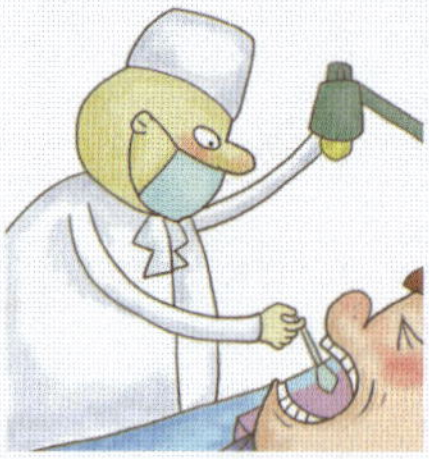

发音代言人

car

[kɑː] 小汽车

常见发音字母及字母组合

音标	对应字母	自然发音规则	单词示例
[ɑː]	a	字母a为唯一或重读音节元音时，可发[ɑː]音。	past [pɑːst] 过去

[ɑ:]	ar	字母组合ar可发[ɑ:]音。	dark [dɑ:k] 黑暗的

[ʌ]

发音要素

发元音[ʌ] 时，嘴巴张开，下嘴唇略低，唇形稍扁，上下齿稍稍分开，露出部分下齿，舌头位于口腔中央与[æ]相似。

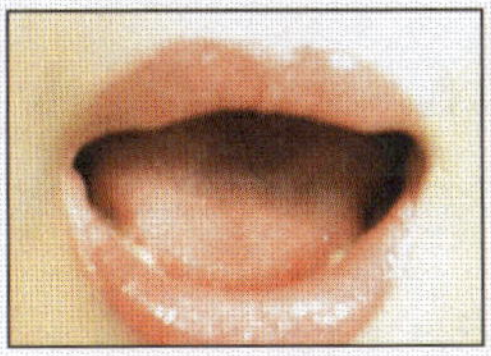

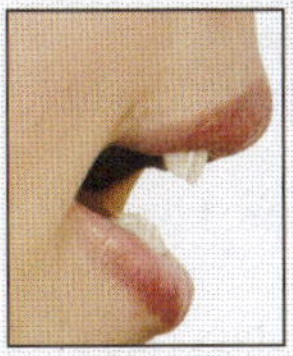

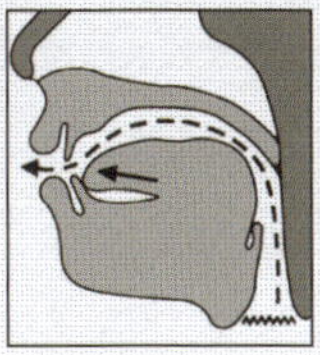

大话发音

突然发现包里的手机丢了，发出“啊”的声音。

走在路上，一摸，包里的手机没了，发出“啊”的声音，发出后马上停止，就是[ʌ]的发音。

啊

发音代言人

duck

[dʌk] 鸭子

常见发音字母及字母组合

音标	对应字母	自然发音规则	单词示例
[ʌ]	u	字母u在重读闭音节中发[ʌ]音。	under ['ʌndə] 在下面
[ʌ]	o	字母o为唯一或重音节元音时，大多发[ʌ]音。	love [lʌv] 爱情
[ʌ]	oo	字母组合oo有时发[ʌ]音。	blood [blʌd] 血液

[ʌ]	ou	字母组合ou有时发[ʌ]音。	**trouble** ['trʌbl] 麻烦

发音操练

[ɑ:]	[ʌ]
glass [glɑ:s] 玻璃	**thumb** [θʌm] 拇指
guitar [gɪ'tɑ:] 吉他	**glove** [glʌv] 手套
park [pɑ:k] 公园	**sun** [sʌn] 太阳
class [klɑ:s] 班级	**flood** [flʌd] 洪水
star [stɑ:] 星星	**cut** [kʌt] 切
card [kɑ:d] 卡片	**fun** [fʌn] 有趣的
bark [bɑ:k]（狗等）吠，叫	**gun** [gʌn] 枪
yard [jɑ:d] 院子	**hug** [hʌg] 拥抱
far [fɑ:] 远的	**luck** [lʌk] 幸运的
half [hɑ:f] 一半	**suck** [sʌk] 吮吸

基础短语

- after ['ɑ:ftə] the party ['pɑ:ti] 聚会过后
- can't [kɑ:nt] dance [dɑ:ns] 不会跳舞
- Master ['mɑ:stə] of Arts [ɑ:ts] 文学硕士
- in harsh [hɑ:ʃ] times 在艰苦的年代
- glance [glɑ:ns] over my report 浏览我的报告
- a very hard [hɑ:d] nut [nʌt] 一个很难对付的人

以句识音

1. He parked [pɑːkt] his car [kɑː] in front of the bar [bɑː] at last [lɑːst].
   他最后把车停在了酒吧前面。
2. Mr. Smith was looking for his glasses [glɑːsɪz] in the dark [dɑːk] classroom ['klɑːsrʊm].
   史密斯先生在黑暗的教室里寻找他的眼镜。
3. His card [kɑːd] is larger ['lɑːdʒə] than his aunt's [ɑːnts].
   他的卡片比他姑姑的大。
4. Mr. Charles' son [sʌn] loves [lʌvz] Mary very much [mʌtʃ].
   查尔斯先生的儿子很爱玛丽。
5. He loves [lʌvz] nothing ['nʌθɪŋ] but [bʌt] money ['mʌnɪ].
   他只爱钱。
6. He is tough ['tʌf] enough [ɪ'nʌf] to crack the nut [nʌt].
   他对付得了这个难题。

经典绕口令（运动你的舌头）

1. The shark's [ʃɑːks] remark [rɪ'mɑːk] on the marble ['mɑːbl] mark [mɑːk] in the market ['mɑːkɪt] **is remarkable** [rɪ'mɑːkəbl].
   骗子关于市场上大理石标记的评论值得关注。
2. In the sparkling ['spɑːklɪŋ] park [pɑːk], the darling ['dɑːlɪŋ] dark [dɑːk] dog barked [bɑːkt] at the embarked [ɪm'bɑːkt] larks [lɑːks].
   在闪着火花的公园里，这只可爱的黑狗对着船上的云雀吠叫。
3. Can you drive the large [lɑːdʒ] car to that far [fɑː] bar [bɑː]?
   你能把这辆大车开到那个很远的酒吧吗？
4. Betty had a bit of better butter ['bʌtə], Betty had a bit of bitter butter ['bʌtə].
   贝蒂有点很好的黄油，贝蒂还有点很苦的黄油。
5. She mixed the bitter butter ['bʌtə] with the better butter ['bʌtə], to make her bitter butter ['bʌtə] better.
   她把苦的黄油和好的黄油混在一起，好让苦黄油变好一点。

影音荟萃

一 听音乐学音标

May It Be
但愿

Enya

May it be an evening star	但愿有一颗暮色之星
Shines down upon you	照耀着你
May it be when darkness ['dɑːknəs] falls	即使黑暗降临
Your heart [hɑːt] will be true	你将揣着一颗真诚的心
You walk a lonely road	孤独地上路
Oh! How far [fɑː] you are from home	噢，离家的路途有多远
Mornie utulie (Quenya: Darkness ['dɑːknəs] has come)	（黑暗已经来临）
Believe and you will find your way	相信你会找到路径
Mornie alantie (Quenya: Darkness ['dɑːknəs] has fallen)	（黑暗已经来临）
A promise lives within you now	如今希望在你心中不泯
May it be the shadow's call	但愿阴影的笼罩
Will fly away	将消逝
May it be your journey on	但愿你足下的旅途
To light the day	走向光明的天日
When the night is overcome	当黑夜逝去时
You may rise to find the sun	愿你起身迎接朝阳
Mornie utulie (Quenya: Darkness ['dɑːknəs] has come)	（黑暗已经来临）
Believe and you will find your way	相信你会找到路径

Mornie alantie (Quenya: Darkness ['dɑːknəs] has fallen)　（黑暗已经降临）

A promise lives within you now　如今希望在你心中不泯

A promise lives within you now　如今希望在你心中不泯

歌曲评论

2001年年底，恩雅（Enya）受《魔戒》导演彼得·杰克逊邀请创作了*May It Be*，作为电影的主题曲。*May It Be* 获得了极高的学术荣誉和商业地位，发行后在德国单曲榜成为冠军。在多国下载榜也名列前茅，之后获得奥斯卡“最佳原创歌曲”、金球奖“最佳原创歌曲”和格莱美“最佳电影歌曲”提名。

恩雅一名，来自古代凯尔特的同名女神Enya。出生于民间音乐世家的她，将爱尔兰传统民谣重新编曲，形成具有鲜明特色的音乐创作，实际上是叶芝和乔伊斯在诗歌和小说上成功经验的音乐翻版。20世纪80年代中期以来，恩雅成为国际乐坛上雅俗共赏的新星。她是现在全球唱片销量最高的女歌手之一，同时也是唱片销量最高的爱尔兰女艺人和唱片销量最高的新世纪乐派艺人。

Goodbye to Love

再见爱

Carpenters

I'll say goodbye to love [lʌv]　我将对爱情说再见

No one ever cared if I should live or die　从没人在意我是死是活

Time and time again the chance for love [lʌv] has passed me by　一次又一次　爱情总是在我身边经过

And all I know of love [lʌv] is how to live without it　我已经学会　让它远离我的生活

I just can't seem to find it　我总是与它无缘

So I've made my mind up [ʌp] I must live my life alone　所以我已下定决心　就让我孤独地生活

And though it's not the easy way I guess I've　我知道

always know	要这样做很不容易
I'd say goodbye to love [lʌv]	我要对爱情说再见
There are no tomorrows for this heart of mine	我的心已不寄托于明天
Surely time will lose these bitter memories	时间会冲淡这些苦涩的记忆
And I'll find that there is someone to believe in	我将会找到其他可以信赖的人
And to live for something I could live for	找到其他的生活目标
All the years of useless search	经过多年盲目的追求
Have finally reached an end	切都已经结束
Loneliness and empty days will be my only friend	剩下孤独与空虚成为我唯一的朋友
From this day love [lʌv] is forgotten	从今天起，我的记忆就要擦除爱情
I'll go on as best I can	我会继续坚持我的生活
What lies in the future is a mystery to us all	眼前的未来对谁都是神秘的
No one can predict the wheel of fortune as it falls	命运的转轮谁也不知
There may come a time when I will see that I've been wrong	有天也许我会发现自己错了
But for now this is my song	但现在这就是我要唱的歌
And it's goodbye to love [lʌv]	再见了，爱情
I'll say goodbye to love [lʌv]	再见了，爱情

歌曲评论

卡朋特乐队（Carpenters）是美国歌星理查德·卡朋特和卡伦·卡朋特兄妹二人组成的演唱组合，20世纪70年代和80年代初期风靡一时。卡朋特兄妹于1965年开始组建乐队，1969年11月15日，卡朋特乐队的单曲*Close to You*（《靠近你》）一举走红，其后，他们在整个70年代大获成功。*Yesterday Once More*（《昨日重现》）、*Top of the World*（《世界之巅》）、*Please Mr. Postman*（《请等一下，邮差先生》）等歌曲广为人知。1983年2月4日，卡伦·卡朋特因长期严重神经性厌食症而突然去世，卡朋特乐队随之告终。

Goodbye to Love（《再见爱》）是卡朋特乐队最著名的歌曲之一，收录在专辑*A Song for You*中。

二 看电影学音标

电影简介：

《冰雪奇缘》（*Frozen*）是2013年美国一部以电脑动画技术制成的音乐奇幻喜剧和三维电影，由克里斯·巴克和珍妮弗·李联合导演、珍妮弗编剧、迪士尼动画制作、迪士尼电影公司发行。取材自安徒生童话故事《冰雪女王》，是第53部迪士尼经典动画长片。2013年11月27日于美国上映。该片包揽了2013年度金球奖、安妮奖、奥斯卡最佳动画长片等奖项。

妹妹被姐姐的冰雪魔力所伤，国王和王后带着姐妹俩来找森林中的巨人们。森林里的精灵们在给妹妹疗伤。（节选自《冰雪奇缘》）

—Your Majesty!

—Born with the powers or cursed?

—Born. And they're [ɑː] getting stronger.

—You're [ɑː] lucky it wasn't her heart [hɑːt]. The heart [hɑːt] is not so easily changed. But the head can be persuaded.

—Do what you must.

—国王陛下!

—是生来就有还是中了恶咒?

—生来就有，而且法力越来越强了。

—幸好伤到的不是她的心，心不容易恢复，头却不难治好。

—请你尽力。

电影简介：

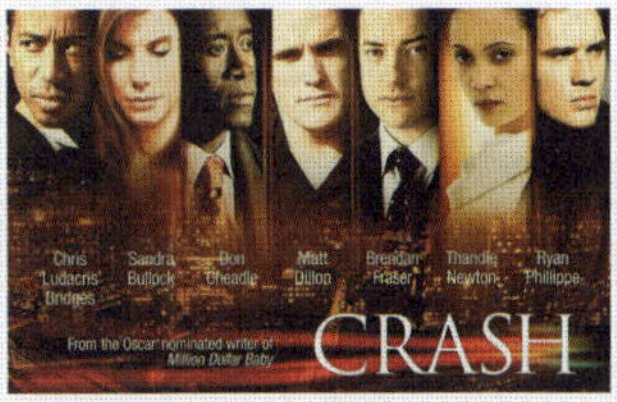

《撞车》（*Crash*）是一部美国彩色剧情电影。由导演保罗·哈吉斯倾力打造，马特·狄龙、桑迪·牛顿、莱恩·菲利普等主演。2004年开始全球上映。该片曾获得第78届奥斯卡金像奖最佳影片。

一对黑人夫妇在路上出了交通事故，警察正在调查事故。（节选自《撞车》）

—It's the sense of touch [tʌtʃ].

—What?

—Any real city, you walk, you know you brush [brʌʃ] past people. People bump [bʌmp] into you. In L.A., nobody touches ['tʌtʃɪz] you. We're always behind this metal and glass. I think we miss that touch [tʌtʃ] so much [mʌtʃ] that we crash into each other ['ʌðə] just so we can feel something ['sʌmθɪŋ].

—You guys okay?

—I think he hit his head.

—You don't think that's true?

—Stay in your car.

—这就是触碰的感觉。

—什么?

—穿梭在城市之中，你知道吗?你和人们擦肩而过，不期而遇。在洛杉矶，没有人触摸你。我们总是躲在冰冷的建筑物后面。我想我们十分想念那种触碰的感觉。我们彼此碰撞，只为了感受到彼此的存在。

—你们还好吧?

—他撞到了他的头。

—你不认为那是真的吗?

—待在你的车里。

Unit 2 [u:] & [ʊ]

[u:]

发音要素

发后元音[u:]时，舌后部尽量抬起，舌位比[ʊ]高，双唇收圆并突出，口腔肌肉始终保持紧张状态。口型比[ʊ]稍小。

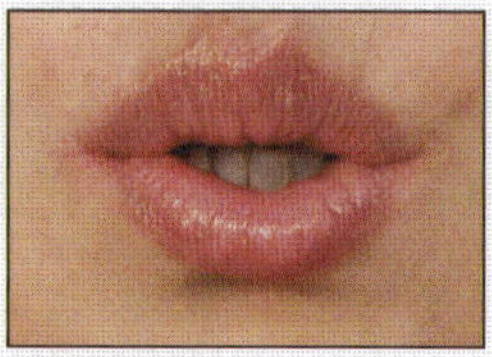

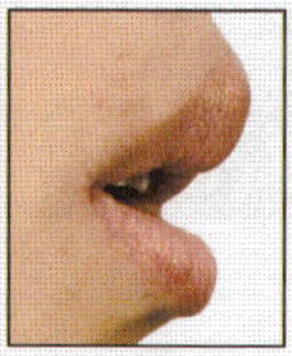

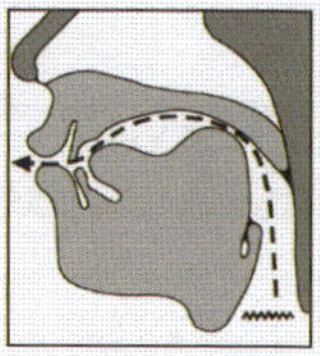

大话发音

火车来了，就会发出“呜……”的声音。

小孩子做游戏，想象火车来了，鸣起长笛，各个嘴巴都会张得圆圆的，这时就会发出[u:]这个音。

呜

发音代言人

moon

[mu:n] 月亮

常见发音字母及字母组合

音标	对应字母	自然发音规则	单词示例
[u:]	o	字母o为唯一或重读音节元音时，可发[u:]音。	who [hu:] 谁

[u:]	u	字母u为唯一或重读音节元音时，可发[u:]音。	**ruler** ['ru:lə] 直尺
[u:]	oo	字母组合oo可发[u:]音。	**boot** [bu:t] 靴子
[u:]	ou	字母组合ou可发[u:]音。	**soup** [su:p] 汤
[u:]	ue	字母组合ue位于词尾可发[u:]音。	**glue** [glu:] 胶水
[u:]	ui	字母组合ui可发[u:]音	**fruit** [fru:t] 水果

[ʊ]

发音要素

发后元音[ʊ]时，舌后部抬起，舌身后缩，舌尖离开下齿。双唇收圆，稍突出。

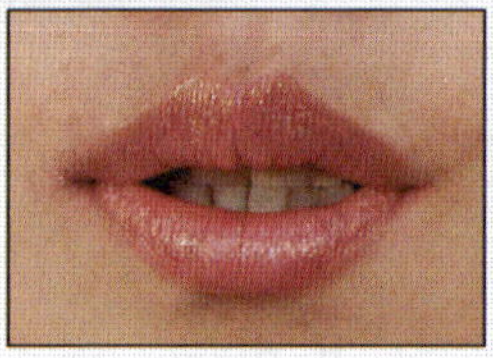

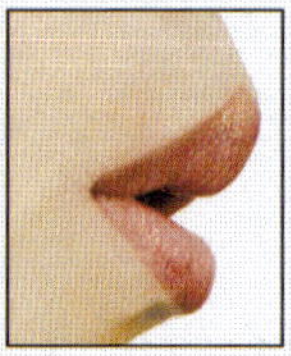

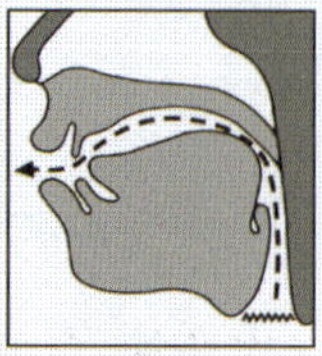

大话发音

后元音 [ʊ] 和普通话“乌”相似

小乌鸦口渴了，“乌”发得更短更急促，就是[ʊ]的发音。

乌

发音代言人

book

[bʊk] 书

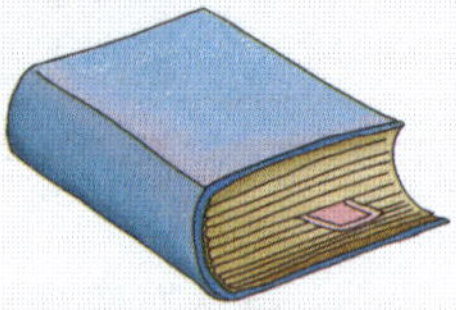

常见发音字母及字母组合

音标	对应字母	自然发音规则	单词示例
[ʊ]	u	字母u在重读闭音节中发[ʊ]音。	**sugar** ['ʃʊgə] 砂糖
[ʊ]	oo	字母组合oo有时发[ʊ]音。	**good** [gʊd] 好的
[ʊ]	ou	字母组合ou有时发[ʊ]音。	**could** [kʊd] 可以

发音操练

[u:]	[ʊ]
do [du:] 做	**wool** [wʊl] 羊毛
June [dʒu:n] 六月	**foot** [fʊt] 脚
tool [tu:l] 工具	**bull** [bʊl] 公牛
goose [gu:s] 鹅；傻瓜	**full** [fʊl] 满的
juice [dʒu:s] 果汁	**hook** [hʊk] 钩子
noodle ['nu:dl] 面条	**would** [wʊd] 愿意
rule [ru:l] 规则	**should** [ʃʊd] 应该
true [tʃu:] 真的	**butcher** ['bʊtʃə] 屠夫
stool [stu:l] 凳子	**bush** [bʊʃ] 灌木
lose [lu:z] 丢失	**wood** [wʊd] 木头

基础短语

- a very good [gʊd] book [bʊk] 一本很好的书
- put [pʊt] some sugar ['ʃʊgə] in the soup [su:p] 在汤里放些糖
- pull [pʊl] it out 把它拉出来

- at the foot [fʊt] of the mountain　在山脚下
- play the bully ['bʊli]　恃强凌弱
- a cook [kʊk] cooking ['kʊkɪŋ] a goose [gu:s]　正在烧鹅的厨师

以句识音

1. July [dʒu'laɪ]'s usually hotter than June [dʒu:n].
七月通常比六月更热。

2. Choose [tʃu:z] your new shoes [ʃu:z].
选一双新鞋。

3. Blue [blu:] suits you.
蓝色适合你。

4. The woman ['wʊmən] put [pʊt] her foot [fʊt] on the stool [stu:l].
那个女人把脚放在凳子上。

5. This book [bʊk] is full [fʊl] of crooks [krʊks].
这本书充满了欺骗。

6. No one could [kʊd] stop the butcher ['bʊtʃə].
没人能够阻止那个屠夫。

经典绕口令（运动你的舌头）

1. If Stu [stu:] chews [tʃu:z] shoes [ʃu:z], should [ʃʊd] Stu [stu:] choose [tʃu:z] the shoes [ʃu:z] he chews [tʃu:z]?
如果斯图咬鞋，斯图会选择他咬的鞋吗？

2. Roofs [ru:fs] of mushrooms ['mʌʃrʊmz] rarely mush too much.
蘑菇顶端很少能长太高。

3. Blue [blu:] glue [glu:] gun, green glue [glu:] gun.
蓝胶枪，绿胶枪。

4. I would [wʊd] if I could [kʊd], and if I couldn't ['kʊdnt], how could [kʊd] I? You couldn't ['kʊdnt], unless you could [kʊd], could [kʊd] you?
我会做的话就会做的，如果我不会做，我还怎么做？你不会做的，除非你会，你会么？

5. She is a very good [gʊd] cook [kʊk]. She has a good [gʊd] cookbook ['kʊkbʊk]. When she is cooking ['kʊkɪŋ], she takes a good [gʊd] look [lʊk] at the book [bʊk]. When she cooks [kʊks] soup [su:p], she always puts [pʊts] some sugar ['ʃʊgə] in the soup. When she has time, she would [wʊd] take a walk in the nearby bush [bʊʃ].

她是一个很棒的厨师。她有一本很好的烹饪书。当她做饭的时候，她会认真看看这本书。当她煮汤的时候，她总是在汤里加些糖。当她空闲的时候，她会去附近的树林里散步。

影音荟萃

一 听音乐学音标

Gloomy Sunday
忧郁的星期天

Sarah Brightman

Sunday is gloomy ['glu:mi]	星期天令我忧郁
My hours are slumberless	时光流逝，我辗转难眠
Dearest, the shadows I live with are numberless	亲爱的，我活在永无止尽的阴影里
Little white flowers will never awaken you	洁白的小花无法唤醒你
Not where the black coach of sorrow	悲哀的死灵之车更不可能
has taken you	将你带回
Angels have no thought of ever returning you	既然天使未尝想让你重返
Would [wʊd] they be angry if I thought of	我若想加入你的行列
joining you	他们是否会愤怒
Gloomy ['glu:mi] Sunday	忧郁的星期天
Sunday is gloomy ['glu:mi]	星期天令我忧郁
With shadows I spend it all	阴影始终围绕着我
My heart and I have decided to end it all	我的心意已决将这一切都结束

Soon [su:n] there'll be flowers and prayers that are sad
I know, let them not weep
Let them know that I'm glad to go
Death is no dream
For in death I'm caressing you
With the last breath of my soul I'll be blessing you
Gloomy ['glu:mi] Sunday

我知道不久之后就会有蜡烛和吊唁
这些都令人感到悲伤
但请他们别为我哭泣
让他们知道我走得心甘情愿
死亡不是虚无的梦
因为唯有死亡我才能与你缠绵
在我灵魂的最后一次呼吸中
我为你祝福
忧郁的星期天

Dreaming
I was only dreaming
I wake and I find you asleep in the deep of my heart
Dear
Darling, I hope that my dream never haunted you
My heart is telling you how much I wanted you
Gloomy ['glu:mi] Sunday

梦
我不过是在做梦罢了
梦醒时分我发觉你深深地沉睡在我心田
亲爱的
我希望我的梦
没惊扰了你
我的心正向你倾诉我是多么想你
忧郁的星期天

歌曲评论

《忧郁的星期天》是由两位匈牙利人Rezso Seress（作曲）和Laszlo Javor（作词）在1933年创作的歌曲。作曲家是为他的前女友创作的这首歌。因为这首歌被认为和许多自杀事件有关，所以曾一度禁播。作曲者本人也于1968年自杀。

When a Man Loves a Woman
当男人爱上女人

Michael Bolton

When a man loves a woman
Can't keep his mind on nothing else
He'd trade the world
For a good [gʊd] thing he's found
If she is bad, he can't see it

当男人爱上女人
会不能专心于别的事
他用世界交换
他发现的心爱之物
即使她是坏人，他也看不见

She can do [du:] no wrong	她做的事情没有错的
Turn his back on his best friend	如果他最好的朋友贬低她
If he puts her down	他会掉头离开
When a man loves a woman ['wʊmən]	当男人爱上女人
Spend his very last dime	会花掉他剩下的最后一毛钱
Trying to [tu:] hold on to [tu:] what he needs	努力抓牢他所需要的
He'd give up all his comforts	他会放弃所有安逸
And sleep out in the rain	睡在雨水里
If she said that's the way	只要她说这种方式
It ought to [tu:] be	是应当的
When a man loves a woman ['wʊmən]	当男人爱上女人
I give you everything I got (yeah)	我会给你我拥有的一切
Trying to [tu:] hold on	努力抓牢
To [tu:] your precious love	你珍贵的爱
Baby please don't treat me bad	宝贝请不要对我不好
When a man loves a woman	当男人爱女人
Deep down in his soul	爱到了灵魂里
She can bring him such misery	她会带给他这样的不幸
If she is playing him for a fool	如果她把他当成傻瓜戏弄
He's the last one to [tu:] know	他会是最后一个知道的人
Loving eyes can never see	恋爱中的眼睛永远看不见
Yes when a man loves a woman ['wʊmən]	是的，当男人爱上女人
I know exactly how he feels	我完全懂得他的感受
'Cause baby, baby, baby	因为宝贝，宝贝，宝贝
I am a man	我是一个男人
When a man loves a woman ['wʊmən]	当男人爱上女人

歌曲评论

迈克尔 · 波顿（Michael Bolton）是20世纪80年代到90年代乐坛备受欢迎的巨星。一路走来，他创下了全球超过5200万张的唱片销量。凭着《没有你我怎么活》以及《当男人爱上女人》两首脍炙人口的歌曲，成为两届格莱美音乐奖的最佳流行男歌手得主，并获得4次格莱美的提名。迈克尔 · 波顿凭借独特的演绎和声线，以及极富创意的作词、作曲的才华，赢得了乐迷的欣赏。

二 看电影学音标

电影简介：

电影《燕麦饼干店》（*Flakes*）是关于一个老嬉皮士的故事。他独自开了一家只卖燕麦饼干的小店，每天他都花费大量的时间制作燕麦饼干，连休闲时光也是在和当地人谈论燕麦饼干的历史以及制作方法中度过的。他就这样自得其乐地创造了一个属于自己的乌托邦王国。

一位男士走进了燕麦饼干店，可他好像不是普通的顾客，他似乎对开燕麦饼干这种风味小吃店很感兴趣。店里的人展开了一场关于谷物食品的讨论。（节选自《燕麦饼干店》）

Neal: How are you?

Man: Good. Great. So, uh. This is like a, uh…, like a cereal bar, or…

Neal: Yeah.

Man: Cool [ku:l]. Cool [ku:l] idea. Cool [ku:l]. Cool [ku:l]. Cool [ku:l]. Um, what's the most popular?

Neal: Uh, in here, it's anything cocoa. We got a lot of stoners in here. I think, nationally, it's Corn Flakes.

尼尔：你好。

男士：很好。很好。那么，嗯。这就像，嗯……就像压缩饼干，或者……

尼尔：是的。

男士：酷，好主意。好。好。很好。嗯，什么最受欢迎？

尼尔：呃，在这儿，只要带可可的都不错。我们这儿有很多可可的忠实消费者。当然，我想，玉米片最受欢迎。

电影简介:

电影《一个购物狂的自白》（*Confessions of a Shopaholic*）根据英国畅销书作家索菲·金塞拉的“购物狂”系列改编而成。索菲被誉为“女性都会小说”的代表人物，通过她幽默又深刻的笔触，活泼可爱的购物狂丽贝卡跃然纸上，成为无数女性读者喜爱的角色。曾经制作过《绝地战警》、《空中监狱》、《极速60秒》、《珍珠港》《黑鹰坠落》等无数佳片的好莱坞王牌制片人杰瑞·布鲁克海默看中了索菲的作品，决定要把这个人见人爱的购物狂搬上大银幕。

购物狂丽贝卡又被商店里的一条绿丝巾吸引住了，不过想到自己的账单，她又望而却步了。这时佩戴着绿丝巾的模特却开口和丽贝卡说话了，丽贝卡又一次经不住诱惑了。（节选自《一个购物狂的自白》）

—It would [wʊd] make your eyes look [lʊk] bigger.

—Mmm… It would make my haircut look [lʊk] more beautiful.

—You'd wear it with everything.

—It would [wʊd] be an investment.

—You would [wʊd] walk into ['ɪntʊ] that interview confident.

—Confident.

—And poised.

—Poised.

—The girl in the green scarf.

—它会让你的眼睛看起来更大。

—嗯……它会让我的发型看上去更漂亮。

—它配什么都好看。

—这是一项投资。

—这样你面试时会充满自信。

—自信。

—而且泰然自若。

—泰然自若。

—那个围着绿色围巾的女孩。

Unit 3 [i:] & [ɪ]

[i:]

发音要素

[i:] 是前元音，长元音，发音时，舌尖抵下齿，前舌尽量抬高，舌位高于[ɪ]，没有摩擦，口形扁平。

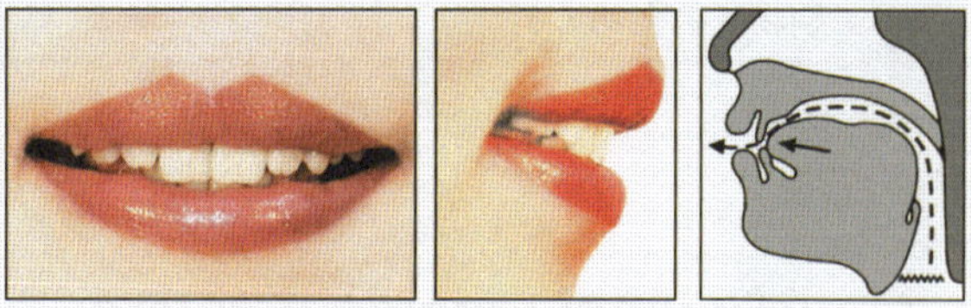

大话发音

数数时第一个数“壹”，类似 [i:] 的发音。

大家在数数时，要从第一个数字数起，拖长些，就是[i:]的发音。

壹

发音代言人

bee

[bi:] 蜜蜂

常见发音字母及字母组合

音标	对应字母	自然发音规则	单词示例
[i:]	e	字母e为唯一或重读音节时，可发[i:]音。	Peter['pi:tə] 彼得（人名）

[iː]	ea	字母组合ea为唯一或重读音节时，可发[iː]音。	**eat** [iːt] 吃
[iː]	ee	字母组合ee为唯一或重读音节时，可发[iː]音。	**sheep** [ʃiːp] 绵羊
[iː]	ie	字母组合ie可发[iː]音。	**thief** [θiːf] 小偷
[iː]	ei	字母组合ei可发[iː]音。	**receive** [rɪ'siːv] 收到
[iː]	ey	字母组合ey可发[iː]音。	**key** [kiː] 钥匙

[ɪ]

发音要素

[ɪ]是前元音，发音时，舌尖抵下齿，舌前部抬高，舌两侧抵上齿两侧，口形扁平。

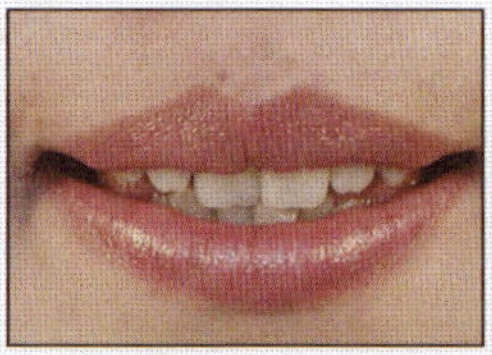

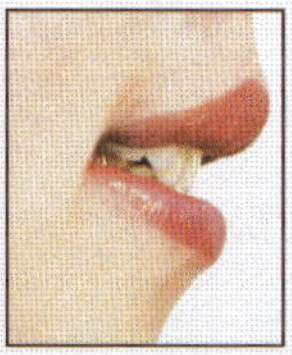

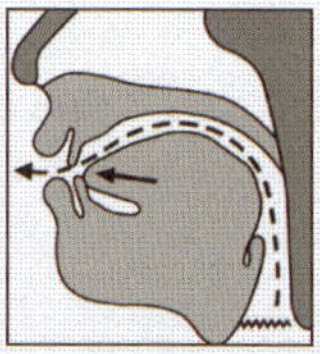

大话发音

英语中的这个音和汉语中的“衣”相似，但发音时要短促有力。

在发这个音的时候，感觉声音像是撞到墙壁上迅速弹回来一样，不能拖长，不能抬高或压低。

衣

发音代言人

pig

[pɪg] 猪

常见发音字母及字母组合

音标	对应字母	自然发音规则	单词示例
[ɪ]	i	字母i在唯一或重读闭音节中大多发[ɪ]音。	**fish** [fɪʃ] 鱼
[ɪ]	y	字母y在单词结尾时，大多发[ɪ]音。	**lady** ['leɪdi] 女士
[ɪ]	u	字母u有时发[ɪ]音。	**busy** ['bɪzi] 忙的
[ɪ]	e	字母e有时发[ɪ]音。	**prepare** [prɪ'peə] 准备

发音操练

[iː]	[ɪ]
Steve [stiːv] 斯蒂夫（人名）	**little** ['lɪtl] 小的
beef [biːf] 牛肉	**big** [bɪg] 大的
seed [siːd] 种子	**ticket** ['tɪkɪt] 票
meat [miːt] 肉	**happy** ['hæpi] 高兴的
meal [miːl] 饭	**family** ['fæməli] 家庭
green [griːn] 绿色的	**story** ['stɔːri] 故事
clean [kliːn] 干净的	**silk** [sɪlk] 丝绸
pea [piː] 豌豆	**lid** [lɪd] 盖子
leaf [liːf] 树叶	**tin** [tɪn] 罐头
knee [niː] 膝盖	**minute** ['mɪnɪt] 分钟

基础短语

- a key [kiː] on a seat [siːt] 座位上的一把钥匙

- trembling like a leaf [li:f]　浑身打哆嗦
- peeping ['pi:pɪŋ] into ['ɪntu:] the street [stri:t]　溜到大街上
- in [ɪn] a few minutes ['mɪnɪts]　几分钟之后
- live [lɪv] in a big [bɪg] city ['sɪtɪ]　住在大城市里
- feel [fi:l] home sick [sɪk]　很想家

以句识音

1. I believe [bɪ'li:v] eating ['i:tɪŋ] too much meat [mi:t] is very harmful.
我认为吃太多肉很不好。

2. He has little ['lɪtl] sleep [sli:p].
他睡得很少。

3. A friend in [ɪn] need [ni:d] is a friend indeed [ɪn'di:d].
患难见真情。（英谚）

4. Keep [ki:p] it [ɪt] between [bɪ'twi:n] you and me [mi:].
不要对别人讲。

5. Seeing ['si:ɪŋ] is believing [bɪ'li:vɪŋ].
眼见为实。（英谚）

6. It's a pity ['pɪti] that he [hi:] missed [mɪst] the film [fɪlm].
真可惜他错过了这场电影。

经典绕口令（运动你的舌头）

1. Some teachers' ['ti:tʃəz] teaching ['ti:tʃɪŋ] pleases ['pli:zɪz] some people. But other people feel [fi:l] the same teaching ['ti:tʃɪŋ] isn't pleasing ['pli:zɪŋ].
有些老师的教学受一些人欢迎，但是另一些人则觉得这种教学不是令人满意的。

2. Mr. Green [gri:n] seldom eats [i:ts] meat [mi:t], but he [hi:] keeps [ki:ps] eighteen [eɪ'ti:n] sheep [ʃi:p]. He [hi:] loves the sheep [ʃi:p] and feeds [fi:dz] them with tree [tri:] leaves [li:vz] every day.
格林先生很少吃肉，但是他养了十八只羊。他喜欢这些羊，每天用树叶喂它们。

3. Will [wɪl] you sit [sɪt] still [stɪl], Bill [bɪl]? I'll sit [sɪt] still [stɪl] as a hill [hɪl].

比尔，你能安静地坐着吗？我会坐着，像山一样岿然不动。

4. We [wiː] eat [iːt] to live [lɪv] but not live [lɪv] to eat [iːt].

我们吃饭是为了活着，但活着并不是为了吃饭。

5. You see [siː], I'm a little ['lɪtl] bee [biː], flying from the west to the east [iːst], when you eat [iːt] sweets [swiːts] with tea [tiː], don't forget me [miː].

你瞧，我是一只小蜜蜂，从西飞到东，当你喝茶吃甜点的时候，千万别忘了我。

影音荟萃

一 听音乐学音标

Heal the World

拯救世界

Michael Jackson

There's a place in [ɪn] your heart	你心中有一方沃土
And I know that it [ɪt] is [ɪz] love	我深知那便是爱的苗圃
And this [ðɪs] place could be [biː]	它比明天还要
Much brighter than tomorrow	光彩夺目
And if [ɪf] you really try	如果你努力尝试
You'll find there's no need to cry	你会发现没有必要哭泣
In [ɪn] this [ðɪs] place	在这片沃土上
You'll feel there's no hurt or sorrow	你将永远感受不到伤害和愁苦
There are ways to get there	通往这片沃土有许许多多的路
If [ɪf] you care enough for the living ['lɪvɪŋ]	如果你真对生命关注
Make a little ['lɪtl] space	那就留给他们一点空间
Make a better place	创造一个更美好的家园
Heal the world	拯救世界
Make it [ɪt] a better place	创一片仙园丽境
For you and for me [miː] and	为你也为我
The entire [ɪn'taɪə] human race	为那芸芸众生

There are people dying	有人还在遭逢死难
If [ɪf] you care enough for the living ['lɪvɪŋ]	如果你真对生命关怜
Make a better place	那就创造一个更美好的家园
For you and for me [mi:]	为你也为我
If [ɪf] you want to know why	如果你想获知原因
There's a love that cannot lie	有一种不会撒谎的爱心
Love is [ɪz] strong	这爱是如此挚深
It [ɪt] only cares of joyful giving ['gɪvɪŋ]	它只念及甘于奉献的真情
If [ɪf] we try we shall see [si:]	试一试，你便会眼见为实
In [ɪn] this [ðɪs] bliss [blɪs] we cannot feel [fi:l]	在这片乐天福地
Fear or dread	我们不会感到恐惧
We [wi:] stop existing [ɪg'zɪstɪŋ] and start living	苟且偷生将至此为止
['lɪvɪŋ]	新的生活将由此开始
Then it [ɪt] feels [fi:lz] that always	这就好像
Love's enough for us growing ['grəuɪŋ]	爱是我们成长中的全部营养
So make a better world	所以创造一个美丽的世界
Make a better world	创造一个人间天堂
Heal the world	拯救世界
Make it [ɪt] a better place	创一片仙园丽境
For you and for me [mi:] and	为你也为我
The entire [ɪn'taɪə] human race	为那芸芸众生
There are people dying ['daɪɪŋ]	有人还在遭逢死难
If [ɪf] you care enough for the living ['lɪvɪŋ]	如果你真对生命关怜
Make a better place	那就创造一个更美好的家园
For you and for me [mi:]	为你也为我
And the dream we were conceived [kən'si:vd] in [ɪn]	我们抱定的理想
Will [wɪl] reveal [rɪ'vi:l] a joyful face	会展露欢欣的笑颜
And the world we once believe [bɪ'li:v] in [ɪn]	我们信任的世界
Will [wɪl] shine again in [ɪn] grace	会闪耀恩慈的光艳
Then why do we [wi:] keep [ki:p] strangling	那为何我们还要继续
['stræŋglɪŋ] life	绞杀生命
Wound this [ðɪs] earth	蹂躏家园

Crucify ['kru:sɪfaɪ] its [ɪts] soul	将无辜的苍生钉向十字架前
Though it's [ɪts] plain to see [si:]	尽管一切都显而易见
This [ðɪs] world is [ɪz] heavenly ['hevnli]	这颗星球是上帝仁爱的造物
Be [bi:] god's glow	是上帝万丈荣光的凝练
We could fly so high	我们能振翅高飞
Let our spirits ['spɪrɪts] never die in [ɪn] my heart	让灵魂永生永垂
I feel [fi:l] you are all my brothers	在我心中，万民都是兄弟姐妹
Create [kri'eɪt] a world with [wɪð] no fear	创造一个没有恐惧的世界
Together we'll [wi:] cry happy tears	让我们喜极而泣
See [si:] the nations	看看这些国家
Turn their swords into plowshares	让它们和平共处吧
We [wi:] could really get there	我们的目标一定会实现
If [ɪf] you cared enough for the living ['lɪvɪŋ]	如果你真对生命关注
Make a little ['lɪtl] space	那就留给它们一点空间
To make a better place	创造一个更美好的家园
Heal the world	拯救世界
Make it [ɪt] a better place	创一片仙园丽境
For you and for me [mi:] and	为你也为我
The entire human race	为那芸芸众生
There are people dying ['daɪɪŋ]	有人还在遭逢死难
If [ɪf] you care enough for the living ['lɪvɪŋ]	如果你真对生命关怜
Make a better place	那就创造一个更美好的家园
For you and for me [mi:]	为你也为我
Make a better place	那就创造一个更美好的家园
For you and for me [mi:]	为你也为我

歌曲评论

迈克尔·杰克逊（Michael Jackson），1958年8月29日在美国印第安纳州加里市出生，美国歌手、舞蹈家、表演家、慈善家、音乐家、人道主义者、和平主义者、慈善机构创办人。迈克尔的歌曲或展示梦想，或激发潜能，或揭穿谎言，或痛斥“黑暗”，他的内心深处，有一种渴求“平等”的力量。迈克尔·杰克逊在音乐上的贡献还有对黑人种族、美国社会和文化的贡献。

《拯救世界》是一首呼唤世界和平的歌曲，这首歌曲被许多人称为迈克尔·杰克逊的公益性歌曲三部曲之一，更被誉为“世界上最动听的歌曲”。

Big Big World
大千世界

Emilia

I'm a big [bɪg] big [bɪg] girl	我是个重要的女孩
In [ɪn] a big [bɪg] big [bɪg] world	在这个大千世界里
It's [ɪts] not a big [bɪg] big [bɪg] thing [θɪŋ] if you leave me	如果你离开我，对我来说不是什么重大的事
But I do do feel	但我真的真的感到
that I do do will [wɪl] miss [mɪs] you much	我真的真的会很想念你
Miss [mɪs] you much	很想念你
I can see the first leaf falling	我看见第一片叶子落下
It's [ɪts] all yellow and nice	完全变得金黄，看起来这样美好
It's [ɪts] so very cold outside	外面是那么的冷
Like the way I'm feeling inside [ˌɪn'saɪd]	如同我内心的感受
I'm a big [bɪg] big [bɪg] girl	我是个重要的女孩
In [ɪn] a big [bɪg] big [bɪg] world	在这个大千世界里
It's [ɪts] not a big [bɪg] big [bɪg] thing [θɪŋ] if [ɪf] you leave me	如果你离开我，对我来说不是什么重大的事
But I do do feel	但我真的真的感到
that I do do will [wɪl] miss [mɪs] you much	我真的真的会很想念你
Miss [mɪs] you much	很想念你
Outside it's [ɪts] now raining	如今外面正在下雨
And tears are falling from my eyes	而眼泪正从我眼中滑落
Why did [dɪd] it [ɪt] have to happen	这一切为何要发生
Why did [dɪd] it [ɪt] all have to end	这一切为何要结束
I'm a big [bɪg] big [bɪg] girl	我是个重要的女孩

In a big [bɪg] big [bɪg] world	在这个大千世界里
It's not a big [bɪg] big [bɪg] thing [θɪŋ] if [ɪf] you leave me	如果你离开我，对我来说不是什么重大的事
But I do do feel	但我真的真的感到
that I do do will [wɪl] miss [mɪs] you much	我真的真的会很想念你
Miss [mɪs] you much	很想念你
I have your arms around me warm like fire	你的手臂环绕着我，温暖如火
But when I open my eyes	但当我睁开眼睛时
You're gone	你却已经离开
I'm a big [bɪg] big [bɪg] girl	我是个重要的女孩
In [ɪn] a big [bɪg] big [bɪg] world	在这个大千世界里
It's [ɪts] not a big [bɪg] big [bɪg] thing if you leave me	如果你离开我，对我来说不是什么重大的事
But I do do feel	但我真的真的感到
that I do do will miss you much	我真的真的会很想念你
Miss you much	很想念你
I'm a big [bɪg] big [bɪg] girl	我是个重要的女孩
In [ɪn] a big [bɪg] big [bɪg] world	在这个大千世界里
It's not a big big thing [θɪŋ] if [ɪf] you leave me	如果你离开我，对我来说不是什么重大的事
But I do feel I will [wɪl] miss [mɪs] you much	但我真的真的感到，我会很想念你
Miss [mɪs] you much	很想念你

歌曲评论

《大千世界》（*Big Big World*）是一首1998年的民谣歌曲，由来自瑞典的Emilia Rydberg演唱，拉塞·安德森参与编写。曲风伤感，风靡一时。这首歌于1998年年底发布。即一炮打响，在欧洲达到了第一名，在许多国家成名。

Emilia Rydberg 1978年1月5日生于瑞典的斯德哥尔摩，全家现定居于美国纽约市。她长着欧美轮廓，拥有巧克力肤色。父亲是爵士乐乐手，他对Emilia的音乐影响是不言而喻的，10岁时她便进入了斯德哥尔摩的音乐学校就读，潜心古典课程，在学校期间Emilia自组乐团演唱灵魂乐。18岁时，她便开始了自己风格独特的词曲创作，从一个小姑娘的视角和观念出发，记述豆蔻年华的女孩的敏感、自信、迷惑和种种的不服输，她的声音更是灵性毕现又不乏童真。因为在乐坛这种小姑娘的情调早已很鲜有，所以Emilia就显得格外吸引人。

二 看电影学音标

电影简介：

影片《穿普拉达的女王》（*The Devil Wears Prada*）是根据劳伦·魏丝伯格（Lauren Weisberger）的同名小说改编而成，由大卫·弗兰科尔执导，梅丽尔·斯特里普、安妮·海瑟薇和艾米莉·布朗特联袂出演。影片于2006年6月30日在美国上映。影片讲述一个刚离开校门的女大学生进入了一家顶级时尚杂志社当主编助理的故事，她从初入职场的迷惑到从自身出发寻找问题的根源，最后成为一个出色的职场与时尚的达人。

米兰达正在进行挑选会，也就是为杂志拍摄图片挑选合适的服装。她对衣服的款式和风格提出了自己独特的看法。（节选自《穿普拉达的女王》）

Miranda: No. And I've seen [siːn] all this before.

Clerk: Theyskens is trying to reinvent [ˌriːɪn'vent] the drop waist, so actually it's…

Miranda: Where are all the other dresses?

Clerk: We have some right here.

Niger: Stand, watch and listen.

Clerk: And I think it can be [biː] very interesting.

Miranda: No. No, I just, it's just baffling to me [miː]. Why is it so impossible to put together a decent ['diːsnt] run-through? You people have had hours and hours to prepare. It's just so confusing to me [miː]. Where are the advertisers?

Clerk: We have some pieces from Banana Republic.

Miranda: No, we need [niːd] more, don't we? Oh. This is, this might be [biː]. What do you think of?

Niger: Yeah, well, you know me [miː]. Give me [miː] a full ballerina skirt and a hint of saloon and I'm on board.

米兰达：不行，都过时了。

职员：西斯肯斯正准备重造一下下摆，所以事实上……

米兰达：其他裙子呢？

职员：这里还有一些。

奈吉尔：站着，边看边听。

职员：我认为这样很时髦。

米兰达：不，不，我真搞不懂。你们怎么就不能安排一个好点的预览呢？你们有这么多的时间准备，真让我搞不懂。广告部的人呢？

职员：我们从Banana Republic 品牌那拿来这些。

米兰达：我们还需要更多，不是吗？哦，这个，这个可以……你们觉得呢？

奈吉尔：是啊。你知道我这个人，一条芭蕾舞裙加一点造型，我绝对赞成。

电影简介：

《漂亮女人》（*Pretty Women*）（又称《麻雀变凤凰》）是朱莉娅·罗伯茨的成名作，是一部典型的讲述出身经历低俗的女子如何与身份悬殊的男人相遇相爱并结婚的现代灰姑娘故事。

维维安要陪爱德华参加一个重要的晚宴，可是她不熟悉高级西餐的礼仪，所以她正在请酒店经理巴尼给她讲解西餐用餐规矩。（节选自《漂亮女人》）

Vivian: Barney!

Barney: It [ɪt] didn't fit [fɪt].

Vivian: Oh, no, no, no, no, no. Uh, I've got a little problem.

Barney: All right, Miss [mɪs] Vivian ['vɪvɪən], one more time. Dinner ['dɪnə] napkin ['næpkɪn]. Laid gently in the lap.

Vivian: Dinner ['dɪnə] napkin ['næpkɪn], laid gently in the lap.

Barney: Good. Elbows off the table. Don't slouch. Shrimp [ʃrɪmp] fork, salad fork, dinner ['dɪnə] fork.

Vivian: I definitely ['defɪnɪtlɪ] have the salad fork. The rest of the silverware ['sɪlvəweə] is a little ['lɪtl] confusing.

Barney: All right, if [ɪf] you get nervous, just count the tines. Four tines: dinner ['dɪnə] fork. And sometimes there are three tines in the salad fork. And sometimes…

维维安：巴尼！

巴尼：不合胃口？

维维安：不，我有点小问题。

巴尼：好，维维安小姐，再一次，餐巾。将餐巾轻轻地放在大腿上。

维维安：将餐巾轻轻地放在大腿上。

巴尼：很好，手肘别放在桌子上，不要弯腰驼背，这是吃海鲜的叉子，这是吃沙拉的叉子，正餐用这个叉子。

维维安：沙拉叉我没问题，其他的餐具，我有一些弄不清楚。

巴尼：若是你弄不清，那你数数叉子上的尖！四个尖的是正餐叉子。吃沙拉的叉子有时有三个尖，有时候……

Unit 4 [ɜː] & [ə]

[ɜː]

发音要素

发元音[ɜː]时，舌中部向硬腭部分稍稍抬起，舌尖须向后向上稍稍卷起，双唇扁平。

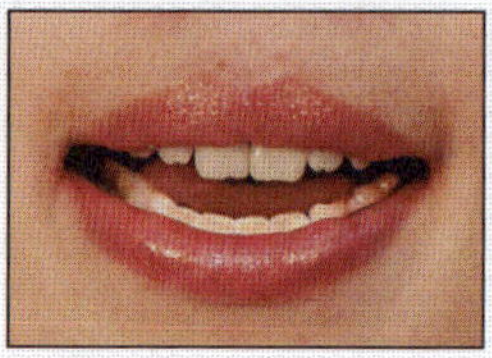

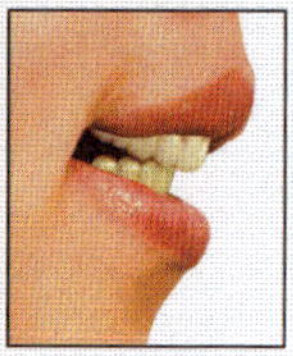

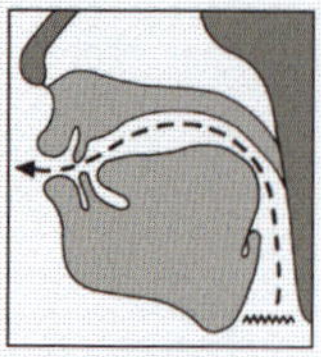

大话发音

这个音和汉语普通话“饿”拖长的音相同。一般在思考问题时发出这种声音。

在汉语中“饿”的发音短促，把它稍稍延长就是[ɜː]的发音。

饿

发音代言人

bird

[bɜːd] 小鸟

常见发音字母及字母组合

音标	对应字母	自然发音规则	单词示例
[ɜː]	er	字母组合er可发[ɜː]音。	term [tɜːm] 学期

[ɜː]	ir	字母组合ir可发[ɜː]音。	**shirt** [ʃɜːt] 衬衫
[ɜː]	or	字母组合or可发[ɜː]音。	**word** [wɜːd] 单词
[ɜː]	ur	字母组合ur可发[ɜː]音。	**fur** [fɜː] 皮毛
[ɜː]	our	字母组合our可发[ɜː]音。	**journey** ['dʒɜːni] 旅行;旅途
[ɜː]	ear	字母组合ear可发[ɜː]音。	**earth** [ɜːθ] 地球;土壤

[ə]

发音要素

发元音[ə]时，舌身平放，舌中部略隆起，双唇扁平。

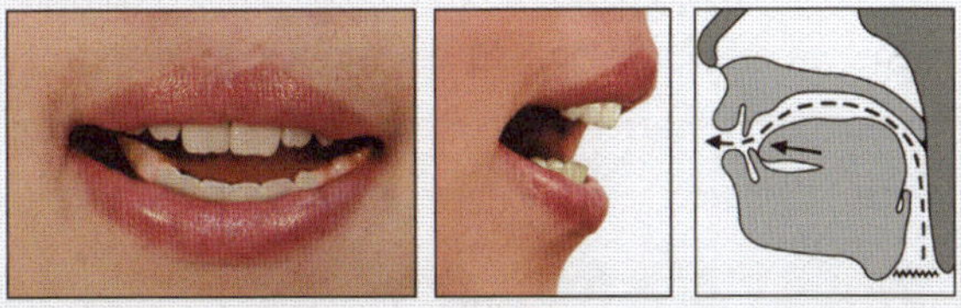

大话发音

吃饱了，人打嗝时，发出“呃”的声音。

这个音和人们吃饱后打饱嗝时的发音很相似，再发得清晰有力点，就是[ə]的发音。

呃

发音代言人

banana

[bə'nɑːnə] 香蕉

常见发音字母及字母组合

音标	对应字母	自然发音规则	单词示例
[ə]	a	字母a通常在单词开头或非重读音节中发[ə]音。	**pizza** ['pi:tsə] 比萨饼
[ə]	o	字母o可发[ə]音。	**o'clock** [ə'klɒk] ……点钟
[ə]	u	字母u有时发[ə]音。	**suppose** [sə'pəuz] 猜想
[ə]	e	字母e有时发[ə]音。	**them** [ðəm] 他们
[ə]	or	字母组合or在非重读音节中发[ə]音。	**actor** ['æktə] 演员
[ə]	er	字母组合er在非重读音节中发[ə]音。	**teacher** ['ti:tʃə] 老师
[ə]	ur	字母组合ur在非重读音节中发[ə]音。	**surprise** [sə'praɪz] 惊讶
[ə]	ar	字母组合ar在非重读音节中发[ə]音。	**sugar** ['ʃugə] 糖
[ə]	ou	字母组合ou在非重读音节中发[ə]音。	**famous** ['feɪməs] 著名的

发音操练

[ɜ:]	[ə]
skirt [skɜ:t] 短裙	**ago** [ə'gəu] 在……以前
world [wɜ:ld] 世界	**butter** ['bʌtə] 黄油
worker ['wɜ:kə] 工人	**farmer** ['fɑ:mə] 农夫
nurse [nɜ:s] 护士	**mother** ['mʌðə] 妈妈
church [tʃɜ:tʃ] 教堂	**distance** ['dɪstəns] 距离
burn [bɜ:n] 燃烧	**committee** [kə'mɪti] 委员会成员
curtain ['kɜ:tn] 窗帘	**federal** ['fedərəl] 联邦的
perfume ['pɜ:fju:m] 香水	**forget** [fə'get] 忘记

German ['dʒɜːmən] 德语	company ['kʌmpəni] 公司
girl [gɜːl] 女孩	water ['wɔːtə] 水

基础短语

- a [ə] very clever ['klevə] girl [gɜːl] 一个非常聪明的女孩
- around [ə'raʊnd] ten o'clock [ə'klɒk] 大约十点钟
- a [ə] drop of water ['wɔːtə] 一滴水
- across [ə'krɒs] the world [wɜːld] 全世界
- a [ə] bird [bɜːd] and a [ə] worm [wɜːm] 一只鸟和一条虫
- the manager ['mænɪdʒə] of a [ə] company ['kʌmpəni] 一个公司的经理

以句识音

1. He was born to achieve [ə'tʃiːv].
   他天生就是个有成就的人。
2. Were [wɜː] you ever ['evə] hurt [hɜːt] in an [ən] accident ['æksɪdənt]?
   你有在事故中受伤过吗？
3. He cursed [kɜːst] the nurse [nɜːs] for her [hɜː] bad service ['sɜːvɪs].
   他咒骂了那个服务质量极差的护士。
4. The [ðə] early ['ɜːli] bird [bɜːd] catches the [ðə] worm [wɜːm].
   早起的鸟儿有虫吃。（英谚）
5. The driver's ['draɪvəs] younger ['jʌŋgə] sister ['sɪstə] is a pop singer ['sɪŋə].
   那个司机的妹妹是流行歌手。
6. First [fɜːst] come, first [fɜːst] served [sɜːvd].
   先到先得。（英谚）

经典绕口令（运动你的舌头）

1. The first [fɜːst] person in a dirty ['dɜːti] shirt [ʃɜːt] works in the third [θɜːd] firm [fɜːm].
   那个穿脏衬衫的第一个人在第三个公司工作。

2. The girl [gɜːl] celebrated her birthday ['bɜːθdeɪ] with the other ['ʌðə] children ['tʃɪldrən] in the kingdom ['kɪŋdəm] garden ['gɑːdn].
   那个女孩在王国的花园里和其他小朋友一起庆祝了她的生日。

3. The actor ['æktə] performs [pə'fɔːms] wonderfully ['wʌndəfəli].
   那个演员表演得很棒。

4. The birds' [bɜːdz] feathers ['feðəz] are dirty ['dɜːti].
   那些鸟的羽毛是脏的。

5. Whether ['weðə] the weather ['weðə] be fine, or whether ['weðə] the weather ['weðə] be not; Whether ['weðə] the weather ['weðə] be cold or whether ['weðə] the weather ['weðə] be hot; We will weather ['weðə] the weather ['weðə] whatever [wɒt'evə] the weather ['weðə] whether ['weðə] we like it or not.
   无论天气好还是不好，无论天气是冷还是热，我们都要经受风霜雨露，无论什么天气，无论我们喜欢与否。

影音荟萃

一 听音乐学音标

Can You Help Me
你能帮帮我吗

Usher

Ooh why...	噢，为什么呢
Living on the edge out of control	人在边缘 失去控制
And the world [wɜːld] just won't let me slow down	世界不会让我失望
But in my biggest picture	但是我最大的照片

Was a photo of you and me	就是你和我的合影
Girl you know I try	女孩 你知道我已尽力了
I work [wɜːk] hard to provide	我努力工作添置
all the material things that I thought	我们所需要的东西
Would make you happy	我以为这样会令你快乐
I'm confused can you make me understand	现在我很迷茫 你能告诉我吗
Cause I try to give you the best of me	因为我已尝试 把最好的东西给你
I thought we were [wɜː] cool maybe I was blind	我以为我们很好 可能是我瞎了眼
But never took time to see	从没有花时间去考虑
Can you help me	你能帮帮我吗
Tell me what you want from me	告诉我 你到底想要什么
Can you help me	你能帮帮我吗
Tell me why you wanna leave	告诉我你为什么想要离开
Baby help me	宝贝帮帮我吧
Without you my whole world [wɜːld] is falling apart	没有你 我的世界都要崩溃了
And I'm going crazy	我都快疯了
Life's a prison when you're in love alone	当你单相思时 生活就是一座监狱
Ooh girl [gɜːl] I love you	噢 女孩 我爱你
I need you to come back home	我想你回家
You know I need you	你知道我需要你
I don't wanna be alone	我不想孤独一人
Girl [gɜːl] I put your love up on the shelf	女孩 是我把你的爱 放在了一边
And I guess I just left it to die	我想 是我让这份爱慢慢死去
Now we're not together	现在我们已经不在一起
Cause I hurt [hɜːt] you too many times	因为我已伤害你太多
And now you're not around	现在你不在我身边
I wish for every moment of time	我渴望回到
that got wasted	我不曾珍惜的每一刻
We used it to make sweet love	我们曾经愉快地亲热
Baby be my guide please take my hand	宝贝给我指引吧 请牵着我的手
Want you to know that I got you	我想让你知道

If you need it	只要你需要我就会给你
Don't want to be on the outside looking in	我不想在围城外做个看客
I gotta have you girl [gɜːl] can't you see	我必须拥有你 你知道吗
Can you help me	你能帮帮我吗
Tell me what you want from me	告诉我 你要的到底是什么
Can you help me	你能帮帮我吗
Tell me why you wanna leave	告诉我你为什么想要离开
Baby help me	宝贝帮帮我吧
Cause without you my whole world [wɜːld] is falling apart	没有你 我的世界都要崩溃了
And without you I'm going crazy	没有你我都快疯了
Life's a prison when you're in love alone	当你单相思时 生活就是一座监狱
Ooh girl [gɜːl] I love you	噢 女孩 我爱你
I need you to come back home	我想你回家
(you know I need you)	（你知道我需要你）
I don't wanna be alone	我不想孤独一人
Baby would you please listen to me oh	宝贝你能听到我的心声吗
Please stay don't go I don't want you to go	别离开我
Give me another chance I wanna be your man	请给我多一次机会吧 我想做你的男人
Girl [gɜːl] you've got me down here on my knees	女孩 我已为你下跪
Crying begging pleading	哭着乞求你
I'll do anything for your love	我会为你做任何事
Oh	噢……
Would you help me [help me]	你能帮帮我吗
Tell me what you want from me [help me]	告诉我 你要的到底是什么
Can you tell me [ueah]	你能告诉我吗
I don't understand I'm just a man	我是男人 不了解女孩的心思
[Just stay don't go I don't want you to leave]	别离开我
Help me Baby help me	帮帮我吧 宝贝帮帮我吧
I'm going crazy	我都快疯了

Would you help me	你能帮帮我吗
Without you my whole world [wɜːld] is falling apart	没有你 我的世界都要崩溃了
And without you I'm going crazy	没有你我都快疯了
Life's a prison without your love	没有你的爱 生活就是一座监狱
Can you help me, tell me why	你能帮帮我吗，告诉我为什么
Can you help me	你能帮帮我吗
Can you help me	你能帮帮我吗
Tell me why why why why why	告诉我为什么……
Can you help me	你能帮帮我吗
Girl I'll never stop cuz you're	女孩 我的爱不会停止 因为你是
All I got	我的所有
Can you help me	你能帮帮我吗
Help me understand why I can't be a man	帮我了解我为什么成不了你的男人
It's driving me crazy (crazy crazy crazy)	这让我快疯了
Ohhh baby, ohhhh no nooh girl [gɜːl] I love you	噢…… 女孩我爱你
Said I love you, you know I need you	我爱你 你知道我需要你
Ohhhh ohh ohh I need you	噢…… 我需要你
Can't live without you	不能离开你
I can't go one day without you oh girl [gɜːl]	一天也不能离开你
I love you, you know I need you	噢 女孩我爱你 你知道我需要你
Can't live without you	不能离开你
Ohh girl [gɜːl] I love you, you know I need you	噢 女孩我爱你 你知道我需要你
Can't live without you	不能离开你
Oh girl [gɜːl] I love you, you know I need you	我爱你 你知道我需要你
Can't live without you	不能离开你
You know I need you	你知道我需要你
Yeahhhhh yeahh yeah yeah	耶……

歌曲评论

Usher是当今美国流行乐界最受欢迎的R&B男歌星，也是一名年少成名的R&B歌星，特别是他在2001年度和2002年度第44和第45届格莱美颁奖典礼上连续两年获得了最佳R&B男歌手奖之后，他的受欢迎程度更是突破了评论界，并且直观地表现在了唱片的市场销量上，成为了被广泛欢迎的2004年头号R&B男歌星，并且一举打破了R&B男歌手的单周专辑销售纪录。

More than I Can Say
爱你在心口难开

Leo Sayer

Wow wow yeah yeah	哦……
I love you more than [ðən] I can [kæn] say	我爱你在心口难开
I'll love you twice as much tomorrow [tə'mɒrəʊ]	我对你的爱一天胜似一天
Wow wow love you more than [ðən] I can [kæn] say	哦，爱你在心口难开
Wow wow yeah yeah	哦……
I miss you every single day	我每一天都在思念着你
Why must my life be filled with sorrow	为什么我的人生必须充满悲伤
Wow wow love you more than [ðən] I can [kæn] say	哦，爱你在心口难开
Don't you know I need you so	啊，难道你不知道我是多么需要你
Tell me please I gotta know	请告诉我，我必须知道
Do you mean to make me cry	你是不是有意要让我哭
Am I just another [ə'nʌðə] guy	又或者说我仅是你追求者之一
Wow wow yeah yeah	哦……
I miss you more than [ðən] I can [kæn] say	我想你在心口难开
Why must my life be filled with sorrow	为什么我的人生必须充满悲伤
Wow wow love you more than I can say	哦，爱你在心口难开
Don't you know I need you so	哦，难道你不知道我是多么需要你
Tell me please I gotta know	请告诉我，我必须知道
Do you mean to make me cry	你是不是有意要让我哭
Am I just another [ə'nʌðə] guy	又或者说我仅是你追求者之一
Wow wow yeah yeah	哦……
I love you more than [ðən] I can [kæn] say	我爱你在心口难开
I'll love you twice as much tomorrow [tə'mɒrəʊ]	我对你的爱一天胜似一天
Wow wow love you more than [ðən] I can [kæn] say	哦，爱你在心口难开

歌曲评论

《爱你在心口难开》（*More Than I Can Say*）是杰瑞·埃利森（Jerry Allison）和桑尼·柯蒂斯（Sonny Curtis）创作的，产生于20世纪60年代初期，开始是由Bobby Vee在1971年唱红的，后来Leo Sayer于1980年将之重新诠释。此曲因此成为20世纪80年代男女吐露恋爱心声的抒情经典，1980年分别获得金唱片奖第二名、美国排行榜6周亚军、成人抒情榜3周冠军和英国榜亚军单曲。

二 看电影学音标

电影简介：

《音乐之声》（*The Sound of Music* ）是美国一部家喻户晓的音乐类电影，公认的好作品，讲述了一个修女来到一个富人家里当家庭教师的故事。

对生活充满信心的玛丽亚初涉尘俗来到特拉普上校家里做家庭教师，在那里她和特拉普上校进行了第一次对话。谈话内容涉及玛丽亚的衣着。（节选自《音乐之声》）

Captain: In the future, you're kind of to remember that certain [ˈsɜːtn] rooms in this house which are not to be disturbed [dɪˈstɜːbd].

Maria: Yes, Captain, sir.

Captain: Why do you stare at me that way?

Maria: Well, you don't look at all like a sea Captain, sir.

Captain: I'm afraid you don't look very much like a governess. Turn [tɜːn] around, please.

Maria: What?

Captain: Turn [tɜːn]. Hat off. It's the dress. You have to put on another one before you meet the children.

上校：以后请你记住，这房子里有些房间是不能乱闯的。

玛丽亚：是，上校，先生。

上校：为什么这样盯着我？

玛丽亚：先生，你看起来一点都不像海军上校。

上校：恐怕你也不怎么像家庭教师。请转过身去。

玛丽亚：什么？

上校：　转身，脱帽。衣服不对劲。在和孩子们见面之前，你得换套衣服。

电影简介：

《后天》（*The Day after Tomorrow*）为20世纪福克斯公司的年度科幻巨片，投资1.25亿美元，由曾经执导《独立日》、《爱国者》等影片的导演罗兰·艾默里奇执导，新生代偶像丹尼斯·奎德、杰克·吉伦哈尔、艾米·罗森、莎拉·沃德等主演。影片讲述温室效应造成地球气候异变，全球即将陷入第二次冰河纪的故事。《后天》的意义，不仅仅在于思考灾难来临之时，对人类的伤害，还在于反思人类对自然的伤害，最终会毁灭人类自身。这是一部充满人文关照的影片。

新德里联合国全球气候变暖会议上，豪尔教授正在发言。（节选自《后天》）

—What we have found locked in these ice cores is evidence ['evɪdəns] of a cataclysmic [ˌkætə'klɪzmɪk] climate shift, which occurred [ə'kɜːd] around 10,000 years ago [ə'gəʊ]. The concentration of these natural ['nætʃrəl] greenhouse gases in the ice cores indicates that runaway ['rʌnəweɪ] warming pushed Earth into an [ən] ice age which lasted two centuries.

—我们在这些冰芯中发现了将近一万年前，灾难性气候迁移的证据。这些温室效应气体在冰芯中的凝聚，表明了失控性的气候变暖把全球推向冰川时代，而这个时代一直持续了两个世纪。

Unit 5 [ɔː] & [ɒ]

[ɔː]

发音要素

发元音[ɔː] 时，舌后部抬得比[ɒ]高，双唇收得更圆更小，并向前突出。

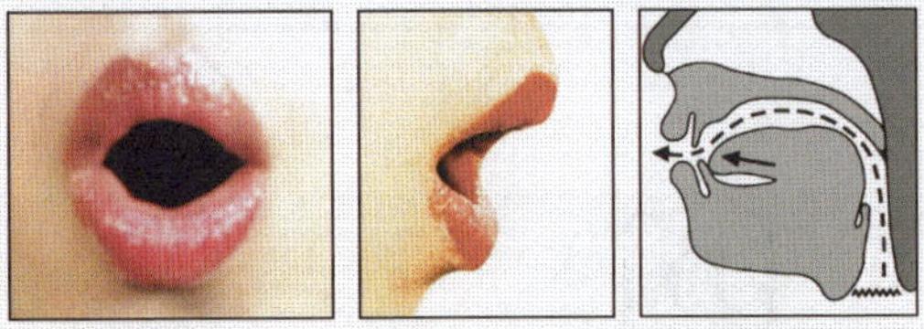

大话发音

这是一个需要技巧的发音“哦”。

发这个音的时候要把双唇向前凸起，双唇间的缝隙很小，连个小手指都几乎放不进去。

哦

发音代言人

ball

[bɔːl] 球

常见发音字母及字母组合

音标	对应字母	自然发音规则	单词示例
[ɔː]	a	字母a可发[ɔː]音。	**water** ['wɔːtə] 水
[ɔː]	o	字母o可发[ɔː]音。	**off** [ɔːf] < 美音 > 从……离开

[ɔː]	or	字母组合or可发[ɔː]音。	**fork** [fɔːk] 叉子
[ɔː]	al	字母组合al可发[ɔː]音。	**chalk** [tʃɔːk] 粉笔
[ɔː]	aw	字母组合aw可发[ɔː]音。	**lawn** [lɔːn] 草坪
[ɔː]	au	字母组合au可发[ɔː]音。	**cause** [kɔːz] 原因；借口
[ɔː]	oar	字母组合oar可发[ɔː]音。	**board** [bɔːd] 木板
[ɔː]	our	字母组合our可发[ɔː]音。	**four** [fɔː] 四
[ɔː]	oor	字母组合oor可发[ɔː]音。	**door** [dɔː] 门
[ɔː]	ough	字母组合ough可发[ɔː]音。	**thought** [θɔːt] 想法

[ɒ]

发音要素

发元音[ɒ]时，口张大，舌身尽量降低并后缩，双唇稍稍收圆。

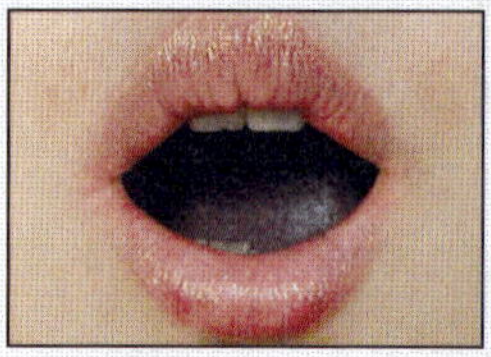

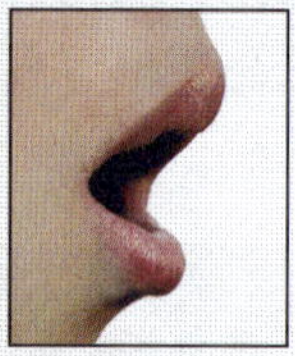

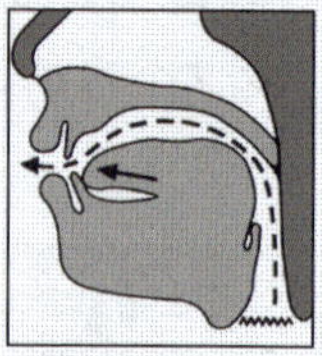

大话发音

与汉字中凹陷的“凹”的声音相似。

在汉语中，我们发“凹”时，短促一些，就会发出[ɒ]的音。

凹

发音代言人

fox

[fɒks] 狐狸

常见发音字母及字母组合

音标	对应字母	自然发音规则	单词示例
[ɒ]	o	字母o在重读音节中发[ɒ]音。	dog [dɒg] 狗
[ɒ]	a	字母a为唯一或重读音节元音时，可发[ɒ]音。	what [wɒt] 什么

发音操练

[ɔ:]	[ɒ]
horse [hɔ:s] 马	hot [hɒt] 热的
lord [lɔ:d] 领主	lock [lɒk] 锁
talk [tɔ:k] 谈话	bottle ['bɒtl] 瓶子
walk [wɔ:k] 走路	box [bɒks] 盒子
floor [flɔ:] 地板	pot [pɒt] 壶
course [kɔ:s] 课程；进程	boss [bɒs] 老板
cause [kɔ:z] 原因；借口	job [dʒɒb] 工作
salt [sɔ:lt] 盐	mop [mɒp] 拖把
wall [wɔ:l] 墙	hobby ['hɒbi] 爱好
more [mɔ:] 更多的	tomorrow [tə'mɒrəʊ] 明天

基础短语

- walk [wɔ:k] on the lawn [lɔ:n] 在草坪上散步
- a dog [dɒg] and a fox [fɒks] 一只狗和一只狐狸
- a watchman ['wɒtʃmən] and a lawyer ['lɔ:jə] 一个警卫和一个律师
- in the corner ['kɔ:nə] 在角落

- talk [tɔːk] to the Board [bɔːd]　向董事会报告
- the boss [bɒs] of the shop [ʃɒp]　一个商店的老板

以句识音

1. He has lots [lɒts] of cards in his pocket ['pɒkɪt].
   他的口袋里有许多卡片。
2. The man walking ['wɔːkɪŋ] on the lawn [lɔːn] is my boss [bɒs].
   在草坪上散步的那个人是我老板。
3. It's Ford [fɔːd]'s fault [fɔːlt].
   这是福特的错。
4. She is eating a hotdog ['hɒtˌdɒg] at the door [dɔː] way.
   她在门口，吃着热狗。
5. Tom [tɒm] has a lofty ['lɒftɪ] job [dʒɒb] and a lot [lɒt] of hobbies ['hɒbɪz].
   汤姆有一个高尚的职业，还有许多爱好。
6. The scholar ['skɒlə] is going on [ɒn] a holiday ['hɒlədeɪ].
   那个学者正在度假。

经典绕口令（运动你的舌头）

1. I thought [θɔːt] a thought [θɔːt]. But the thought [θɔːt] I thought [θɔːt] wasn't the **thought [θɔːt] I thought [θɔːt].**
   我有一个想法。但是这个想法并不是我认为我所想的那个想法。
2. A little pot [pɒt] is soon getting hot [hɒt].
   壶小易热，肚小易怒。（英谚）
3. Tall [tɔːl] Paul [pɔːl] ate some awful ['ɔːfl] corn [kɔːn] sauce [sɔːs].
   高高的保罗吃了一些难吃的玉米汁。
4. Bob [bɒb] took a hot [hɒt] pot [pɒt] but he overturned the pot [pɒt] and the hot [hɒt] water ['wɔːtə] spattered on the floor [flɔː].
   鲍勃拿了一个热锅，他把锅打翻了，热水溅在了地板上。
5. Froggy ['frɒgi] boggy ['bɒgi] sat on [ɒn] a rock [rɒk]. Froggy ['frɒgi] boggy ['bɒgi] had

a great shock [ʃɒk]. Froggy ['frɒgi] boggy ['bɒgi] fell off [ɒf] the top [tɒp]. Into the pond [pɒnd] he fell with a pop [pɒp].

小青蛙，坐石上，受了惊，吓一跳，从岩石上面掉下来，扑通一声进池塘。

影音荟萃

一 听音乐学音标

Se a Vida é
这便是生活

Pet Shop Boys

Come outside and see a brand new day
The troubles in your [jɔː] mind will blow away
It's easy to believe they here to stay
but you won't find them standing in your [jɔː] way

走出小房间，看看崭新的一天，
脑海中的愁绪定能随风飘散。
相信并不难，这良辰将留驻你身边，
却又不会阻碍你向前。

Se a vida é, I love you
Come outside and feel the morning ['mɔːnɪŋ] sun
Se a vida é, I love you
Life is much more [mɔː] simple when you're young
Come on essa vida é
That's the way life is That's the way life is

生活就是这样，我爱你在心上。
快快走出来，感受这新一轮朝阳。
生活就是这样，我爱你在心上。
当你依旧青春，生活是多么单纯。
来吧，
生活就是这样，生活就是这样。

Although we see the world through different eyes
We share the same idea of paradise
So don't search in the stars for signs of love
Look around your [jɔː] life you'll find enough
Se a vida é, I love you
Come outside and feel the morning ['mɔːnɪŋ] sun

尽管我们的世界观不同，
对天堂却怀有相同的憧憬。
所以不要把爱的希望寄托在星空，
蓦然环顾，身边就有真情涌动。
生活就是这样，我爱你在心上。
快快走出来，感受这新一轮朝阳。

Se a vida é, I love you	生活就是这样，我爱你在心上。
Life is much m**ore** [mɔː] simple when you're young	当你依旧青春，生活是多么单纯。
Come on essa vida é	来吧，
That's the way life is That's the way life is	生活就是这样，生活就是这样。
Why do you want to sit alone in gothic gloom	你为何要独坐空房，
surrounded by the ghosts of love	任爱情的魑魅在哥特式的
that haunt y**our** [jɔː] room	阴郁中游荡。
Somewhere there's a different d**oor** [dɔː]	总有一个地方，
to open wide	一扇全新的门会向你开敞。
You gotta throw those skeletons	你该抛开往日的不快，
out of y**our** [jɔː] closet	走出忧伤。
And come outside	到外面来吧，
So you will see a brand new day	看看崭新的一天，
The troubles in your mind will blow away	脑海中的愁绪定能随风飘散。
It's easy to believe they're here to stay	相信并不难，这良辰将留驻你身边，
but you find them standing in y**our** [jɔː] way	却又不会阻碍你向前。
Se a vida é, I love you, Se a vida e	生活就是这样，我爱你在心上。
Come outside and feel the m**or**ning ['mɔːnɪŋ] sun	快快走出来，感受这新一轮朝阳。
Se a vida é, I love you	生活就是这样，我爱你在心上。
Life is much m**ore** [mɔː] simple when you're young	当你依旧青春，生活是多么单纯。
Come on essa vida é That's the way life is	来吧，生活就是这样，
That's the way life is	生活就是这样。

歌曲评论

“宠物店男孩”成立于1981年，是一支英国流行音乐组合。成员只有两个——1954年7月10日出生的主唱尼尔·坦南特(Neil Tennant)和比他小5岁的键盘手克里斯·罗(Chris Lowe)。因为对电子舞曲的共同爱好，这两个人一见如故，并且马上有了合组一支乐队的打算。由于他们有一位朋友在一家宠物店工作，于是乐队便有了一个奇特而好记的名字——“宠物店男孩”。

1985年，他们签约EMI公司，和《西区女孩》一样，他们的第二首单曲《机会（我们来赚大钱）》(*Opportunities <Let's Make Lots of Money>*)也没有引起什么反响。1986年，他们请制作人斯蒂芬·哈格（Stephen Hague）重新制作了《西区女孩》，结果这首只有催眠性质的歌曲打上了英国排行榜，并慢慢爬上了英、美两个国家的排行榜冠军位置。1987年，乐队推出了专辑《事实上》（Actually），这张广受欢迎的专辑创下了他们的唱片销量之最。

Miss You
想你

Westlife

I can't sleep, I just can't breathe
When your shadow is all over me baby
I don't wanna ['wɒnə] be, a fool in your eyes
Cause what [wɒt] we had was built on [ɒn] lies
And when our love seems to fade away
Listen to me hear what [wɒt] I say
I don't wanna ['wɒnə] feel the way that I do
I just wanna ['wɒnə] be right here with you
I don't wanna ['wɒnə] see, see us apart
I just wanna ['wɒnə] say it straight from [frɒm]
my heart
I miss you

What [wɒt] would it take, for you to see
to make you understand that I'll
always believe
You and I, can make it through
And I still know, I can't get over you
Cause when our love seems to fade away
Listen to me hear what [wɒt] I say
I don't wanna ['wɒnə] feel the way that I do
I just wanna ['wɒnə] be right here with you
I don't wanna ['wɒnə] see, see us apart
I just wanna ['wɒnə] say it straight from [frɒm]
my heart
Oh baby I miss you, I do

Cause when our love always fades away
Listen to me hear what [wɒt] I say
I don't wanna ['wɒnə] feel the way that I do
I just wanna ['wɒnə] be right here with you

我无法入睡，我甚至无法呼吸
当你的身影经过我心里，宝贝
我不想成为你眼中的一个傻瓜
因为我们拥有的一切都是基于谎言
当我们的爱似乎在流逝
请聆听我说的话
我不想感到这样的痛苦
我只是想待在你身边
我不愿意看到，看到我们分开
我只是想
径直说出藏在我心底的话
我想你

如何能让你看到
让你懂得
我一直相信
你和我，可以共渡难关
因为我仍然知道，我不能离开你
因为当我们的爱似乎在流逝
请聆听我说的话
我不想感到这样的痛苦
我只是想待在你身边
我不愿意看到，看到我们分开
我只是想
径直说出藏在我心底的话
哦宝贝，我想你，真的想你

因为当我们的爱似乎在流逝
请聆听我说的话
我不想感到这样的痛苦
我只是想待在你身边

I don't wanna ['wɒnə] see, see us apart	我不愿意看到，看到我们分开
I just wanna ['wɒnə] say it straight from [frɒm]	我只是想
my heart	径直说出藏在我心底的话
I miss you... I miss you... I do	我想你，我想你，真的想你
I don't wanna feel	我不想感受
The way that I do	这样的痛苦
I just wanna ['wɒnə] be	我只是想
Right here with you	待在你身边
I don't wanna ['wɒnə] see	我不愿意看到
See us apart	看到我们分开
I just wanna ['wɒnə] say it straight from [frɒm]	我只是想
my heart	径直说出藏在我心底的话
Oh baby I miss you, I do	哦宝贝，我想你，真的想你

歌曲评论

《想你》（*Miss You*）是爱尔兰男子歌唱团体西城男孩（Westlife）的第一张同名专辑中的一首歌曲，很动听的一首歌，喜欢音乐的朋友可以听一下，我相信你们不会忘记这首歌的。

西城男孩来自于爱尔兰，1998年12月份第一次演出，1999年正式出道。成员：主唱是Shane（尚恩）、Mark（马克）、Bryan（布莱恩）（2004年已单飞离队）、合音是Kian（奇恩）、Nicky（尼基）。他们是英国金榜史上首支连创7首空降冠军单曲的艺人，而且获得英国14首单曲冠军的纪录仅次于猫王埃尔维斯·普雷斯利（Elvis Presley）和甲壳虫乐队（The Beatles），位居英国第3位年度唱片。分别以1999年的*Flying Without Wings*、2000年的*My Love*、2003年的*Mandy*、2005年的*You Raise Me Up*四次成为获得年度唱片最多的艺人。

二 看电影学音标

电影简介：

在上一单元我们已经介绍过《后天》（*The Day After Tomorrow*）这部电影。影片讲述温室效应造成地球气候异变，全球即将陷入第二次冰河纪的故事。

新德里联合国全球气候变暖会议上，豪尔教授正在发言。他在向大家讲述全球变暖的危害。（节选自《后天》）

—I'm confused. I thought [θɔ:t] you were talking ['tɔ:kɪŋ] about global warming ['wɔ:mɪŋ] , not an ice age.

—Yes, it is a paradox, but global warming ['wɔ:mɪŋ] can trigger a cooling trend. Let me explain. The Northern ['nɔ:ðən] Hemisphere owes its climate to the North [nɔ:θ] Atlantic Current. Heat from the sun arrives at the equator and is carried north [nɔ:θ] by the ocean. But global warming ['wɔ:mɪŋ] is melting the polar ice caps and disrupting this flow. Eventually it will shut down. And when that occurs there goes our warm [wɔ:m] climate...

—我被你搞糊涂了。我还以为你是在讨论全球变暖问题而不是冰川时代……

—是有点自相矛盾。但是全球变暖会导致气候冷却的趋势。我来解释一下。北大西洋暖流直接影响北半球气候。来自太阳的热量到达赤道后再由洋流传送到北方，但是全球变暖正在融化极地的冰川，而这干扰了这个洋流。最后它会慢慢停下来，到那时候，我们温暖的天气就消失了……

电影简介:

美国影片《缘分天注定》（*Serendipity*）由约翰·库萨克、凯特·贝金赛尔等主演，被评为“必须要看的十大经典浪漫爱情电影”之一。讲述的是一对男女一见钟情的故事。

几年后，萨拉和好朋友在酒店门口分别，朋友问她打算怎么办，并建议她最好就在这里等待和乔纳森再次相遇，要真的相信缘分天注定。（节选自《缘分天注定》）

—So what are you gonna ['gɒnə] do?	—你打算怎么做?
—I don't know. I guess I'm just gonna ['gɒnə] try and find him or something.	—不知道。我想我会试着找到他。
—I don't think you should do that. I really don't.	—我认为你不该再找了。
—Well, what [wɒt] do you think I should do?	—那我该怎么做?
—Just be here. I feel it. I feel it in the air.	—在这里等着。我有预感。
—Eve, what's [wɒts] happened to you? You've become your own worst nightmare right there.	—伊芙，你怎么了？怎么也开始迷信了?
—Bye.	—再见。
—And please put a jacket on [ɒn]. It's freezing out here.	—拜托你穿上外套，外面很冷呢。

Unit 6 [æ] & [e]

[æ]

发音要素

发音时，舌尖抵下齿，双唇向两边平伸，呈扁平行，张开牙床至上下齿之间可以容纳食指和中指的宽度。

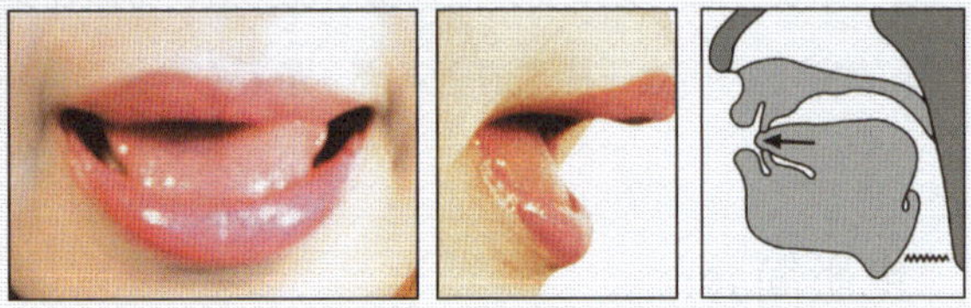

大话发音

汉语中没有和这个音完全一致的发音，但类似汉字“安”去掉后半部分鼻音“n”，只留前半部分的音。发这个音时嘴巴张大，脸部肌肉紧张。

发这个音是有窍门的，你的嘴巴张开的大小以上下齿之间的距离衡量大概是两个手指平放的宽度为准。

安

发音代言人

flag

[flæg] 旗

常见发音字母及字母组合

音标 对应字母	自然发音规则	单词示例

[æ]	a	字母a在闭音节或重读闭音节中发[æ]音。	cat [kæt] 猫

[e]

发音要素

发元音[e]时，舌尖抵下齿，舌前部稍抬起，比[i:]低，双唇稍扁。

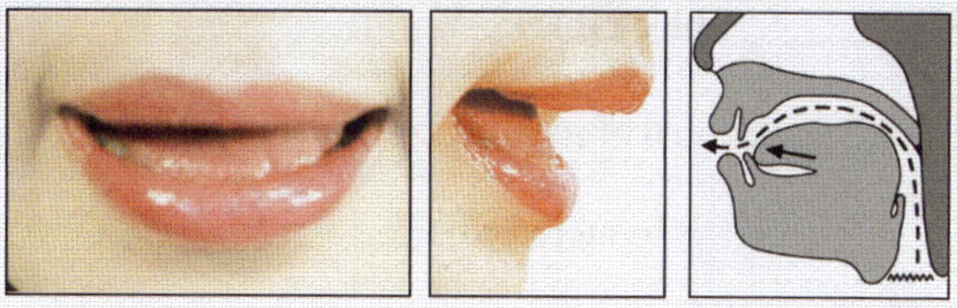

大话发音

[e] 类似于汉字“哎”的发音。

在夸奖别人时，会说“哎呀，你真棒”，“哎”的音，跟[e]这个音很相似，发这个音时，嘴巴张开的大小大约为上下齿间的距离只有一个手指平放的宽度。

哎

发音代言人

bed

[bed] 床

常见发音字母及字母组合

音标	对应字母	自然发音规则	单词示例
[e]	e	字母e在单词中可发[e]音。	men [men] 人；男人
[e]	ea	字母组合ea在单词中可发[e]音。	head [hed] 头

发音操练

[æ]	[e]
rabbit ['ræbɪt] 兔子	desk [desk] 书桌
van [væn] （有棚的）货车	bench [bentʃ] 长椅
tractor ['træktə] 拖拉机	tent [tent] 帐篷
black [blæk] 黑色的	red [red] 红色的
dad [dæd] 爸爸	letter ['letə] 信
hand [hænd] 手	help [help] 帮忙
glad [glæd] 高兴的	best [best] 最好的
fat [fæt] 胖的	tell [tel] 告诉
sad [sæd] 悲伤的	dress [dres] 穿着
bank [bæŋk] 银行	chess [tʃes] 象棋

基础短语

- a glad [glæd] hand [hænd] 乐于助人
- get [get] mad [mæd] 发疯
- traffic ['træfɪk] accidents ['æksɪdənts] 交通事故
- a bad [bæd] apple ['æpl] 一个坏蛋
- a fat [fæt] cat [kæt] 一个特别有钱的大亨
- seldom ['seldəm] forget [fə'get] 很少忘记

以句识音

1. I shall never ['nevə] forget [fə'get] the lesson ['lesn].

我永远不会忘记这个教训。

2. It's very bad [bæd] of you to talk back [bæk] to your dad [dæd].
你竟然和你爸爸顶嘴，真是太无礼了。

3. Who is that [ðæt] fat [fæt] man [mæn] standing ['stændɪŋ] at the back [bæk]?
站在后面的那个胖子是谁？

4. The heavier ['heviə], the better ['betə].
越重越好。

5. Better ['betə] late than never ['nevə].
亡羊补牢，未为迟也。（英谚）

6. East or west [west], home is best [best].
金窝银窝，不如自己的狗窝。（英谚）

经典绕口令（运动你的舌头）

1. How many ['meni] yaks [jæks] could a yak [jæk] pack [pæk] pack [pæk] if a yak [jæk] pack [pæk] could pack [pæk] yaks [jæks]?
如果一个牦牛包可以装牦牛的话，一个牦牛包可以装多少头牦牛？

2. We need a plan [plæn] to fan [fæn] a pan [pæn]; find a pan [pæn] to fan [fæn], then find a fan [fæn] to fan [fæn] the pan [pæn], then fan [fæn] the pan [pæn].
我们需要一个计划来扇平底锅，找个要扇的锅，然后找把扇子来扇锅，然后扇锅。

3. Ted [ted] sent [sent] Fred [fred] ten [ten] hens [henz] yesterday ['jestədei] so Fred's [fredz] fresh [freʃ] bread [bred] is ready ['redi] already [ɔ:l'redi].
特德昨天给弗莱德送去了十只母鸡，所以弗莱德的新鲜面包已经准备好了。

4. Of all the felt [felt] I ever ['evə] felt [felt], I never ['nevə] felt [felt] a piece of felt [felt] which felt [felt] as fine as that [ðæt] felt [felt] felt [felt], when first I felt [felt] that felt [felt] hat's [hæts] felt [felt].
在我所触摸过的毡子中，我从未触摸过一块如此舒适的毡子，直至我试过这顶毡帽的毡子为止。

5. Peter Pepper ['pepə] picked a peck [pek] of pickled pepper ['pepə];
A peck [pek] of pickled pepper ['pepə] Peter Pepper ['pepə] picked;
If Peter Pepper ['pepə] picked a peck [pek] of pickled pepper ['pepə],
Where is the peck [pek] of pickled pepper ['pepə] Peter Pepper ['pepə] picked?
皮特 · 派珀捏起一撮泡菜；

一撮皮特·派珀捏起的泡菜；
如果皮特·派珀捏起的是一撮泡菜；
那么皮特·派珀捏起的泡菜在哪儿？

影音荟萃

一 听音乐学音标

Alone Again Naturally

再度孤独

Gilbert O'Sullivan

In a little while from now	再过一会儿
If I'm not feeling any less sour	若没有感觉好受一点
I promise myself to treat myself	我向自己保证
And visit a nearby tower	就去附近的高塔
And climbing to the top	爬到制高点
Will throw myself off	然后释放自己
In an effort to, make it clear to who-	努力向某人表明
Ever what its like when you're shattered ['ʃætəd]	当一个人崩溃时是怎样的状态
Left standing ['stændɪŋ] in the lurch, at a church	摇晃不定站在教堂
Where people saying My God	那里的人们说，天啊
That's tough, she's stood him up	太糟了，她放了他鸽子
No point in us remaining	我们之间没有沟通
We may as [æz] well go home	我们还是回家吧
As [æz] I did on my own	像我之前一样独自一人
Alone again, naturally ['nætʃrəli]	再度孤独 自然而然
To think that [ðæt] only yesterday	想起就在昨日
I was cheerful bright and [ænd] gay	我还欢喜雀跃
Looking forward to, but who wouldn't do	期待着，任谁都不会像我这样
The role I was about to play	做我所担当的角色

But as [æz] if to knock me down	而真相到来时
Reality came around	仿佛要把我击垮
And [ænd] without so much as [æz] a mere touch	不需要太多，仅仅一个轻轻的触碰
Cut me into little pieces	就把我剪得粉碎
Leaving me to doubt	让我怀疑
Talk about God in his mercy, who if	让我探讨上帝和他的仁慈
He really does exist	如果他真的存在
Why did he desert me	为何要抛弃我
In my hour of need, I truly am indeed	就在我最需要他的时刻
Alone again, naturally ['nætʃrəli]	再度孤独，自然而然
It seems to me that [ðæt] there are more hearts	看来在这世上
broken in the world, that [ðæt] can't [kænt] be	还有更多破碎的心灵
mended	它们无法被修复
Left unattended	被遗弃
What do we do? What do we do?	我们能做什么？我们能做什么？
Alone again, naturally ['nætʃrəli]	再度孤独，自然而然
Now looking back [bæk] over the years	回顾过去的这些年
And [ænd] whatever [wɒt'evə] else that [ðæt]	还有什么事情发生
appears	
I remember I cried, when my father died	我记得我为父亲的去世而哭泣
Never wishing to hide the tears	仍由眼泪落下
And [ænd] at [æt] sixty-five years old	在母亲65岁之际
My mother God rest her soul	她永远睡去
Couldn't understand why the only man [mæn]	无法理解，为什么
She had [hæd] ever loved had been taken	她唯一爱过的男人会被上帝带走
Leaving her to start with a heart	剩下她独自一人重新开始
So badly ['bædli] broken	心灵破碎不堪
Despite encouragement from me	尽管我尽力安慰
No words were ever spoken	她还是再也没有开口说过话
And when she passed away	而当她去世的时候
I cried and [ænd] cried all day	我终日哭泣
Alone again naturally ['nætʃrəli]	再度孤独，自然而然
Alone again naturally ['nætʃrəli]	再度孤独，自然而然

歌曲评论

爱尔兰音乐人Gilbert O'Sullivan在1972年发行的单曲《再度孤独》（*Alone Again Naturally*），获得美国单曲榜的冠军，英国单曲榜的第三名。

Gilbert O'Sullivan，爱尔兰著名歌手以及作曲人，1946年12月1日出生于爱尔兰沃特福德县。以其70年代初的热门歌曲 *Alone Again Naturally*、*Clair*、*Get Down* 以及其独一无二的短裤、低底圆帽和布丁盆发型为世人所熟知，并由此拓宽了他在国际上演艺事业的发展。英国音乐杂志 *Record Mirror* 评选他为1972年英国最佳歌手。

Crying in the Rain
在雨中哭泣

Carole King

I'll never ['nevə] let [let] you see	我不会让你看到
The way my broken heart is hurting me	破碎的心给我带来的伤
I've got my pride and I know how to hide	我有尊严 我知道如何去隐藏
All the sorrow and pain	所有的悲伤疼痛
I'll do my crying in the rain	我会在雨中哭泣
If I wait for cloudy skies	我在期盼着暴风雨的来临
You won't know the rain from the tears in my eyes	这样你就不会知道这泪是从我眼中流出的
You'll never ['nevə] know that I still love you	你就不会知道我依旧如此爱你
So though the heartaches remain	心还是那么疼痛
I'll do my crying in the rain	我会在雨中哭泣
Raindrops falling from heaven ['hevn]	那来自天堂的雨滴落下
Could never ['nevə] wash away my misery	从来没有带走我的伤悲
But since we're not together [tə'geðə]	自从我们分手
I'll look for stormy weather ['weðə]	我会挑暴风雨的天气
To hide these tears I hope you'll never ['nevə] see	去隐藏我希望你永远不会见到的泪光
Someday when [wen] my crying's done	也许泪水有干涸的一日

I'm gonna wear a smile and walk in the sun	我会带着微笑走在阳光下
I may be a fool	我或许有点笨
But till then [ðen], darling, you'll never ['nevə]	然而到那时，亲爱的，你绝不会看到
see me complain	我抱怨
I'll do my crying in the rain	我会在雨中哭泣
I'll do my crying in the rain	我会在雨中哭泣

歌曲评论

卡萝尔·金（Carole King，出生于1942年2月9日）是美国歌手及作曲人。她和丈夫格里·戈芬（Gerry Goffin）在20世纪60年代写了20多首热门歌曲。她的专辑《挂毯》（*Tapestry*）于1971年高居美国音乐专辑榜榜首15个星期，并留在专辑榜超过6年。1959年，她17岁的时候与格里·戈芬写了她第一首流行榜排行第一的作品 *Will You Love Me Tomorrow*。她赢得了4个格莱美奖并入选了创作人名人堂（Songwriters Hall of Fame）和摇滚名人堂（Rock and Roll Hall of Fame）。她拥有女歌手在Billboard 200上连续获得冠军时间最长的纪录。

Crying in the Rain 是她2005年出品的专辑 *Speeding Time* 中的第三首歌曲。

二 看电影学音标

电影简介：

《律政俏佳人2》（*Legally Blonde 2*）是由查尔斯·赫曼·温菲尔德导演，瑞茜·维瑟斯庞、卢克·威尔逊、莎莉·菲尔德、鲍伯·纽哈特主演的喜剧电影。2003年7月2日首映。

金发美女艾丽回来了！从哈佛法学院毕业后，艾丽在一家法律事务所工作，并开始筹备自己的盛大婚礼，当然是和在哈佛意外结识的艾默特。艾丽正在给艾默特打电话告诉他在棒球场举行婚礼的好消息。（节选自《律政俏佳人2》）

—Infield. What are you talking about?

—OK. It turns out the starting pitcher for the Red Sox has [hæz] an unfortunate unibrow problem. Anyway he goes to Nedia, my waxer ['wæksə], so the team pulled some strings with the site manager ['mænɪdʒə] and we're getting married ['mærid] at Fenway!

—Are you serious? I mean are you sure this is what you want to do? I can get married ['mærid] anywhere and it wouldn't matter ['mætə]. That's a lie. I'm getting married ['mærid] under the Green Monster.

—在场地上。你在说什么?
—好了。红短袜的第一个投手不幸有个一字眉。他去找娜迪亚，我的上蜡师，所以球队帮助拉上了关系。我们要在芬威结婚了。
—你是当真的吗？我是说，你真的想那样做吗？我可以在任何地方结婚，这没什么关系。你撒谎。我要在记分板下结婚了!

电影简介:

《阿甘正传》(*Forrest Gump*)，是一部根据同名小说改编的美国电影，小说作者是温斯顿·格鲁姆（Winston Groom），电影荣获1995年奥斯卡最佳影片奖、奥斯卡最佳男主角奖、奥斯卡最佳导演奖等6项大奖。

阿甘又一次出于爱，用自己的方式帮助了珍妮，阿甘深爱着珍妮，但珍妮却不爱他。（节选自《阿甘正传》）

—Polly, get [get] out here! Shut up yourself [jɔː'self]. Just shut up.
—Forrest! What are you doing here? What are you doing? Let [let] me down.
You can't keep doing this, Forrest. You can't keep trying to rescue ['reskjuː] me all the time.
—They were trying to grab you.
—A lot of people try to grab me. Just … You can't keep doing this all the time.
—I can't help [help] it. I love you.
—Forrest, you don't know what love is.

—波莉，快走！你闭嘴！闭嘴!
—福里斯特，你来干什么？你干什么，放下我!
你不能老是这样做，福里斯特，你别老是想着要救我。
—他们在占你便宜。
—很多人想要占我便宜，可是你不能老是这样做。
—我忍不住。我爱你。
—福里斯特，你不知道什么是爱。

Unit 7 [eɪ]

[eɪ]

发音要素

发双元音[eɪ]时，先发[e]音，然后滑向[ɪ]音。双唇稍扁，口形从半开到合。

[e]

[ɪ]

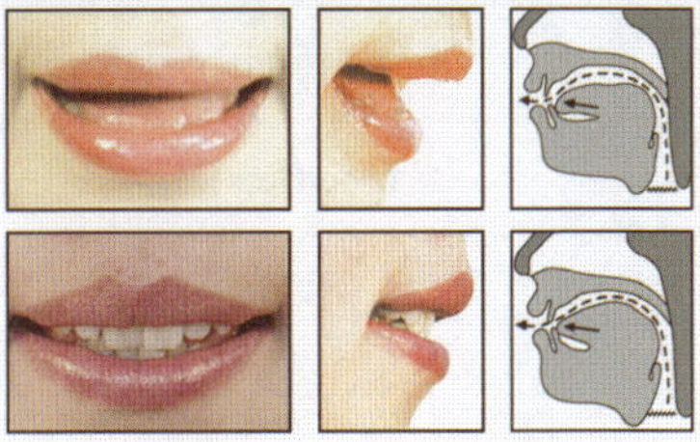

大话发音

此音类似于英文字母“A”、汉字“诶”的发音。不过发这个音时要注意前一个音长而强，后一个音短而弱，两个音的滑动过渡要自然流畅。

诶

发音代言人

cake

[keɪk] 蛋糕

常见发音字母及字母组合

音标	对应字母	自然发音规则	单词示例
[eɪ]	a	字母a在开音节单词中发[eɪ]音。	name [neɪm] 名字
[eɪ]	ay	字母组合ay可发[eɪ]音。	ray [reɪ] 光束；光线

[eɪ]	ai	字母组合ai可发[eɪ]音。	**rain** [reɪn] 雨
[eɪ]	ea	字母组合ea可发[eɪ]音。	**great** [greɪt] 伟大的
[eɪ]	ey	字母组合ey可发[eɪ]音。	**hey** [heɪ] 喂；嘿

发音操练

[eɪ]	
fame [feɪm] 名声	**late** [leɪt] 迟到
face [feɪs] 脸	**plate** [pleɪt] 盘子
hay [heɪ] 干草	**day** [deɪ] 一天；白天
bay [beɪ] 港湾	**complain** [kəm'pleɪn] 抱怨
famous ['feɪməs] 著名的	**stain** [steɪn] 褪色；被玷污；污染

基础短语

- for the sake [seɪk] of 为了……的缘故
- a birthday ['bɜːθdeɪ] cake [keɪk] 一个生日蛋糕
- make [meɪk] a silly mistake [mɪs'teɪk] 犯了一个不该犯的错误
- leave a space [speɪs] 留一个空间
- call a spade [speɪd] a spade [speɪd] 直言不讳
- in the same [seɪm] way [weɪ] 以同样的方式

以句识音

1. She works at the railway ['reɪlweɪ] station ['steɪʃn].

她在火车站工作。

2. I'm sorry for coming late [leɪt] again.

很抱歉我又来晚了。

3. On the same [seɪm] day [deɪ] another plane [pleɪn] crash happened.

在同一天还发生了另一起飞机坠毁事件。

4. No pains [peɪnz], no gains [geɪnz].

不劳则无获。（英谚）

5. A penny saved [seɪvd] is a penny gained [geɪnd].

积少成多。（英谚）

6. You should play [pleɪ] it safe [seɪf] and not make [meɪk] haste [heɪst].

你应该慎重，不要操之过急。

经典绕口令（运动你的舌头）

1. Here's an easy game [geɪm] to play [pleɪ]. Here's an easy name [neɪm] to say [seɪ].

这是一个容易玩的游戏；这是一个容易说的名字。

2. The great [greɪt] Greek grape [greɪp] growers grow great [greɪt] Greek grapes [greɪps].

伟大的希腊葡萄种植者种出了伟大的希腊葡萄。

3. Today [tə'deɪ] is a grey [greɪ] day [deɪ], not a rainy ['reɪni] day [deɪ].

今天是个阴沉的日子，但不是个下雨天。

4. Rain [reɪn], rain [reɪn], go away, come again another day [deɪ]. Little children want to play [pleɪ], rain [reɪn], rain [reɪn], go away.[ə'weɪ]

雨啊，雨啊，请走开，还是改天你再来；小朋友们要玩耍，雨啊，雨啊，别下啦。

5. Today [tə'deɪ], today [tə'deɪ], is the first of May [meɪ]; on this happy day [deɪ] in May [meɪ], boys and girls dance and play [pleɪ].

今天，今天，是五月的第一天；在这个五月的快乐的一天，孩子们快乐地跳舞玩耍。

影音荟萃

一 听音乐学音标

Hey Jude
嘿！裘德

The Beatles

Hey [heɪ] Jude, don't make [meɪk] it bad	嘿！裘德！别沮丧
Take a sad song and make [meɪk] it better	找一首哀伤的歌把它唱得更快乐
Remember to let her into your heart	记得将她唱入你的心田
Then you can start to make [meɪk] it better	然后你就可以唱得更快乐
Hey [heɪ] Jude, don't be afraid [ə'freɪd]	嘿！裘德！别害怕
You were made [meɪd] to go out and get her	你天生就要勇于去追求她
The minute you let her under your skin	当你将她深埋于心底那一刻
Then you begin to make [meɪk] it better	然后你就可以唱得更快乐
And anytime you feel the pain [peɪn]	当你感受痛苦的滋味
Hey [heɪ] Jude, refrain [rɪ'freɪn]	嘿！裘德！要忍耐
Don't carry the world upon your shoulders	别把世界的重担都往肩上扛
For well you know that it's a fool	你知道那些愚蠢的人
who plays [pleɪz] it cool	总是装作不在乎
By making ['meɪkɪŋ] his world a little colder	把自己的世界弄得很冷酷
Na Na Na Na Na Na-Na-Na-Na-Na	Na na na na na na na na na na
Hey [heɪ] Jude, don't let me down	嘿！裘德！别让我失望
You have found her, now go and get her	既然找到真爱就要勇敢追求
Remember to let her into your heart	记住要将她揽入你的心房
Then you can start to make [meɪk] it better	那样世界就能开始好转
So let it out and let it in	所以啊，让你的爱自由来去

Hey [heɪ] Jude, begin	嘿！裘德！开始啊
You're waiting ['weɪtɪŋ] for someone to perform with	你期待有个人与你同台表演
And don't you know that it's just you	你不知道那个人就是你自己吗
Hey [heɪ] Jude, you'll do	嘿！裘德！你会办到
The movement you need is on your shoulder	下一步该怎么做就全看你自己
Na Na Na Na Na Na-Na-Na-Na-Na	Na na na na na na na na na na
Hey [heɪ] Jude, don't make [meɪk] it bad	嘿，裘德！别灰心
Take [teɪk] a sad song and make [meɪk] it better	找一首哀伤的歌把它唱得更快乐
Remember to let her under your skin,	记得将她深藏于心
Then you'll begin to make [meɪk] it better	然后你就可以唱得更快乐
Na na na, na-na-na-na, na-na-na-na, hey [heɪ] Jude...	Na na na，na na na na，na na na na，嘿，裘德
Na na na, na-na-na-na, na-na-na-na, hey [heɪ] Jude...	Na na na，na na na na，na na na na，嘿，裘德
Na na na, na-na-na-na, na-na-na-na, hey [heɪ] Jude...	Na na na，na na na na，na na na na，嘿，裘德
Na na na, na-na-na-na, na-na-na-na, hey [heɪ] Jude...	Na na na，na na na na，na na na na，嘿，裘德

歌曲评论

《嘿！裘德》（*Hey Jude*）是披头士乐队成员保罗·麦卡特尼创作的一首歌，于1968年发行。原本计划收录进同名专辑 *The Beatles*，后来作为单曲发行，并迅速成为当年的冠军单曲。*Hey Jude*原曲长7分10秒。这首歌的原名是 *Hey Julian*，后来改为 *Hey Jules*，最终变成 *Hey Jude*。虽然它比一般的单曲长了两倍，但还是广受欢迎，并且很快就成了英国和荷兰的歌曲排行榜冠军。短短两个星期后就出人意料地售出了两百万张，并且在美国Billboard 榜首位置上停留了9个星期。*Hey Jude* 在全球的销量超过了八百万张。

这支诞生于英国利物浦的传奇乐队，保持着世界上各种唱片销量统计的最高纪录，其唱片销量在世界拥有压倒性的数字——数以亿计，并且至今每年仍有数百万张的增幅，大大领先于“猫王”埃尔维斯·普雷斯利。披头士乐队还曾经获得过八次格莱美奖。保罗·麦卡特尼个人在乐坛上的卓越贡献也让他在1990年获得格莱美奖终身成就奖。

二 看电影学音标

电影简介：

《居家男人》（*Family man*）是2000年的美国电影，由著名影星尼古拉斯·凯奇主演。

今天是杰克和凯特的结婚周年纪念日，杰克带凯特去高级餐馆吃饭来庆祝他们的结婚周年纪念日。（节选自《居家男人》）

Kate: Jack, can we afford this place?

Jack: I'm taking ['teɪkɪŋ] my baby ['beɪbi] out for our anniversary, damn the costs.

Waiter: May [meɪ] I have your order now?

Jack: We'll have the terrine of quail breast with shitake mushrooms, to start. Then the veal medallions in raspberry truffle sauce and the sea scallops with pureed artichoke hearts.

Waiter: Very good, sir. And may [meɪ] I say [seɪ] those are excellent selections?

Jack: You may [meɪ]. Also, we'll have a bottle of Lafite '82.

Kate: Honey, that's an $800 bottle of wine.

Jack: We'll just have some red wine by the glass.

凯特：杰克，这里不会太贵吧？

杰克：我们庆祝纪念日，管它贵不贵。

侍者：来点什么？

杰克：先来一份砂锅鹌鹑肉煮蘑菇，然后薄片小牛肉淋覆盆子酱汁，然后鲍鱼煮朝鲜蓟花苞。

侍者：很好，先生。您真会点菜。

杰克：过奖，再来一瓶82年的拉菲。

凯特：亲爱的，一瓶要800美元呢。

杰克：那就两杯红葡萄酒吧。

Unit 8 [aɪ]

[aɪ]

发音要素

发双元音[aɪ]时，先发[a]音，然后滑向[ɪ]音。舌尖抵住下齿。发此音的关键是要把[a]音发足，注意从开到合的滑动。

[a]

[ɪ]

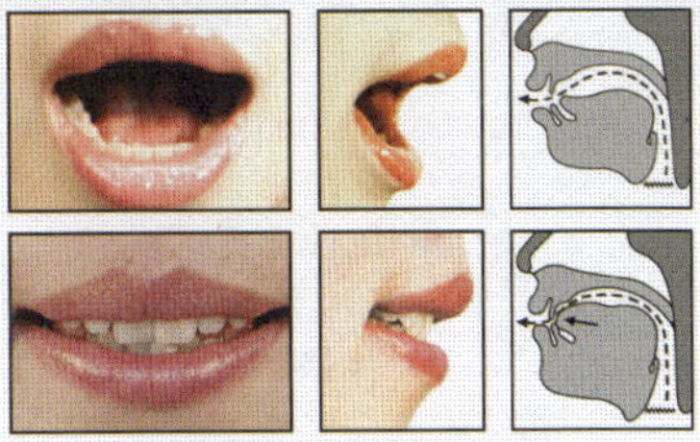

大话发音

这个音和汉语中的“爱”音相似，不过口形要更大更圆，而后转小。

这是英语中嘴巴张得最大的一个音了，注意要发得圆润饱满啊。

爱

发音代言人

eye

[aɪ] 眼睛

常见发音字母及字母组合

音标	对应字母	自然发音规则	单词示例
[aɪ]	i	字母i在开音节单词中发[aɪ]音。	kite [kaɪt] 风筝
[aɪ]	y	字母y在单词中可发[aɪ]音。	sky [skaɪ] 天空

[aɪ]	ie	字母组合ie可发[aɪ]音。	lie [laɪ] 说谎
[aɪ]	ye	字母组合ye可发[aɪ]音。	goodbye [ˌgʊd'baɪ] 再见
[aɪ]	igh	字母组合igh可发[aɪ]音。	high [haɪ] 高的
[aɪ]	eye	字母组合eye可发[aɪ]音。	eye [aɪ] 眼睛

发音操练

[aɪ]	
I [aɪ] 我	like [laɪk] 喜欢
wife [waɪf] 妻子	shy [ʃaɪ] 害羞的
style [staɪl] 风格	die [daɪ] 死
night [naɪt] 夜晚	fight [faɪt] 打斗
ride [raɪd] 骑	mind [maɪnd] 头脑

基础短语

- a quiet ['kwaɪət] night [naɪt] 一个安静的夜晚
- widen ['waɪdən] my horizon [hə'raɪzn] 开阔了我的视野
- at the sight [saɪt] of 一见到……
- pay a price [praɪs] 付出代价
- swim with the tide [taɪd] 随波逐流
- tigers ['taɪgəz] and lions ['laɪənz] 老虎和狮子

以句识音

1. Prices ['praɪsɪz] are sky-high ['skaɪ'haɪ] these days.

这些日子物价高得不得了。

2. I don't know why [waɪ] she is on her high [haɪ] horse.
我不知道她为什么如此趾高气扬。

3. He is light [laɪt]-hearted but short-sighted ['saɪtɪd].
他无忧无虑但目光短浅。

4. She is only telling a white [waɪt] lie [laɪ].
她只是说了一个善意的谎言。

5. Time [taɪm] and tide [taɪd] wait for no man.
时不我待。（英谚）

6. Out of sight [saɪt], out of mind [maɪnd].
眼不见，心不烦。（英谚）

经典绕口令（运动你的舌头）

1. I like [laɪk] to ride [raɪd] my light [laɪt] white [waɪt] bike [baɪk], and fly [flaɪ] a white [waɪt] light [laɪt] kite [kaɪt] with my wife [waɪf].
我喜欢和我妻子一起边骑着那白色的轻型车边放白色的轻风筝。

2. Mike [maɪk] likes [laɪks] to write [raɪt] by the bright [braɪt] light [laɪt] at night [naɪt].
麦克喜欢夜晚在一盏明亮的灯下写作。

3. A tidy ['taɪdi] tiger ['taɪgə] tied [taɪd] a tie [taɪ] tighter ['taɪtə] to tidy ['taɪdi] her tiny ['taɪni] tail.
一只整洁的老虎将领带系紧，清洁它的小尾巴。

4. A writer ['raɪtə] named Wright [raɪt] was instructing his little son how to write [raɪt] Wright [raɪt] right [raɪt]. He said: "It is not right [raɪt] to write [raɪt] Wright [raɪt] as 'rite' [raɪt]—try[traɪ] to write [raɪt] Wright [raɪt] aright [ə'raɪt]!"
一个名叫"Wright"的作家正在指导他年幼的儿子怎样把"Wright"写对。他说："把'Wright'写成'rite'是不对的—要把'Wright'写正确！"

5. There's no need to light [laɪt] a night [naɪt] light [laɪt], on a light [laɪt] night [naɪt] like tonight [tə'naɪt]; for a night [naɪt] light's[laɪts] just a slight [slaɪt] light [laɪt], on a light [laɪt] night [naɪt] like tonight [tə'naɪt].
没有必要点燃一盏夜灯，在一个像今晚这样明亮的夜晚；因为在今晚这样明亮的夜晚，夜灯的光已经微不足道了。

影音荟萃

一 听音乐学音标

Goodbye
再见

Air Supply

I can see the pain living in your eyes [aɪz]	我看得见你眼中的痛楚
And I know how hard you try [traɪ]	我也晓得你曾努力尝试
You deserve to have so much more	你应该得到更多
I can feel your heart and I sympathize ['sɪmpəθaɪz]	我能感同身受，心有所悯
And I'll never criticize ['krɪtɪsaɪz] all you've	你在我生命中的意义
ever meant to my life [laɪf]	我绝不多做评断
I don't want to let you down	我不想让你失望
I don't want to lead you on	不想带领你走
I don't want to hold you back	我不想挽回你
From where you might [maɪt] belong	从你归属的地方
You would never ask me why [waɪ]	你从来不问我原因
My heart is so disguised [dɪs'gaɪzd]	我的内心充满伪装
I just can't live a lie [laɪ] anymore	我不能再活在谎言中
I would rather hurt myself	我宁愿伤害自己
Than to ever make you cry [kraɪ]	也不愿让你哭泣
There's nothing left to say but goodbye[ˌgʊd'baɪ]	除了再见，还能说什么
You deserve the chance at the kind of love	你该拥有爱的机会
I'm not sure I'm worthy of	我不确定自己是否值得
Losing you is painful to me	失去你，我十分痛苦
I don't want to let you down	我不想让你失望
I don't want to lead you on	不想带领你走
I don't want to hold you back	我不想挽回你

From where you might [maɪt] belong	从你归属的地方
You would never ask me why [waɪ]	你从来不问我原因
My heart is so disguised [dɪs'gaɪzd]	我的内心充满伪装
I just can't live a lie [laɪ] anymore	我不能再活在谎言中
I would rather hurt myself	我宁愿伤害自己
Than to ever make you cry [kraɪ]	也不愿让你哭泣
There's nothing left to say but goodbye [ˌgʊd'baɪ]	除了再见，还能说什么

You would never ask me why [waɪ]	你从来不问我原因
My heart is so disguised [dɪs'gaɪzd]	我的内心充满伪装
I just can't live a lie [laɪ] anymore...	我不能再活在谎言中……
I would rather hurt myself	我宁愿伤害自己
Than to ever make you cry [kraɪ]	也不愿让你哭泣
There's nothing left to try [traɪ]	已没有机会可以再试了
Now it's gonna hurt us both	虽然这将会伤害我俩
It's no other way than to say goodbye [ˌgʊd'baɪ]	除了说再见，别无他路

歌曲评论

Air Supply（空中补给合唱团）是在20世纪70~80年代享誉全球的慢摇滚组合。1976年成立于澳洲，1980年进军美国乐坛，当年即取得惊人成绩，首张专辑《迷失爱中》（*Lost in Love*）先后有九首歌曲打入当年流行音乐排行榜前10名，从而使其走向了超级乐队的地位。乐队由主要从事创作的格雷厄姆·拉塞尔（Graham Russell）和主唱歌手拉塞尔·希契科克（Russell Hitchcock）组成。

Air Supply有着近30年音乐路程，*Goodbye* 是其经典歌曲之一。情感纯粹、音乐简洁、旋律抒情优美是Air Supply最大的特点。因为纯净，所以强烈直击人心。在渴望简洁的今天，全世界又掀起Air Supply的热潮。Air Supply天使般纯净而激情的歌声，已经成为我们内心最深处的风景，与我们的生命同行。

二 看电影学音标

电影简介：

《舞出我人生3》（*Step Up 3*）由朱浩伟执导，瑞奇·马兰博瑞和沙妮·文森主演。故事讲述了街舞爱好者卢克、娜塔莉和纽约舞蹈大学新生摩斯组成一队参加地下比舞大赛。和前几部不同，这次影片采用了3D立体电影形式，可以让观众有身临其境的感觉。

卢克向舞蹈爱好者们问了一个问题：“你为什么跳舞？”听听大家是怎么回答的吧。（节选自《舞出我人生3》）

—Why do you dance?

—Because it’s like [laɪk] breathing, it’s like [laɪk] walking to me.

—I’m [aɪm] not pretending, and when I [aɪ] dance, I [aɪ] don’t pretend.

—I’m [aɪm] more myself [maɪ'self] when I [aɪ] dance than any other moment in the day.

—I [aɪ] dance to become someone else.

—你为什么跳舞？

—对于我来说，舞蹈就是呼吸，就是走路。

—不做作。跳舞时，我毫不做作。

—一天当中，跳舞时，我比任何时候都更像自己。

—我跳舞是想成为另一个自己。

Unit 9 [ɔɪ]

[ɔɪ]

发音要素

发双元音[ɔɪ]时，双唇从圆到扁，口形从开到合。发好这个音的关键是先要把短元音[ɒ]发足，然后滑向[ɪ]音。

[ɒ]

[ɪ]

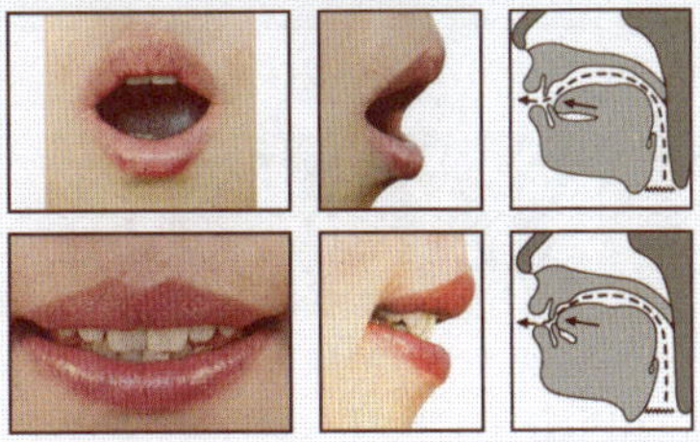

大话发音

这个音类似于“哦咦”的发音。

先发出“哦”的音，再发出“咦”的音，连在一起，就是这个双元音的发音了。

哦咦

发音代言人

boy

[bɔɪ] 男孩

常见发音字母及字母组合

音标	对应字母	自然发音规则	单词示例
[ɔɪ]	oi	字母组合oi在单词中发[ɔɪ]音。	coin [kɔɪn] 硬币
[ɔɪ]	oy	字母组合oy在单词中可发[ɔɪ]音。	toy [tɔɪ] 玩具

发音操练

[ɔɪ]	
boil [bɔɪl] 煮沸	soil [sɔɪl] 土壤
oil [ɔɪl] 油	choice [tʃɔɪs] 选择
join [dʒɔɪn] 参加	joy [dʒɔɪ] 欢乐
soy [sɔɪ] 大豆	annoy [ə'nɔɪ] 打扰；使烦恼
enjoy [ɪn'dʒɔɪ] 喜欢	oyster ['ɔɪstə] 牡蛎

基础短语

- an office boy[bɔɪ] 一个办公室勤杂工
- boiling ['bɔɪlɪŋ] point [pɔɪnt] 沸点
- toil [tɔɪl] and moil [mɔɪl] 辛辛苦苦地工作
- spoil [spɔɪl] the child 溺爱孩子
- point [pɔɪnt] by point [pɔɪnt] 逐点逐条
- a joyful ['dʒɔɪfl] voyage ['vɔɪɪdʒ] 一次愉快的旅行

以句识音

1. The boy [bɔɪ] enjoys [ɪn'dʒɔɪz] playing with the toys [tɔɪz].
   那个男孩喜欢玩这些玩具。
2. Nobody wants to employ [ɪm'plɔɪ] the spoiled [spɔɪld] boy [bɔɪ].
   没人喜欢雇用被宠坏的孩子。
3. I was quite annoyed [ə'nɔɪd] by his casual attitude.
   我很讨厌他那种漫不经心的态度。
4. Roy [rɔɪ] toiled [tɔɪld] on the soil [sɔɪl].
   罗伊在地里辛勤劳作。

5. Spare the rod, spoil [spɔɪl] the child.
不打不成才。（英谚）

6. One man's meat is another man's poison ['pɔɪzn].
你喜欢的东西，别人不一定喜欢。（英谚）

经典绕口令（运动你的舌头）

1. Roy [rɔɪ] is a spoiled [spɔɪld] boy [bɔɪ].
罗伊是个被宠坏的男孩。

2. One boy [bɔɪ] is a boy [bɔɪ]; two boys [bɔɪz] half a boy [bɔɪ]; three boys [bɔɪz] no boy [bɔɪ].
一个和尚有水喝，两个和尚抬水喝，三个和尚没水喝。

3. Come on boys [bɔɪz] and girls, clap your hands and join [dʒɔɪn] me.
来吧，男孩女孩们，拍拍小手来参加。

4. Come on and join [dʒɔɪn] into the game.
来吧，快来做游戏。

5. Let's join [dʒɔɪn] hands and play a joyful ['dʒɔɪfl] game for boys [bɔɪz] and girls.
大家一起手拉手，做个我们都喜欢的游戏吧。

影音荟萃

一 听音乐学音标

Pretty Boy
漂亮男孩

M2M

I lie awake at night
See things in black and white
I've only got you inside my mind
You know you have made me blind

晚上我躺在床上没有一点睡意
有的故事在脑海里如黑白电影般掠过
你的形象无时无刻不在我脑中闪动
我的眼里只有你

I lie awake and pray	我清醒地躺在床上祈祷
That you will look my way	祈祷你会看见我
I have all this longing in my heart	我的心中充满渴望
I knew it right from the start	一开始我就知道
Oh my pretty pretty boy [bɔɪ] I love you	我的漂亮男孩，我爱你
Like I never ever loved no one before you	在你之前我从未这样爱过一个人
Pretty pretty boy [bɔɪ] of mine	我的漂亮男孩
Just tell me you love me too	告诉我你也爱我
Oh my pretty pretty boy [bɔɪ] I need you	我的漂亮男孩，我需要你
Oh my pretty pretty boy [bɔɪ] I do	我的漂亮男孩，我真的需要你
Let me inside make me stay right beside you	让我进入你的心里，留在你身边
I used to write your name	我曾写下你的名字
And put it in a frame	并把它框起来
And sometimes I think I hear you call	有时我以为我听见你的呼唤
Right from my bedroom wall	从我卧室的墙上
You stay a little while	你待了一会儿
And touch me with your smile	用你的微笑打动我的心
And what can I say to make you mine	我该说什么才能赢得你的心
To reach out for you in time	才能及时掳获你
Oh my pretty pretty boy [bɔɪ] I love you	我的漂亮男孩，我爱你
Like I never ever loved no one before you	在你之前我从未这样爱过一个人
Pretty pretty boy [bɔɪ] of mine	我的漂亮男孩
Just tell me you love me too	告诉我你也爱我
Oh my pretty pretty boy [bɔɪ] I need you	我的漂亮男孩，我需要你
Oh my pretty pretty boy [bɔɪ] I do	我的漂亮男孩，我真的需要你
Let me inside	让我进到你心里
Make me stay right beside you	让我留在你身旁
Oh pretty boy [bɔɪ], pretty boy [bɔɪ], pretty boy [bɔɪ]	我的漂亮男孩
Say you love me too	说你也爱我
Oh my pretty pretty boy [bɔɪ] I love you	我的漂亮男孩，我爱你
Like I never ever loved no one before you	在你之前我从未这样爱过一个人
Pretty pretty boy [bɔɪ] of mine	我的漂亮男孩
Just tell me you love me too	告诉我你也爱我

Oh my pretty pretty boy [bɔɪ] I need you	我的漂亮男孩，我需要你
Oh my pretty pretty boy [bɔɪ] I do	我的漂亮男孩，我真的需要你
Let me inside	让我进到你心里
Make me stay right beside you	让我留在你身旁

歌曲评论

这首歌是M2M组合（窈窕美眉）演唱的处女专辑 *Shades of Purple* 中的主打歌，也是M2M最火的歌曲。M2M是由两个来自挪威的小女孩玛莉特及玛莉安所组成的乐团组合，她们小时候就是很好的伙伴，热爱音乐，所以就组成了这个组合。由于两人名字都是M开头，所以就叫M2M。现在这个组合的成员已单飞。

二 看电影学音标

电影简介：

《禁闭岛》（Shutter Island）是根据美国小说家丹尼斯·勒翰（Dennis Lehane）的同名小说改编的电影。1954年，联邦警官泰迪（莱昂纳多·迪卡普里奥饰）和搭档查克（马克·鲁弗洛饰）乘船来到波士顿附近的禁闭岛精神病犯监狱调查一桩离奇失踪案。泰迪极度怕水，坐船时晕船。泰迪的妻子在火灾中被熏死了。两人聊起了发生在禁闭岛精神病犯监狱里的离奇案件。（节选自《禁闭岛》）

—You okay, boss?	—没事吧，老大？
—Yeah, I'm fine. I just, I just can't... can't stomach the water. You're my new partner.	—没事，就是……，就是有点……受不了这水。你是我的新搭档。
—That's right.	—没错。
—Not the best way to meet, with my head halfway down the toilet ['tɔɪlət].	—头次跟你见面就吐了，有点不好意思。
—Doesn't exactly square with "Teddy Daniels, the man, the legend". I'll give you that.	—与“传奇人物泰迪·丹尼尔斯”确实不怎么相称。恕我直言。
—The legend? What the hell you boys [bɔɪz] smoking over there in Portland, anyway?	—传奇人物？你们这些家伙在波特兰成天瞎扯什么呢？

Unit 10 [aʊ]

[aʊ]

发音要素

发双元音[aʊ]时，由前元音[a]滑向后元音[ʊ]。舌位由低到高，口形由大到小。注意将音发足。

[a]

[ʊ]

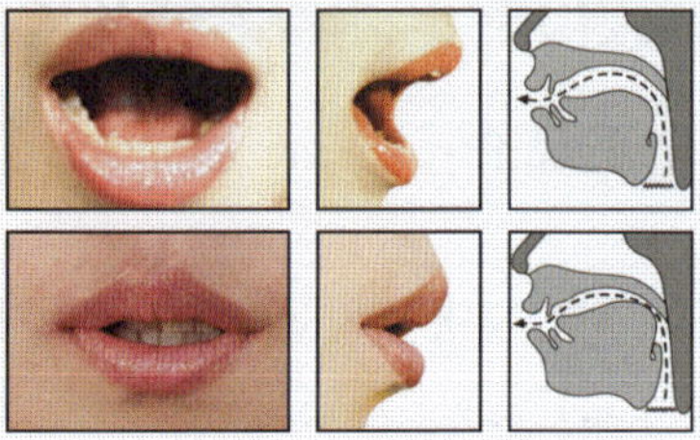

大话发音

这个双元音和汉字“啊呜”的发音相似。

老虎要吃猎物的时候，张开血盆大口，“啊呜”一口吞下去。

啊呜

发音代言人

cow

[kaʊ] 奶牛

常见发音字母及字母组合

音标	对应字母	自然发音规则	单词示例
[aʊ]	ou	字母组合ou在单词中可发[aʊ]音。	**house** [haʊs] 房子
[aʊ]	ow	字母组合ow在单词中可发[aʊ]音。	**town** [taʊn] 城镇

发音操练

[aʊ]

loud [laʊd] 大声的	**south** [saʊθ] 南方
mountain ['maʊntən] 山	**proud** [praʊd] 骄傲的
shout [ʃaʊt] 喊叫	**how** [haʊ] 怎么；如何
crowd [kraʊd] 人群	**now** [naʊ] 现在
flower ['flaʊə] 花	**tower** ['taʊə] 塔；高楼

基础短语

- how [haʊ] about [ə'baʊt] 怎样
- shout [ʃaʊt] out [aʊt] 大声喊叫
- from mouth [maʊθ] to mouth [maʊθ] 口口相传
- cowboy ['kaʊˌbɔɪ] and cowhouse ['kaʊhaʊs] 牛仔和牛舍
- downtown ['daʊn'taʊn] area 闹市区
- bow down [daʊn] 鞠躬

以句识音

1. Open your mouth [maʊθ] and round [raʊnd] your lips.
   张开嘴，嘴张成圆形。
2. What about [ə'baʊt] going to the south [saʊθ] for the holiday?
   去南方度假怎么样？
3. She is very proud [praʊd] of her new house [haʊs].
   她很为她的新房子骄傲。
4. A fountain ['faʊntən] spouts [spaʊts] water into the air.
   喷泉将水喷向空中。

5. Mr. Brown [braʊn] spends hours ['aʊəz] after hours ['aʊəz] among his flowers ['flaʊəz].
布朗先生在花房中可以废寝忘食。

6. March wind and April showers ['ʃaʊəz] bring May flowers ['flaʊəz].
三月的风，四月的雨，迎来五月的鲜花。

经典绕口令（运动你的舌头）

1. Round [raʊnd] and round [raʊnd] the house [haʊs] went the crowd [craʊd].
人群围着房子转来转去。

2. That's how [haʊ] you pronounce [prə'naʊns] the word "plough" [plaʊ].
那就是你发"plough"这个音的方式。

3. Some sounds ['saʊndz] are pronounced [prə'naʊnst] with the mouth [maʊθ] well open.
有些音发音时要把嘴完全张开。

4. The crowd [kraʊd] gathered around [ə'raʊnd] the house [haʊs] and shouted ['ʃaʊtɪd] slogans.
人们聚集在房子周围喊着口号。

5. We had no doubt ['daʊt] about [ə'baʊt] the result as it had been tested a thousand ['θaʊznd] times.
我们对结果毫不怀疑，因为它已经被检验上千次了。

影音荟萃

一 听音乐学音标

The Sound of Silence
寂静之声

Paul Simon & Garfunkel

Hello darkness, my old friend
I've come to talk with you again
Because a vision softly creeping
Left its seeds while I was sleeping

嘿，黑夜啊，我的老友
我又来找你聊天了
因为有种幻觉正悄悄向我袭来
趁我熟睡时暗暗播下了种子

And the vision that was planted in my brain
Still remains
Within the sound [saʊnd] of silence

这种幻觉在我脑海中生根发芽
萦绕盘旋不去
在寂静无声的此刻

In restless dreams I walked alone
Narrow streets of cobblestone
'Neath the halo of a street lamp
I turned my collar to the cold and damp
When my eyes were stabbed by the flash of a neon light
That split the night
And touched the sound [saʊnd] of silence

在无数不安的梦中我茕茕独行
行走在狭窄的鹅卵石街道上
头顶上街灯的光晕将我笼罩
我竖起衣领以抗御这湿冷的夜
当我的眼睛为耀眼的霓虹灯光
所迷时
它也划破了夜空
打破了黑夜的寂静

And in the naked light I saw
Ten thousand ['θaʊznd] people, maybe more
People talking without speaking
People hearing without listening
People writing songs that voices never share
And no one dare
Disturb the sound [saʊnd] of silence

在炫目的灯光下
我看到人头攒动
有的人说而不言
有的人听而不闻
有的人在写着那些从不会被传唱的歌
但没有人敢于去
打破这份寂静

Fools said I, you do not know
Silence like a cancer grows
Hear my words that I might teach you
Take my arms that I might reach you
But my words like silent raindrops fell
And echoed in the wells of silence

我说道：愚蠢的人啊，你们不知道
寂静如同顽疾滋长
听我说的话，让我来教导你
抓紧我的手，让我来救你
但是我的话却如寂静无声的雨点落下
徒然回响在沉静的井里

And the people bowed [baʊd] and prayed
To the neon god they made
And the sign flashed out its warning
In the words that it was forming
And the sign said, the words of the prophets
Are written on the subway walls
And tenement halls
And whisper'd in the sounds [saʊndz] of silence

人们仍然顶礼膜拜着
自己塑造的霓虹灯神
灯光中闪烁出告诫的语句
在字里行间指明
它告诉人们:先知的话语
已被写在地铁的墙上以及
出租公寓的走廊上
也在无声的寂静中被轻声传诵

歌曲评论

《寂静之声》（*The Sound of Silence*）是20世纪60年代民谣二人组Paul Simon & Garfunkel的成名作，在1967年作为美国电影《毕业生》的主题歌，非常受欢迎。1964年，西蒙和卡尔方灌制了这首曲子，之后迪夫·古鲁吉把这首曲子巧妙地电影音乐化了。

西蒙和卡尔方是现代历史上最重要的民谣先驱之一。他们清新纯净的民谣作品将长久地在喜爱的人中闪光。这个双人组合因参与舞台剧《爱丽丝梦游仙境》的演出而结识，并成立于1960年。1966年他们为达斯汀·霍夫曼主演的电影《毕业生》创作原声带，主题曲《*Mrs. Robinson*》与原声带双双夺冠，获得年度唱片和最佳流行唱片两座格莱美奖。

二 看电影学音标

电影简介：

《辣妈辣妹》（*Freaky Friday*）是迪士尼1976年推出的电影，故事根据玛丽·罗杰斯的小说改编，后来迪士尼又对该经典老片进行了翻拍并于2003年8月推出。本片的主要人物是一个中产家庭的母女俩，由于个性和修养的截然不同，母亲和女儿对调身体以后因不能适应，而闹出了一连串的笑话。

柯夫人和她的未婚夫莱恩带着孩子们去“旧中国城”餐馆吃饭，未来的继父很想讨安娜高兴，可安娜却似乎不领情。（节选自《辣妈辣妹》）

Owner: Hello. How [haʊ] are you?	店主：柯医生，你好啊。
Mrs. Coleman: Hello, Pei-Pei.	柯夫人：你好，佩佩。
Owner: Anna, Harry, you're so big now [naʊ]. What happened? Are you happy for your mommy?	店主：安娜，哈利，你们现在已经长这么大了啊。发生什么事了？你们为自己的妈妈高兴吗？
Anna: About [ə'baʊt] what?	安娜：高兴什么？
Owner: Oh. She's such a joker. Who's catering? Chinese food good luck.	店主：噢！她真爱开玩笑。宴席谁办？中国菜能带来好运。
Mrs. Coleman: Actually, It's all planned already.	柯夫人：其实全都计划好了。
Owner: Okay, how [haʊ] about [ə'baʊt] me?	店主：找我吧。

Unit 11 [əʊ]

[əʊ]

发音要素

发双元音[əʊ]时，由中元音[ə]滑向后元音[ʊ]，舌位由半低到高，口形由半开到小。注意将音发足。

[ə]

[ʊ]

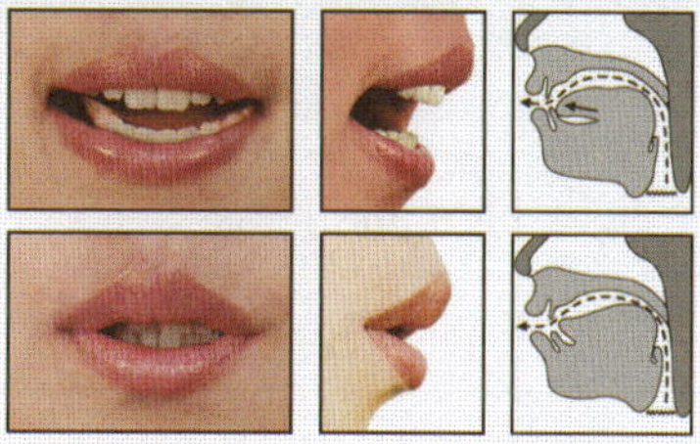

大话发音

[əʊ] 也是两个音的组合，好像汉语的“欧”，但发音更圆润一些。

在发“欧”音的时候，一定要把这个字的音拖得更长一些。

欧

发音代言人

boat

[bəʊt] 小船

常见发音字母及字母组合

音标	对应字母	自然发音规则	单词示例
[əʊ]	o	字母o在单词中可发[əʊ]音。	home [həʊm] 家
[əʊ]	ow	字母组合ow在单词中可发[əʊ]音。	snow [snəʊ] 雪

[əʊ]	oa	字母组合oa在单词中可发[əʊ]音。	**goat** [gəʊt] 山羊
[əʊ]	oe	字母组合oe在单词中可发[əʊ]音。	**toe** [təʊ] 脚趾

发音操练

[əʊ]	
hope [həʊp] 希望	**cold** [kəʊld] 冷的
gold [gəʊld] 黄金	**post** [pəʊst] 职位
low [ləʊ] 低的	**show** [ʃəʊ] 显示
blow [bləʊ] 一击；打击	**road** [rəʊd] 路
poem [pəʊɪm] 诗歌	**foe** [fəʊ] 敌人

基础短语

- go [gəʊ] home [həʊm] 回家
- no [nəʊ] hope [həʊp] 没有希望
- make a toast [təʊst] 祝酒
- on the road [rəʊd] 在路上
- in a hole [həʊl] 处于困境
- Holy ['həʊli] Ghost [gəʊst] 圣灵

以句识音

1. He feels cold [kəʊld], and lonely ['ləʊnli], too.
他感到很冷，也很孤独。

2. They rowed [rəʊd] the boat [bəʊt] along the coast [kəʊst].
他们沿着海岸线划船。

3. He rose [rəʊz] to propose [prə'pəʊz] the toast [təʊst].
他站起来祝酒。

4. He smokes [sməʊks] roasted ['rəʊstɪd] tobacco [tə'bækəʊ].
他抽烤烟。

5. Little stroke [strəʊk] fell great oaks [əʊks].
水滴石穿。（英谚）

6. A rolling ['rəʊlɪŋ] stone [stəʊn] gathers no [nəʊ] moss.
滚石不生苔；转行不聚财。（英谚）

经典绕口令（运动你的舌头）

1. Are our oars oak [əʊk]?
我们的桨是橡木吗？

2. You know [nəʊ] I know [nəʊ] that you know [nəʊ]. I know [nəʊ] that you know [nəʊ] that I know [nəʊ].
你明白我知道你知道这件事。我也知道你了解我所知道的。

3. Amid the mists and coldest ['kəʊldɪst] frosts,
With barest wrists and stoutest boasts [bəʊsts],
He thrusts his fists against the posts [pəʊsts],
And still insists he sees the ghosts [gəʊsts].
雾蒙蒙，冰霜冻，
手腕儿空空，话儿涌，
只见他猛将拳头往柱子上砸，
直说自己把鬼碰。

4. If you notice ['nəʊtɪs] this notice ['nəʊtɪs] you will notice ['nəʊtɪs] that this notice ['nəʊtɪs] is not worth noticing ['nəʊtɪsɪŋ].
若你看到这张告示，你会发现这张告示是不值得留意的。

5. Moses ['məʊzɪz] supposes [sə'pəʊzɪz] his toes [təʊz] are roses ['rəʊzɪz], but Moses ['məʊzɪz] supposes [sə'pəʊzɪz] erroneously [ɪ'rəʊnɪəslɪ]. For Moses ['məʊzɪz], he knows [nəʊz] his toes [təʊz] aren't roses ['rəʊzɪz] as Moses ['məʊzɪz] supposes [sə'pəʊzɪz] his toes [təʊz] to be!
摩西假设他的脚趾是玫瑰，可是，摩西的假设错了。摩西知道他的脚趾并不是玫瑰，因为他只是假设它们是玫瑰。

影音荟萃

一 听音乐学音标

Love Story
爱的故事

Taylor Swift

We were both [bəʊθ] young when I first saw you
I close [kləʊz] my eyes and the flashback starts
I'm standing there on a balcony in summer air

See the lights, see the party, the ball gowns
See you make your way through the crowd
and say hello [he'ləʊ], little did I know [nəʊ]
that you were Romeo ['rəʊmiəʊ]
You were throwing ['θrəʊɪŋ] pebbles
And my daddy said, "Stay away from Juliet."
And I was crying on the staircase
Begging you, "Please, don't go [gəʊ]."
And I said,
"Romeo ['rəʊmiəʊ], take me somewhere we can be alone [ə'ləʊn]
I'll be waiting; all there's left to do is run

You'll be the prince and I'll be the princess"

It's a love story, baby, just say "Yes."

当我第一次见到你的时候，我们都还年轻
我闭上眼睛，一幕幕往事又在脑海中重现
我站在阳台上，空气里，浓浓的，是夏天的味道

看见灯火，看见热闹的舞会，华丽的盛装
看见你穿过拥挤的人群
对我打招呼问好，至少让我知道了你的名字叫“罗密欧”
你（对着我家的窗户）扔小石子儿
我爸爸气急败坏地叫你离我远一点
（可是这时）我却蜷坐在楼梯间里偷偷地抹眼泪
在心底里祈求你不要离开
我说：
“罗密欧，带我走吧，去一个我们可以相依相偎的地方
我一直在等待（这一天），现在唯一能做的就是逃离

（到那时）我们就可以像王子和公主一样（快乐地在一起）”

这是多么美好的爱情故事呀，亲爱的，答应我吧

So I sneak out to the garden to see you	于是，我偷偷摸摸地溜到小花园去见你
We keep quiet ’cause we’re dead if they knew	我们压抑着声息，被他们发现我们就完蛋了
So close [kləuz] your eyes	所以，请闭上你的双眼
escape this town for a little while	逃避这个喧嚣的尘世，即使只有如此短暂的一刻
’Cause you were Romeo ['rəumiəu]	正因为你的出现
I was a scarlet letter	我的生命才有了如此鲜艳的光彩
And my daddy said, “Stay away from Juliet.”	我爸爸气急败坏地叫你离我远一点
But you were everything to me	但你对我来说是我的全部
I was begging you, “Please, don’t go [gəu].”	于是，我无时无刻不在祈求你不要离开
And I said	我说:
“Romeo ['rəumiəu], take me somewhere we can	“罗密欧，带我走吧，去一个我们可以相依
be alone [ə'ləun]	相偎的地方
I’ll be waiting;	我一直在等待（这一天），
all there’s left to do is run	现在唯一能做的就是逃离
You’ll be the prince	（到那时）我们就可以像王子和公主一样
and I’ll be the princess”	（快乐地在一起）”
It’s a love story, baby, just say “Yes.”	这是多么美好的爱情故事呀，亲爱的，答应我吧
Romeo ['rəumiəu], save me	罗密欧，拯救我痛苦的灵魂吧
They’re tryin’ to tell me how to feel	他们总在试图左右我的思想
This love is difficult, but it’s real	我们的爱情面对着重重的困难，却无比的忠诚坚贞
Don’t be afraid, we’ll make it out of this mess	不要害怕，（我相信）我们终究会冲破困境
It’s a love story, baby, just say “Yes.”	这就是我们的爱情，亲爱的，请答应我
I got tired of waiting	我厌倦了似乎无穷无尽的等待
Wondering if you were ever comin’ around	渐渐开始怀疑你是否会如期出现在我面前
My faith in you was fading	曾经坚定的信念，也渐渐开始动摇
When I met you on the outskirts of town	当我再一次在小镇的郊外与你相会
And I said	我说:
“Romeo ['rəumiəu], save me	“罗密欧，救救我，
I’ve been feeling so [səu] alone [ə'ləun]	我再也无法承受这孤独的煎熬
I keep waiting for you but you never come	我一直在等着你，而你却杳然无踪
Is this in my head?	我脑子里乱糟糟的

I don't know [nəʊ] what to think"
He knelt to the ground and pulled out a ring and said,
"Marry me, Juliet. You'll never have to be alone [ə'ləʊn]
I love you and that's all I really know [nəʊ]
I talked to your dad
Go [gəʊ] pick out a white dress
It's a love story, baby, just say 'Yes.' "

我不知道我在想什么"
梦中的他此时正虔诚地跪在我的面前，拿出手中的戒指，他说：
"嫁给我吧，朱丽叶，你再也不会感受到孤独
我只知道，我爱你
我与你的父亲已经谈过
去挑选嫁衣吧
这就是我们的爱情故事，亲爱的，请答应我"

Oh [əʊ], oh [əʊ]
We were both [bəʊθ] young when I first saw you

噢，我不禁又想起了
我第一次见到你的时候，我们都还年轻

歌曲评论

《爱的故事》（*Love Story*）是由泰勒·斯威夫特（Taylor Swift）作词谱曲，Nathan Chapman制作。*Love Story*作为Taylor第二张专辑*Fearless*的主打曲目，在2008年7月12日由大机器唱片公司（Big Machine Records）发行。*Love Story*一经发布，便在世界各地卖出超过800万次的音乐下载，也因此成为有史以来世界畅销单曲之一，并使得泰勒·斯威夫特在当时成为美国拥有最畅销数字单曲的女歌手。

泰勒·斯威夫特，1989年12月13日出生于美国宾夕法尼亚州，美国乡村音乐创作型女歌手。2006年，泰勒与独立唱片公司Big Machine签约并推出了首支单曲*Tim McGraw*，紧接着推出了首张同名专辑*Taylor Swift*，该专辑获得美国唱片业协会的5倍白金唱片认证。第二张专辑*Fearless*于2008年11月11日发行，在"*Billboard 200*"专辑榜上一共获得11周冠军，并被美国唱片业协会认证为7倍白金唱片，与此同时依靠这张专辑收获无数格莱美奖项。2009年，泰勒被*Billboard*杂志评选为"年度艺人"。

二 看电影学音标

电影简介：

美国电影《诺丁山》（*Notting Hill*）拍摄于1998年，由朱莉娅·罗伯茨、休·格兰特、瑞斯·伊凡斯、迪兰·莫兰、约翰·斯拉普内尔、米莎·巴顿主演。讲述小人物威廉与明星安娜的爱情故事。

威廉在伦敦的诺丁山经营着一家书店，这天大明星安娜·斯科特来光顾他的书店了，所以他心情很好，现在正在帮自己的店员买橙汁，可是不幸又幸运的是，他把橙汁洒到了安娜的衣服上。他们是怎么解决这件事情的呢？（节选自《诺丁山》）

—Another one?

—Yes. No [nəʊ]. Let's go [gəʊ] crazy. I'll have an orange juice.

—Okay [əʊ'keɪ], thanks. Bye-bye.

—See you later.

—Oh [əʊ]! Oh [əʊ]! Shit!

—Oh [əʊ], my God! Bugger!

—还要一杯吗?

—好啊……不。就奢侈一回，我要橙汁。

—好，谢谢！ 再见!

—回见。

—该死!

—哦，对不起，非常抱歉。

Unit 12 [ɪə]

[ɪə]

发音要素

发双元音[ɪə]时，从[ɪ]音滑向[ə]音。前面的[ɪ]发得较清楚，后面的[ə]较弱。双唇始终半开。此音一定要发足。

[ɪ]

[ə]

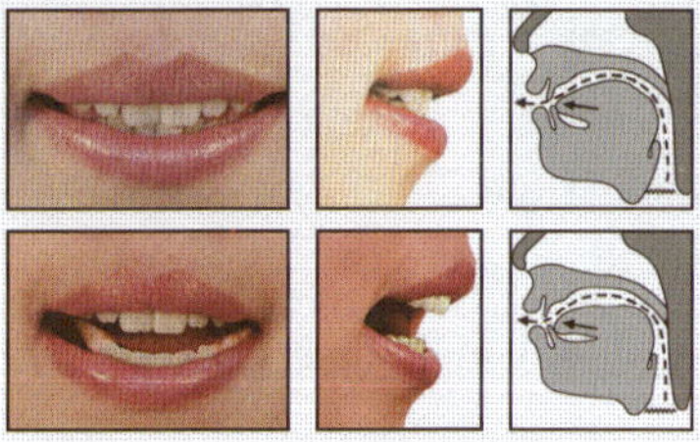

大话发音

[ɪə] 则是"咦"加"呃"。记得要连读。

先发"咦"，再发"呃"，连在一起像"叶儿"。

咦呃

发音代言人

ear

[ɪə] 耳朵

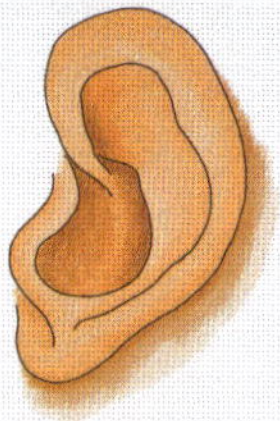

常见发音字母及字母组合

音标	对应字母	自然发音规则	单词示例
[ɪə]	ere	字母组合ere在单词中可发[ɪə]音。	here [hɪə] 这里
[ɪə]	ear	字母组合ear在单词中可发[ɪə]音。	tear [tɪə] 眼泪

[ɪə]	eer	字母组合eer在单词中发[ɪə]音。	**beer** [bɪə] 啤酒
[ɪə]	ea	字母组合ea在单词中可发[ɪə]音。	**real** [rɪəl] 真的
[ɪə]	e	字母e有时在单词中可发[ɪə]音。	**series** ['sɪəri:z] 系列
[ɪə]	iou	字母组合iou在单词中可发[ɪə]音。	**serious** ['sɪərɪəs] 严肃的

发音操练

[ɪə]	
mere [mɪə] 仅仅；只不过	**clear** [klɪə] 清楚的
dear [dɪə] 亲爱的	**hear** [hɪə] 听到；听见
peer [pɪə] 同龄人	**sheer** [ʃɪə] 完全的；十足的
serial ['sɪərɪəl] 连续的；一系列的	**spear** [spɪə] 矛；枪
furious ['fjʊərɪəs] 狂怒的；暴怒的	**area** ['eərɪə] 地区；区域

基础短语

- come here [hɪə] 到这来
- be all ears [ɪəz] 全神贯注地听
- my dearest ['dɪərɪst] 我最亲爱的
- fear [fɪə] nothing 无所畏惧
- shear [ʃɪə] the sheep 剪羊毛
- drink the beer [bɪə] 喝啤酒

以句识音

1. He is quite serious ['sɪərɪəs] and really ['rɪəlɪ] sincere [sɪn'sɪə].
   他是很严肃也很真诚的。
2. Nobody wants to hear [hɪə] his mysterious [mɪ'stɪərɪəs] ideas [aɪ'dɪəz].
   没人想听他的神秘的想法。
3. There is a very good hotel around here [hɪə].
   附近有一家很好的饭店。
4. Things are clear [klɪə] and you don't need to fear [fɪə].
   事情都清楚了，你不必害怕了。
5. Cheers [tʃɪəz]!
   干杯！（祝酒用语）
6. That's a dear [dɪə].
   真是个好孩子。

经典绕口令（运动你的舌头）

1. Real weird [wɪəd] rear [rɪə] wheels.
   真正怪异的后轮胎。
2. I shed tears [tɪəz] for he shears [ʃɪəz] my dear [dɪə] toy deer [dɪə]'s ear [ɪə].
   我哭了，因为他剪了我亲爱的玩具鹿的耳朵。
3. A deer [dɪə] near [nɪə] me burst into tears [tɪəz].
   我旁边的一只鹿突然大哭起来。
4. Near [nɪə] an ear [ɪə], a nearer ['nɪərə] ear [ɪə], a nearly ['nɪəli] eerie ['ɪəri] ear [ɪə].
   靠近耳朵，一只更靠近的耳朵，一只几乎令人恐怖的耳朵。
5. Is there a beer [bɪə] house near [nɪə] here [hɪə]?
   附近有啤酒店吗？

影音荟萃

一 听音乐学音标

Right Here Waiting
此情可待

Richard Marx

Oceans apart day after day	远隔重洋，日复一日
And I slowly go insane	我一步步走向疯狂
I hear [hɪə] your voice on the line	电话里传来你的声音
But it doesn't stop the pain	但这无法让伤痛停止
If I see you next to never	倘若此生再难相见
How can we say forever	又怎能说和你长相厮守
Wherever you go	无论你去哪里
Whatever you do	无论你做什么
I will be right here [hɪə] waiting for you	我会一直在这里等你
Whatever it takes	无论付出什么代价
Or how my heart breaks	无论我多么心碎
I will be right here [hɪə] waiting for you	我会一直在这里等你
I took for granted all the times	我一直坚信
That I though would last somehow	我们一定能坚持到最后
I hear [hɪə] the laughter	回忆起你的欢笑
I taste the tears [tɪəz]	和你动人的泪水
But I can't get near [nɪə] you now	可是此刻却无法接近你
Oh can't you see it baby	哦，你看不见吗，宝贝
You've got me goin' crazy	你让我陷入痴狂
Wherever you go	无论你去哪里
Whatever you do	无论你做什么
I will be right here [hɪə] waiting for you	我会一直在这里等你
Whatever it takes	无论付出什么代价

Or how my heart breaks	无论我多么心碎
I will be right here [hɪə] waiting for you	我会一直在这里等你
I wonder how we can survive	我想知道
This romance	我们如何才能拯救这段感情
But in the end if I'm with you	但只要最终能和你在一起
I'll take the chance	我会奋不顾身
Oh can't you see it baby	哦，你看不见吗，宝贝
You've got me goin' crazy	你让我陷入痴狂
Wherever you go	无论你去哪里
Whatever you do	无论你做什么
I will be right here [hɪə] waiting for you	我会一直在这里等你
Whatever it takes	无论付出什么代价
Or how my heart breaks	无论我多么心碎
I will be right here [hɪə] waiting for you	我会一直在这里等你
waiting for you	等候着你

歌曲评论

理查德 · 马克斯（Richard Marx）不仅歌唱得好，他还能自己创作写歌，《此情可待》（*Right Here Waiting*）就是他自己写的一首名曲。《此情可待》曾在新加坡获得三张白金唱片的荣誉地位。世界上其他地方的歌手也纷纷用他的曲调重新填词翻唱，比如香港歌星钟镇涛的《红叶斜落我心寂寞时》。

理查德是一个集作曲、填词、演唱和音乐制作于一身的摇滚才子。他特别热衷于巡回演出，曾先后在美国、加拿大、日本等地巡回演出。他的大部分歌曲都是摇滚风格的。他自己表示，摇滚乐才是他的真正兴趣所在。

二 看电影学音标

电影简介:

《街角的商店》（*The Shop Around the Corner*）是著名电影喜剧大师刘别谦1940年执导的一部经典喜剧片，由詹姆斯·斯图尔特与玛格丽特·苏利文等主演。讲述一个商店里发生的种种故事。影片刻画小人物的寂寞心灵，有十分温馨动人的戏剧效果。此片被列入美国电影学会评选的“百年百大爱情类电影”，由美国国家电影保护局收藏。

诺瓦克小姐走进一家商店，店里的资深职员克拉里克先生热情地招呼着她。（节选自《街角的商店》）

Mr. Kralik: It’s an imported model. We have it in pigskin, several different colors... and with or without fitted accessories.

Miss Novak: I really ['rɪəli] didn’t come in to buy a bag.

Mr. Kralik: I beg your pardon. What can I show you?

Miss Novak: To tell you the truth, I really ['rɪəli] didn’t come in to buy anything.

Mr. Kralik: That’s perfectly all right. If you wish to look around, make yourself at home.

Miss Novak: Yes, thank you.

克拉里克先生: 这是本公司进口的样式，我们用猪皮制作。有好几种颜色，附不附配件都行。

诺瓦克小姐: 我不是来买袋子的。

克拉里克先生: 请你原谅，小姐。那么你想看什么呢?

诺瓦克小姐: 老实说，我不是来买东西的。

克拉里克先生: 那也没关系，如果你想到处看看，请便。

诺瓦克小姐: 好的，谢谢你。

Unit 13 [ʊə]

[ʊə]

发音要素

发双元音[ʊə]时，发音时，嘴唇从收圆到半开。发好这个音的关键是首先要把[ʊ]音发足，然后滑向[ə]音。

[ʊ]

[ə]

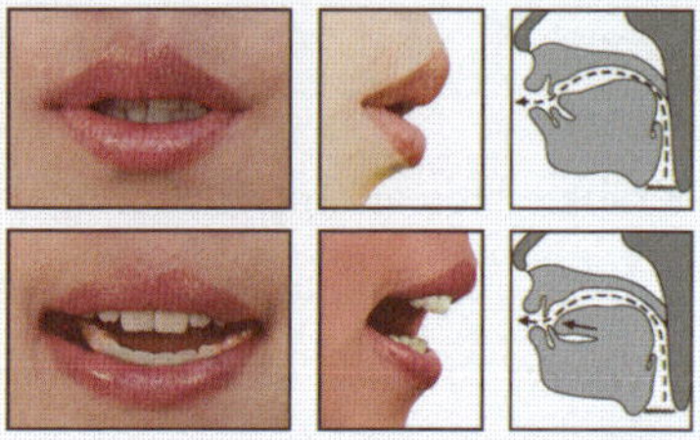

大话发音

这个音很像“呜呃”的发音。

在发“呜呃”的音时，一定要将“呜”的音拖长一些，然后再发出“呃”的音，前长后短。

呜呃

发音代言人

poor

[pʊə] 贫穷的

常见发音字母及字母组合

音标	对应字母	自然发音规则	单词示例
[ʊə]	our	字母组合our在单词中可发[ʊə]音。	tour [tʊə] 旅行
[ʊə]	ure	字母组合ure在单词中可发[ʊə] 音。 与其他音标组合可发[jʊə]音。	sure [ʃʊə] 确信的 pure [pjʊə] 纯净的

[ʊə]	oor	字母组合oor在单词中可发[ʊə]音。	moor [mʊə] 荒野
[ʊə]	ua	字母组合ua在单词中可发[ʊə]音。	casual ['kæʒʊəl] 偶然的

发音操练

[ʊə]	[jʊə]
poor [pʊə] 贫穷的	bureau ['bjʊərəʊ] 局，处
moor [mʊə] 荒野	impure [ɪm'pjʊə] 不纯的
lure [lʊə] 诱饵	cure [kjʊə] 治愈
assure [ə'ʃʊə] 使确信	obscure [əb'skjʊə] 模糊的
spoor [spʊə]（动物的）足迹；臭迹	secure [sɪ'kjʊə] 牢固的；可靠的

基础短语

- a poor [pʊə] lady　一个可怜的妇人
- make sure [ʃʊə]　确保
- a housing bureau ['bjʊərəʊ]　一个房产局
- pure [pjʊə] and simple　纯洁而简单
- a casual ['kæʒʊəl] remark　漫不经心的评价
- be lured [lʊəd] into the impure [ɪm'pjʊə]　受不良思想的诱惑

以句识音

1. The future is obscure [əb'skjʊə].
不知未来会怎样。

2. She is curious to find the cure [kjʊə].
她极想找出解决问题的方法。

3. I am sure [ʃʊə] that he is a very poor [pʊə] man.
我确信他是一个穷人。

4. The tourists ['tʊərɪsts] were attracted by the beautiful garden.
游客们被这座美丽的花园吸引了。

5. I'm sure [ʃʊə] that's pure [pjʊə] gold.
我确信那是纯金。

6. Are you sure [ʃʊə] it's all right?
你确定没事吗?

经典绕口令（运动你的舌头）

1. Are you sure [ʃʊə] the milk is pure [pjʊə]?
你确定这牛奶是纯的吗?

2. The tourists ['tʊərɪsts] were curious to know the story behind the mural ['mjʊərəl].
旅客们对隐藏在壁画后面的故事非常好奇。

3. The tourist ['tʊərɪst] toured ['tʊəd] the moor [mʊə] in February ['februəri].
那个旅游者在二月去荒野旅行了。

4. I can't endure [ɪn'djʊə] this inspection tour [tʊə].
我不能忍受这种巡回检查。

5. I'm not sure [ʃʊə] whether he will endure [ɪn'djʊə] the lure [lʊə] or not.
我不能肯定他是否能忍受得了诱惑。

影音荟萃

一 听音乐学音标

Help the Poor
救救可怜人

Eric Clapton

Help the poor [pʊə] 救救可怜人

Won't you help poor [puə] me | 你难道不救救可怜的我吗

I need help from you baby | 我需要来自你的帮助，宝贝

Need it desperately | 强烈地需要你的帮助

I need you so much | 我是这么需要你

I need your care | 我需要你的关爱

Need all the loving baby you can spare | 需要你能够给予的所有的爱，宝贝

Help the poor [puə] | 救救可怜人

Oh, baby won't you help poor [puə] me | 哦，宝贝，你难道不救救可怜的我吗

Say you will | 说你会的

Say you'll help me on | 说你会救我的

I can't make it no longer | 我不能再承受

In this world alone | 孤单一人在这世界上

Baby I'm begging with tears in my eyes | 宝贝，我满含泪水地乞求

For your love, don't you realize | 你的爱，难道你没有意识到吗

I need help | 我需要帮助

Oh baby, help poor [puə] me | 哦宝贝，救救可怜的我吧

You are my inspiration | 你是我的精神支柱

Baby, that makes me be a king | 宝贝，让我成为王者

But if you don't come to my rescue | 但是如果你不来拯救我

I couldn't ever be anything | 我将一无是处

Help the poor [puə] | 救救可怜人

Won't you help poor [puə] me | 你难道不救救可怜的我吗

Have a heart won't you baby | 发发善心，好吗宝贝

Listen to my plead | 聆听我的请求

Oh, I lost my courage till I found you | 哦，遇到你我失去了勇气

You've got what it takes, baby | 宝贝，你掌控着

To pull me through | 我是否能渡过难关

Help the poor [puə] | 救救可怜人

Oh baby, won't you help poor [puə] me | 哦，宝贝，你难道不救救可怜的我吗

You are my inspiration	你是我的精神支柱
Baby that makes be a king	宝贝，让我成为王者
But if you don't come to my rescue	但是如果你不来拯救我
I couldn't ever be anything	我将一无是处
Help the poor [puə]	救救可怜人
Won't you help poor [puə] me	你难道不救救可怜的我吗
Have a heart wont you baby	发发善心，好吗宝贝
Listen to my plead	聆听我的请求
Oh, I lost my courage till I found you	哦，遇到你我失去了勇气
You got what it takes baby	宝贝，你掌控着
To pull me through	我是否能渡过难关
Help the poor [puə]	救救可怜人
Oh baby, won't you help poor [puə] me	哦，宝贝，你难道不救救可怜的我吗

歌曲评论

英国最伟大的布鲁斯吉他手埃里克·克莱普顿（Eric Clapton），1945年3月30日出生于英国苏里。在他15岁时，祖母送给他第一把吉他。在最初他对布鲁斯音乐的兴趣并不大，可后来开始听瞎子莱蒙·杰夫和桑·豪斯等布鲁斯吉他高手的唱片，跟着学习吉他弹奏，并由此开始了终生对布鲁斯音乐的钟爱。1994年，克莱普顿的唱片《原声作品集》为他赢得6项格莱美奖。在生活中历尽劫难的克莱普顿依然用吉他和歌喉吟唱着，这位布鲁斯乐坛的常青树为世人留下了无数经典的作品。

《救救可怜人》收录在由Eric Clapton和B.B.King两位重量级歌手合作的专辑*Riding With King* 里。这首歌以Eric特有的吉他音色感人肺腑。

二 看电影学音标

电影简介：

《音乐之声》（*The Sound of Music*）是美国一部家喻户晓的音乐类电影，公认的好作品，讲述了一个修女来到一个富人家里当家庭教师的故事。

对生活充满信心的玛丽亚初涉尘俗来到特拉普上校家里做家庭教师，在那里她和特拉普上校进行了第一次对话。谈话内容涉及玛丽亚的衣着。（节选自《音乐之声》）

Maria: But I don't have another one. When we enter the abbey, our worldly clothes are given to the poor [pʊə].

Captain: What about this one?

Maria: The poor [pʊə] didn't want this one.

Captain: Hmm.

Maria: I would've made myself a new dress but there wasn't time. I can make my own clothes.

Captain: Well, I'll see you get some material. Today, if possible. Now, Fraulein... er...

玛丽亚：但是我没有其他衣服。当我们进修道院时，就把平时穿的衣服都送给穷人了。

上校：这一套呢？

玛丽亚：穷人不要这一套。

上校：嗯。

玛丽亚：我本可以给自己做一套新裙子，但是没空。我会自己做衣服。

上校：那么我来给你弄些布料。可能的话，今天就给你。现在，弗劳伦……呃……

Unit 14 [eə]

[eə]

发音要素

发双元音[eə]时，从[e]音滑向[ə]音。发音时舌端抵下齿，前舌略抬起，双唇半开，[ə]音较轻。

[e]

[ə]

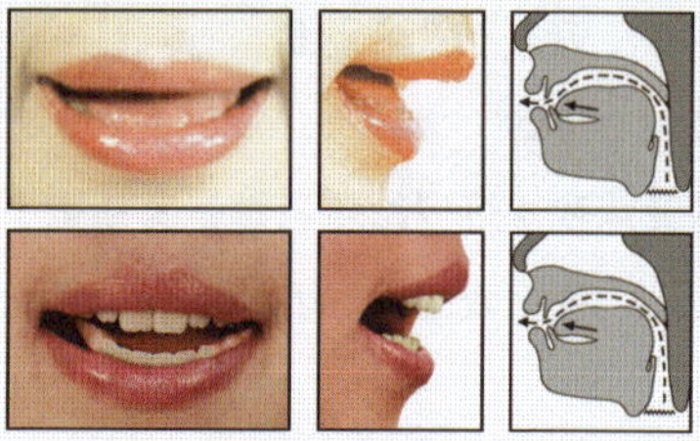

大话发音

[eə] 类似汉语“哎呃”快速连读时的轻声音。

被玫瑰刺了一下，好疼，“哎呃”！记得要快而轻地发这个音，口形不要太大啊。

哎呃

发音代言人

bear

[beə] 熊

常见发音字母及字母组合

音标	对应字母	自然发音规则	单词示例
[eə]	ear	字母组合ear在单词中可发[eə]音。	pear [peə] 梨
[eə]	are	字母组合are在单词中可发[eə]音。	hare [heə] 野兔

[eə]	air	字母组合air在单词中可发[eə]音。	air [eə] 空气
[eə]	ere	字母组合ere在单词中可发[eə]音。	there [ðeə] 那里

发音操练

[eə]	
wear [weə] 穿；戴	bare [beə] 光秃秃的
fare [feə] 车费；票价	care [keə] 关心
chair [tʃeə] 椅子	hair [heə] 头发
mare [meə] 母马；母驴	fair [feə] 公平的
where [weə] 哪里	repair [rɪ'peə] 修理

基础短语

- dare [deə] to say 敢说
- the lion's share [ʃeə] 大部分
- run barefoot ['beəfʊt] 光着脚跑
- out of repair [rɪ'peə] 失修
- spare [speə] some time 抽出一些时间
- here, there [ðeə] and everywhere ['evrɪweə] 这里，那里，到处都是

以句识音

1. Where [weə] there's [ðeəz] a will, there's [ðeəz] a way.
有志者事竟成。（英谚）

2. That's quite another pair [peə] of shoes.
那完全是另外一回事。

3. Tom likes to wear [weə] his hair [heə] long.
汤姆喜欢留长发。

4. Let's share [ʃeə] and share [ʃeə] alike.
咱们平均分配吧。

5. I dare [deə] not say he is not fair [feə] and square [skweə].
我敢说他办事公正。

6. She has done the lion's share [ʃeə] of the job.
这活儿她干了一大半。

经典绕口令（运动你的舌头）

1. The man with fair [feə] hair [heə] dare [deə] not repair [rɪ'peə] their [ðeə] chair [tʃeə] there [ðeə] because there [ðeə] is a bear [beə] there [ðeə].
有着漂亮头发的那个男人不敢在那儿修理他们的椅子，因为那里有一只熊。

2. They are Plague-bearing ['beərɪŋ] prairie ['preəri] dogs.
它们是感染瘟疫的草原犬鼠。

3. Beware [bɪ'weə]! That's a bear [beə] lair [leə].
小心！那是一个熊窝。

4. I gave Mary ['meəri] a pair [peə] of chairs [tʃeəz] and various ['veərɪəs] kinds of pears [peəz].
我给了玛丽一对椅子和各种各样的梨。

5. Once upon a barren moor there dwelt a bear [beə], also a boar. The bear [beə] could not bear [beə] the boar. The boar thought the bear [beə] a bore. At last the bear [beə] could bear [beə] no more of that boar that bored him on the moor, and so one morn he bored the boar — that boar will bore the bear [beə] no more.
从前，在一个贫瘠的荒野里住了一只熊和一只公野猪。熊忍受不了公野猪，公野猪又觉得熊是一只令人讨厌的东西。最后，那只熊再也忍不了那只令它讨厌的公野猪，因此，在一个早上，那只熊把公野猪烦透了——自此以后，公野猪不再令熊烦闷了。

影音荟萃

一 听音乐学音标

Losing Grip
失去力量

Avril Lavigne

Are you aware of what you make me feel, baby?
Right now I feel invisible to you,
like I'm not real
Didn't you feel me lock my arms around you?
Why'd you turn away?
Here's what I have to say:
I was left to cry there [ðeə], waiting outside there [ðeə]
Grinnin' with a lost stare [steə(r)]
That's when I decided

*Why should I care [keə(r)]?
'Cuz you weren't there [ðeə] when I was scared [skeəd]
I was so alone
You, you need to listen!
I'm startin'to trip, I'm losin'my grip
And I'm in this thing alone*
*(repeat)

Am I just some chick you placed beside you
To take somebody's place?
When you turn around can you recognize my face?
You used to love me, you used to hug me
But that wasn't the case
Everything wasn't okay

你知道我对你的感觉吗，宝贝
现在我觉得我对你仿佛隐形
似乎我并不存在
难道你没有感觉到我环绕着你的双臂吗
为何你却转身而去
有些话我不得不说
我被留在外面独自等待，独自哭泣
眼神迷茫，带着苦笑
那一刻我做出了决定

*我为何要在乎呢?
当我惊恐害怕时你却不在我身边
我是如此孤单
你，你听着!
我将踏上征程，我正失去力量
我独自一人，孤军奋战*
*(重复)

难道我只是你放在身边的玩物吗
只是某人的替代品吗?
当你转过身去，你还能认出我的面孔吗
你曾经爱过我，你曾经拥抱我
但是那并不是真的
一切都不对头

I was left to cry there [ðeə], waiting outside there [ðeə]	我被留在外面独自等待，独自哭泣
Grinnin'with a lost stare [steə(r)]	眼神迷茫，带着苦笑
That's when I decided	那一刻我做出了决定
Cryin'out loud	大声哭出来
I'm cryin'out loud	我大声地哭了起来
Cryin'out loud	大声哭出来
I'm cryin' out loud	我大声地哭了起来
Open your eyes	睁开你的眼睛
Open up wide	睁大你的眼睛
Why should I care [keə(r)]?	我为何要在乎呢?
'Cuz you weren't there [ðeə] when I was scared [skeəd]	当我惊恐害怕时你却不在我身边
I was so alone	我是如此孤单
**Why should I care [keə(r)]?	**我为何要在乎呢?
'Cuz you weren't there [ðeə] when I was scared [skeəd]	当我惊恐害怕时你却不在我身边
I was so alone	我是如此孤单
Why should I care [keə(r)]?	我为何要在乎呢?
If you don't care [keə(r)] then I don't care [keə(r)]	你若是不在乎，我也不会在乎
We're not goin' anywhere ['enɪweə(r)]**	我们不会有什么结果**
**(Repeat)	**（重复）

歌曲评论

艾薇儿的音乐跟之前许多才女人文歌手，如艾拉妮丝、珠儿不同。她的音乐并非像那些前辈的那样充满深刻思考，而是充满直觉性的呐喊，破碎的歌词语句符合简略时兴的网络语言，更显爆发力，仿佛受困的猛兽，四处冲撞着现世框架，加上朗朗上口的旋律性、神经质的Vocal，都成为一种迷人的优势，随时让你重温敏感心情，有着“是可忍、孰不可忍”的巾帼气魄，岂不让你感到格外亲切？延续着其一贯的风格，*Losing Grip*一如这位歌手的日记，记录着她的酸甜苦辣。电吉他的丰富表情，配上激越鼓声飙窜整张专辑，给你精神上的电击治疗，器乐配置并不复杂，艾薇儿富于变化的嗓音本身即是可圈可点的器乐，她属于声音实力演技派的歌手。她的歌声不温不火，渐进加温，直到随鼓声营造的逃离步伐，变成嘶吼的挣扎，将既骄傲又痛苦的情绪掌控自如，情感相当澎湃。这张专辑，爱情依然是传达的重点。不过正如艾薇儿自己在内页中的告白，“没有男生可以伤我的心，我是咬着牙这么说的”一样，这张专辑的歌曲虽平易近人但又题材重复，多首歌都是向男友叫嚣，或是强烈表达不妥协的立场。

二 看电影学音标

电影简介：

《幸福终点站》（*The Terminal*）是一部2004年出品的电影，由美国斯蒂芬·斯皮尔伯格导演执导，主要演员有汤姆·汉克斯、凯瑟琳·泽塔-琼斯、斯坦利·塔奇和齐·麦拜特。剧本由沙查·盖华斯、谢夫·内森逊根据安德鲁·尼高尔和沙查·盖华斯的原著故事改编。影片讲述主角前往美国途中家乡发生政变，政府被推翻，所持证件不被美国入境当局承认，被拒绝入境却又不能回国，被迫滞留肯尼迪国际机场期间的故事。

维克多·纳沃斯基终于进入了美国境内，来到纽约市区，他正乘坐出租车到他想去的地方。（节选自《幸福终点站》）

Viktor: Taxi!

Driver: Where [weə] you go?

Viktor: 161, Lexington. Please take Van Wyck Expressway to Queensboro Bridge. It's faster than BQE.

Driver: Where [weə] you from?

Viktor: Krakozhia. Viktor Navorski.

Driver: I'm Goran. Albania.

Viktor: When do you come to New York?

Driver: Thursday.

维克多：出租车!

司机：去哪儿?

维克多：列克星敦161号，走范怀克高速到皇后大桥，比BQE高速要快。

司机：你打哪来?

维克多：克罗西亚。维克多·纳沃斯基。

司机：我是格兰。阿尔巴尼亚人。

维克多：你什么时候来纽约的?

司机：星期四。

Chapter

2

辅音发音

Unit 1 [p] & [b]

[p]

发音要素

[p]是双唇爆破辅音。发音时双唇紧闭，憋住气，然后突然分开，气流冲出口腔，发出爆破音。[p]是清辅音，声带不振动。

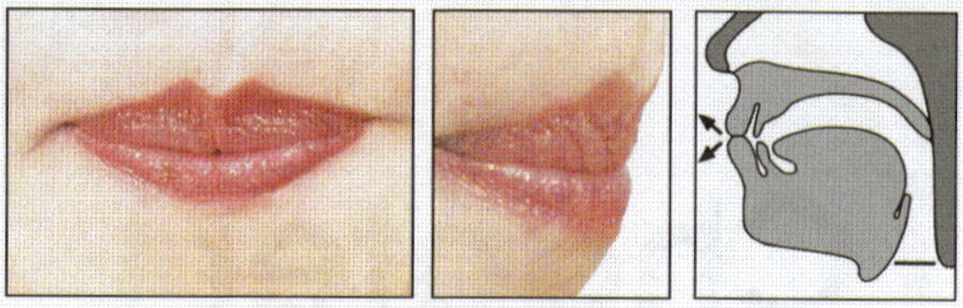

大话发音

[p] 音标和汉语中的“泼”音很相似。不过千万要记得，你的声带不振动。

发这个音时，口形和发汉语的“泼”音一样，不同的是你把手指放在喉咙处，感受不到声带的振动就对了。

泼

发音代言人

cap

[kæp] 帽子

常见发音字母及字母组合

音标	对应字母	自然发音规则	单词示例
[p]	p	字母p在单词中发[p]音。	**pie** [paɪ] 馅饼
[p]	pp	字母组合pp在单词中发[p]音。	**apple** ['æpl] 苹果

[b]

发音要素

[b]是双唇爆破辅音。发音时双唇紧闭，憋住气，然后突然分开，气流冲出口腔，发出爆破音。[b]是浊辅音，声带振动。

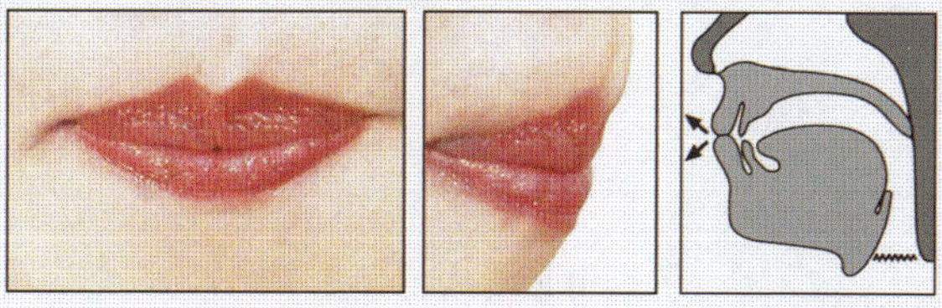

大话发音

[b] 音标和汉语中的“波”音很相似。

记得发这个音时要轻柔短促就行了。

波

发音代言人

cab

[kæb] 出租车

常见发音字母及字母组合

音标	对应字母	自然发音规则	单词示例
[b]	b	字母b在单词中发[b]音。	**bus** [bʌs] 公共汽车
[b]	bb	字母组合bb在单词中发[b]音。	**cabbage** ['kæbɪdʒ] 洋白菜

发音操练

[p]	[b]
pot [pɒt] 罐；锅	buy [baɪ] 买
paper ['peɪpə] 纸	build [bɪld] 建造
pea [pi:] 豌豆	black [blæk] 黑色的
pit [pɪt] 坑	bread [bred] 面包
lap [læp] 膝盖	bulb [bʌlb] 灯泡
lip [lɪp] 嘴唇	boast [bəʊst] 吹牛
park [pɑ:k] 公园	lab [læb] 实验室
plant [plɑ:nt] 植物	tab [tæb] 标签
map [mæp] 地图	rabbit ['ræbɪt] 兔子
happy ['hæpi] 幸福的	shabby ['ʃæbi] 破旧的

基础短语

- basketball ['bɑ:skɪtbɔ:l] player ['pleɪə] 篮球运动员
- push [pʊʃ] the button ['bʌtn] 按按钮
- peace [pi:s]-loving people ['pi:pl] 热爱和平的人民
- a police [pə'li:s] post [pəʊst] 派出所
- a popular ['pɒpjulə] opera ['ɒpərə] 流行歌剧
- buy [baɪ] in bulk [bʌlk] 成批买进

以句识音

1. Practice ['præktɪs] makes perfect ['pəfɪkt].

   熟能生巧。（英谚）

2. Bill [bɪl] broke [brəʊk] his promise ['prɒmɪs].

比尔未能信守诺言。

3. The pickpocket ['pɪkˌpɒkɪt] was peeping ['pi:pɪŋ] into his pocket ['pɒkɪt].

小偷正在偷窥他的口袋。

4. The big [bɪg] building ['bɪldɪŋ] is two blocks [blɒks] away.

到那座大建筑物要过两条马路。

5. Business ['bɪznəs] is business ['bɪznəs].

公事公办。

6. She is baking ['beɪkɪŋ] a pie [paɪ].

她在烤馅饼。

经典绕口令（运动你的舌头）

1. A bloke [bləʊk]'s back [bæk] bike [baɪk] brake [breɪk] block [blɒk] broke [brəʊk].

一个家伙的脚踏车后刹车坏了。

2. A big [bɪg] black [blæk] bug [bʌg] bit [bɪt] a big [bɪg] black [blæk] bear [beə], made the big [bɪg] black [blæk] bear [beə] bleed [bli:d] blood [blʌd]!

大黑虫咬大黑熊，大黑熊流血了！

3. A bitter ['bɪtə] biting ['baɪtɪŋ] bittern ['bɪtən] bit [bɪt] a better ['betə] brother ['brʌðə] bittern ['bɪtən], and the bitter ['bɪtə] better ['betə] bittern ['bɪtən] bit [bɪt] the bitter ['bɪtə] bittern ['bɪtən] back [bæk]. And the bitter ['bɪtə] bittern ['bɪtən], bitten ['bɪtn], by the better ['betə] bitten ['bɪtn] bittern ['bɪtən], said: "I'm a bitter ['bɪtə] biter ['baɪtə] bit [bɪt], alack!"

一只沮丧而尖刻的麻鸦咬了它兄弟一口，而没有它那么沮丧的兄弟又咬了它一口。那只被咬的沮丧的麻鸦对它的兄弟说：“我是一只充满怨恨的麻鸦！我害人终害己了！”

4. Badmin ['bædmɪn] was able ['eɪbl] to beat [bi:t] Bill [bɪl] at billiards ['bɪlɪədz], but [bʌt] Bill [bɪl] always beat [bi:t] Badmin ['bædmɪn] badly ['bædli] at badminton ['bædmɪntən].

巴德明在台球上能够打败比尔，但是打羽毛球比尔常常打败巴德明。

5. A pleasant ['pleznt] peasant ['peznt] keeps [ki:ps] a pleasant ['pleznt] pheasant and both the peasant ['peznt] and the pheasant are having a pleasant ['pleznt] time together.

一位和气的农民养了一只伶俐的野鸡，农民和野鸡在一起度过了一段很美好的时光。

影音荟萃

一 听音乐学音标

Postman Pat
邮递员派特叔叔

Postman ['pəustmən] Pat [pæt], Postman ['pəustmən]	邮递员派特叔叔
Pat,	邮递员派特叔叔
Postman ['pəustmən] Pat [pæt] and his black and	邮递员派特叔叔
white cat	和他的白脸小黑猫
Early in the morning	每天清晨
Just as day is dawning	天刚刚亮
He picks [pɪks] up [ʌp] all the post [pəust] bags	他将所有邮包
in his van	装上车
Postman ['pəustmən] Pat [pæt], Postman ['pəustmən]	邮递员派特叔叔
Pat [pæt]	邮递员派特叔叔
Postman ['pəustmən] Pat [pæt] and his black and	邮递员派特叔叔
white cat	和他的白脸小黑猫
All the birds are singing	鸟儿在歌唱
And the day is just beginning	新的一天刚刚开始
Pat [pæt] feels he's a really happy ['hæpi] man	派特叔叔是一个快乐的人
Everybody knows, his bright red van	大家都知道，他有一辆红色的车子
All his friends will smile as he waves to greet	他向朋友们挥手问候时
them	朋友们会对他微笑
Maybe	也许
You can never be sure	你永远都不知道
There'll be knock	包裹会送到你家门口
Ring	叮咚

Letters through your door　信件就送到了门口

Hay hay　嘿
Postman ['pəustmən] Pat [pæt], Postman ['pəustmən] Pat　邮递员派特叔叔 邮递员派特叔叔
Postman ['pəustmən] Pat [pæt] and his black and white cat　邮递员派特叔叔 和他的白脸小黑猫
All the birds are singing　鸟儿在歌唱
And the day is just beginning　新的一天刚刚开始
Pat [pæt] feels he's a really happy ['hæpi] man　派特叔叔是一个快乐的人
Pat [pæt] feels he's a really happy ['hæpi] man　派特叔叔是一个快乐的人
Pat [pæt] feels he's a really happy ['hæpi] man　派特叔叔是一个快乐的人

歌曲评论

《邮递员派特叔叔》动画由二十年来一直深受大人小孩欢迎的John Cunliffe的故事改编而成，该动画是儿童电视节目的经典之作，在英国是最受欢迎的儿童节目之一，也是国外儿童教育产品的一个著名品牌，其产品涉及视音频、图书、玩具、游戏、服装、日用品等等。该动画的歌曲也很受孩子们喜爱，同名主题曲《邮递员派特叔叔》曾经荣登香港“新城劲爆儿歌榜”第一名。

Because You Live
只因有你

Jesse McCartney

Staring out at the rain with a heavy heart　心情沉重凝视窗外的雨
It's the end of the world in my mind　如同世界末日降临心际
Then your voice calls me back [bæk] like a wake-up call　你的声音把我唤醒 如同晨钟响起
I've been [bi:n] looking for the answer　我一直在寻找答案
Somewhere　在某处
I couldn't see that it was right there　我所不能见的存在
But [bʌt] now I know what I really know　但如今终于清晰

Because [bɪ'kɒz] you live and breathe [bri:ð]	由于你的存在与呼吸
Because [bɪ'kɒz] you make me believe [bɪ'li:v] in	由于你在我无助时
myself when nobody ['nəʊbədi] else can help	让我相信了自己
Because [bɪ'kɒz] you live, girl	由于你的存在，宝贝
My world has twice as many stars in the sky	我的世界有两倍繁星闪烁于星空
It's alright, I survived, I'm alive again	正是如此，我重获生机
'Cause of you, made it through every storm	因为你，让我闯过狂风暴雨
What is life, what's the use if you killed inside	如果心中的你幻灭，生活将会怎样，活着又有何用
I'm so glad I found an angel	如此开心找到了我的天使
Someone	那就是
Who was there when all my hopes fell	当所有希望落空时还在支持我的你
I wanna fly, looking in your eyes	凝望你的眼神，我想腾空飞起
Because [bɪ'kɒz] you live and breathe [bri:ð]	由于你的存在与呼吸
Because [bɪ'kɒz] you make me believe [bɪ'li:v] in	由于你在我无助时
myself when nobody ['nəʊbədi] else can help	让我相信了自己
Because [bɪ'kɒz] you live, girl	由于你的出现，宝贝
My world has twice as many stars in the sky	我的世界有两倍繁星闪烁于星空
Because [bɪ'kɒz] you live, I live	因为你存在，我活着
Because [bɪ'kɒz] you live there's a reason why	我找到了理由，只因有你
I carry on when I lose the fight	当我失败时能够坚持下去
I want to give what you've given me always	我愿永远给你，你曾经的赠予
Because [bɪ'kɒz] you live and breathe [bri:ð]	由于你的存在与呼吸
Because [bɪ'kɒz] you make me believe [bɪ'li:v] in	由于你在我无助时
myself when nobody else can help	让我相信了自己
Because [bɪ'kɒz] you live, girl	由于你的出现，宝贝
My world has twice as many stars in the sky	我的世界有两倍繁星闪烁于星空
Because [bɪ'kɒz] you live and breathe [bri:ð]	由于你的存在与呼吸
Because [bɪ'kɒz] you make me believe [bɪ'li:v] in	由于你在我无助时
myself when nobody ['nəʊbədi] else can help	让我相信了自己
Because [bɪ'kɒz] you live, girl	由于你的出现，宝贝
My world has everything I need to survive	我的世界拥有一切我生存的道理
Because [bɪ'kɒz] you live, I live, I live	我存在，我存在，只因有你

歌曲评论

杰西·麦卡尼出生于纽约，自小就开始参加地区性音乐剧的演出，16岁开始展开个人的音乐事业，2004年发行的首张个人专辑《天使的心》（*Beautiful Soul*），迅速在全球卖出150万张，更在台湾地区的G-Music风云榜、五大金榜都夺下冠军宝座，还连冠Hit FM、飞碟电台、ICRT、KISS Radio四大电台。之后的 *Right Where You Want Me*、*Departure*专辑和其中的单曲亦取得了成功。2013年推出了新歌*Back Together*。

歌曲*Because You Live*收录在2004年由Hollywood Records唱片公司发行的专辑*Beautiful Soul*中。这首歌是《公主日记》(*The Princess Diaries*)续集里的一个插曲。

二 看电影学音标

电影简介：

《电子情书》(*You've Got Mail*)电影描述的是乔·福克斯和凯瑟琳·凯莉同生活和工作在纽约的西北区，同在一家商店购物，又同在一处买咖啡，而且还同沿着一条街道散步，仅仅通过电子邮件沟通，产生了爱情，到真正知道对方是谁后，如何接受对方，最后终成眷侣的故事。

电影画面外是男主角福克斯的信的独白，画面中是女主角凯莉去咖啡店买咖啡。（节选自《电子情书》）

Joe Fox: The whole purpose ['pɜ:pəs] of places ['pleɪsɪz] like Starbucks is for people ['pi:pl] with no decision-making ability whatsoever to make six decisions just to buy one cup [kʌp] of coffee. Short, tall, light, dark, caf, decaf, low-fat, nonfat, etc.

—Mocha frappuccino [ˌfræpʊ'tʃi:nəʊ] grande.

Joe Fox: So people ['pi:pl] who don't know what the hell they're doing or who on earth they are can, for only $2.95 get not just a cup [kʌp] of coffee but an absolutely defining sense of self.

—Tall! Decaf! Cappuccino [ˌkæpʊ'tʃi:nəʊ]!

乔·福克斯：像星巴克这种地方的目的，就是非要让那些没有决策能力的人在买一杯咖啡时做6次选择，小杯、中杯，淡味、浓味，非脱因、脱因咖啡，低脂、脱脂咖啡，诸如此类。

——大杯，摩卡，星杯乐

乔·福克斯：所以那些无所适从的人或是没有自信的人，只需要2.95美元，不仅可以买杯咖啡喝，还可以肯定自我的人生价值。

——大杯，低咖啡因，卡布奇诺。

电影简介：

《诸神之怒》（*Wrath of the Titans*）是由华纳兄弟影业所投拍的电影，影片为2010年卖座影片《诸神之战》(*Crash of the Titans*)的续集。该片于2011年3月正式开机拍摄，延续《诸神之战》的故事情节，讲述败北哈迪斯又卷土重来，联合了泰坦之王克洛诺斯，希望能够活捉宙斯。珀尔修斯再一次踏上了拯救世界的征途，与“海神”之子阿基纳、“火神”赫淮斯托斯一同前往冥界救出宙斯。

宙斯和他的神子阿瑞斯相见。（节选自《诸神之怒》）

—Poseidon.

—**B**rother ['brʌðə].

—It has **b**een [bi:n] an age.

—Indeed, it has.

—Ares, my son.

—Where's my **b**rother ['brʌðə] Perseus? Gone fishing?

—Yes.

—What a **b**rave [breɪv] and no**b**le ['nəʊbl] decision.

—波塞冬。

—兄弟。

—好久不见。

—确实，很久了。

—阿瑞斯，我的孩子。

—我的兄弟珀尔修斯在哪儿？去打鱼了？

—是的。

—多么勇敢而高尚的决定。

Unit 2 [t] & [d]

[t]

发音要素

[t]是舌齿爆破辅音。发音时舌尖抵上齿龈，憋住气，然后突然分开，使气流冲出口腔，发出爆破音。[t]是清辅音，声带不振动。

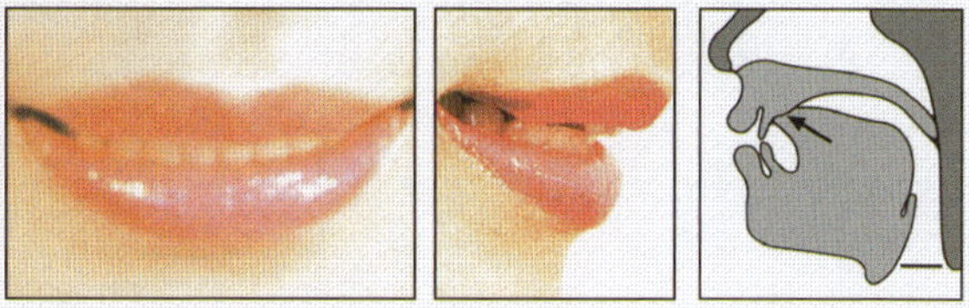

大话发音

女朋友终于答应了他的求婚，他感到“特”幸福，“特”就类似于[t]的发音，只是喉咙处没有振动。

在说出“特”音时，气流冲出后，马上停止，就是[t]的发音。

特

发音代言人

tie

[taɪ] 领带

常见发音字母及字母组合

音标	对应字母	自然发音规则	单词示例
[t]	t	字母t在单词中发[t]音。	tea [tiː] 茶

[t]	tt	字母组合tt在单词中发[t]音。	cotton ['kɒtn] 棉花

[d]

发音要素

[d]是舌齿爆破辅音。发音时舌尖抵上齿龈，憋住气，然后突然分开，使气流冲出口腔，发出爆破音。[d]是浊辅音，声带振动。

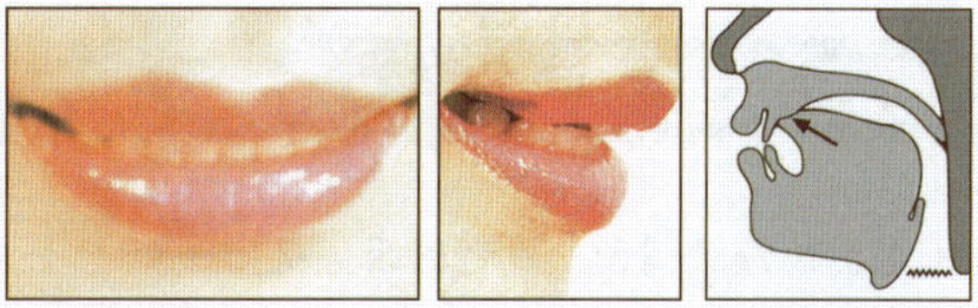

大话发音

马儿奔跑时会发出“嘚、嘚、嘚”的声音。

当骏马驰骋在无边的草原时，轻快的步子在耳边只留下“嘚、嘚、嘚”的马蹄声，就是[d]的发音。

嘚

发音代言人

duck

[dʌk] 鸭子

常见发音字母及字母组合

音标	对应字母	自然发音规则	单词示例
[d]	d	字母d在单词中发[d]音。	card [kɑːd] 卡片
[d]	dd	字母组合dd在单词中发[d]音。	middle ['mɪdl] 中间的

发音操练

[t]	[d]
tide [taɪd] 潮水	die [daɪ] 死
tear [tɪə] 眼泪	dear [dɪə] 亲爱的
team [ti:m] 队	day [deɪ] 日子
two [tu:] 二	do [du:] 做
foot [fʊt] 脚	feed [fi:d] 喂；饲养
let [let] 让	lead [li:d] 领导
neat [ni:t] 整洁的	need [ni:d] 需要
sit [sɪt] 坐	sad [sæd] 悲伤
butt [bʌt] 枪托	board [bɔ:d] 木板
coat [kəʊt] 上衣	code [kəʊd] 编号

基础短语

- stop [stɒp] talking ['tɔ:kɪŋ] 别说话
- not [nɒt] at [æt] all 一点也不
- good [gʊd], better ['betə], best [best] 精益求精
- dirty ['dɜ:ti] water ['wɔ:tə] 脏水

以句识音

1. What [wɒt]'s the date [deɪt] today [tə'deɪ]?
   今天几号？
2. Don't [dəʊt] tell [tel] me what [wɒt] it [ɪt] is.
   别告诉我那是什么。

3. The old [əʊld] lady ['leɪdi]'s daughter ['dɔ:tə] is a doctor ['dɒktə].

那个老太太的女儿是个医生。

4. I get [get] into ['ɪntʊ] bed [bed] at [æt] about [ə'baʊt] 10:30 every day [deɪ].

我每天大约十点半上床休息。

5. Never let [let] it [ɪt] rest [rest].

永不停顿。

6. It [ɪt]'s a duck [dʌk]. It [ɪt]'s a Peking duck [dʌk].

这是一只烤鸭，一只北京烤鸭。

经典绕口令（运动你的舌头）

1. It's better to [tu:] do [du:] it today [tə'deɪ] than to [tu:] do [du:] it tomorrow [tə'mɒrəʊ].

今天做要胜过明天做。

2. Why didn't ['dɪdnt] you do [du:] what [wɒt] I told [təʊld] you to [tu:] do?

为什么你不按照我说的去做呢？

3. Too [tu:] many teenagers ['ti:n,eɪdʒəz] tend [tend] to [tu:] waste [weɪst] their time [taɪm] watching ['wɒtʃɪŋ] television ['telɪvɪʒn].

很多青少年喜欢浪费时间看电视。

4. Betty ['beti] beat [bi:t] a bit [bɪt] of butter ['bʌtə] to make a better ['betə] batter ['bætə].

贝蒂敲打一小块黄油要做一块更好的奶油面。

5. The doctor's ['dɒktəs] daughter ['dɔ:tə] dares [deəz] to clime the tall [tɔ:l] door [dɔ:].

医生的女儿敢去爬那扇很高的门。

影音荟萃

一 听音乐学音标

It's Amazing

如此惊人

Jem

Do it [ɪt], now	现在就这样做
You know who you are	你知道自己是谁
You feel it [ɪt] in your heart [hɑ:t]	你的心里能够感觉得到
And you're burning with ambition	你那强烈的野心

But first [fɜ:st] wait [weɪt]	但首先需要等待
Won't [wəʊnt] get [get] it [ɪt] on a plate [pleɪt]	你不会轻易得到它
You gonna have to [tu:] work for it [ɪt]	你只能努力争取它
Harder and harder	并且要越来越努力
And I know	我知道
Cause I've been there before	因为我也曾经这样过
Knocking on the doors with rejection (rejection)	敲开大门，却只有拒绝
And you'll see (you'll see)	或许你会明白
Cause if it's meant [ment] to [tu:] be	如果命中注定如此
Nothing can compare to [tu:] deserving your	那就无须去比较了
dreams	只要向着自己的梦想

It's amazing it's amazing	这是如此惊人
All that [ðæt] you can do	所有你能做的
It's amazing	都是如此惊人
It [ɪt] makes my heart [hɑ:t] sing	让我用心鸣唱
Now it's up to you	现在就看你的了

Patience, now	现在请耐心
Frustration's in the air	挫折无处不在
And people who don't [dəʊnt] care	没有谁会去在意
Well it's gonna get [get] you down	这会让你失望
And you'll (you'll) fall (fall)	你可能会失败
Cause you will hit [hɪt] a wall	因为你会碰壁
But get [get] back on your feet [fi:t]	但你必须重新站起来
And you'll be stronger and smarter ['smɑ:tə]	你就会变得更强更聪明

And I know	我知道
Cause I've been there before	因为我也曾经这样过

Knocking down the doors	敲开大门
Won't [wəʊnt] take no for an answer	绝不接受拒绝
And you'll see	或许你会明白
Cause if it's meant to be	如果命中注定
Nothing can compare to [tuː] deserving your dreams	那就无须去比较了 只要向着自己的梦想

It's amazing, it's amazing	这是如此惊人
All that [ðæt] you can do	所有你能做的
It's amazing	都是如此惊人
It [ɪt] makes my heart [hɑːt] sing	让我用心鸣唱
Now it's up to [tuː] you	现在就看你的了

It's amazing, it's amazing	这是如此惊人
All that [ðæt] you can do	所有你能做的
It's amazing	都是如此惊人
It [ɪt] makes my heart [hɑːt] sing	让我用心鸣唱
Now it's up to [tuː] you	现在就看你的了

It's amazing, it's amazing	这是如此惊人
All that [ðæt] you can do	所有你能做的
It's amazing	都是如此惊人
It [ɪt] makes my heart [hɑːt] sing	让我用心鸣唱
Now it's up to [tuː] you	现在就看你的了
Ahh-ahh-ahh	啊–啊–啊

歌曲评论

Jem，原名Jemma Griffiths，来自英国威尔士。13岁就开始创作并演唱，29岁才发行了自己的首张专辑*Finally Woken*。被誉为Dido第二的Jem可谓是大器晚成，相比于Dido的飘渺，Jem的音乐多了一种尘世味道。Jem也许并不算是一个美丽的女子，不过听她的音乐，却能感受到她纯净的心灵。

Jem有不少影视中的音乐作品，《欲望都市》（*Sex and the City*）电影版中的这首*It's Amazing*令人过耳不忘。

I Don't Want to Say Goodbye

我不想说再见

Teddy Thompson

I don't [dəʊnt] want to say goodbye [ˌɡʊd'baɪ]	我不想说再见
Let the stars shine through	让繁星照彻天空
I don't [dəʊnt] want to say goodbye [ˌɡʊd'baɪ]	我不想说再见
All I want to do [duː] is live with you	我想做的事就是和你在一起
Just like the light of the morning	就像清晨时的光芒
After the darkness ['dɑːknəs] has gone	在黑暗远离之后
The shadow ['ʃædəʊ] of my love is falling	我的爱降落
On a place where the sun always shone	在太阳所照耀的地方
Don't [dəʊnt] you know that's where our hearts	难道你不知道
both belong	那是我们彼此心灵的归宿
'Cause I don't [dəʊnt] want to say	因为我不想说
goodbye [ˌɡʊd'baɪ]	再见
Let the stars shine through	所以让繁星照彻天空
No, I don't [dəʊnt] want to say goodbye [ˌɡʊd'baɪ]	不，我不想说再见
All I want to do [duː] is live with you	我想做的事就是和你一起
Together our two hearts are strong	当我们一起时，我们的心就无比坚强
Don't [dəʊnt] you know that's where our hearts	难道你不知道
both belong	那是我们彼此心灵的归宿
'Cause I don't [dəʊnt] want to say	因为我不想说
goodbye [ˌɡʊd'baɪ]	再见
Let the stars shine through	所以让繁星照彻天空
I don't [dəʊnt] want to say goodbye [ˌɡʊd'baɪ]	我不想说再见
All I want to do [duː] is live with you	我想做的事就是和你在一起
All I want to do [duː] is live with you	我想做的事就是和你在一起

歌曲评论

Teddy Thompson（泰迪·汤普森），1976年2月19日出生，英国民谣摇滚创作歌手。听他的音乐就像在夏日午后的山谷里，迎面吹来一阵轻风……

《我不想说再见》（*I Don't Want to Say Goodbye*）这首深情感人的歌来自获得第78届奥斯卡最佳导演奖电影《断背山》（*Brokenback Mountain*）。《断背山》在讲述同性恋情的背后，却蕴涵着一种纯净唯美的理想，就是世间任何一种爱都有真性、真情、真恋……人人心中都有一座断背山，我们总是会和最爱的人在那里重逢相遇，无关性别，无关岁月，断背山只有我们的地老天荒!

二 看电影学音标

电影简介:

影片《穿普拉达的女王》（*The Devil Wears Prada*）是根据劳伦·魏丝伯格（Lauren Weisberger）的同名小说改编而成，由大卫·弗兰科尔执导，梅丽尔·斯特里普、安妮·海瑟薇和艾米莉·布朗特联袂出演。

安德里亚要奈吉尔帮忙把自己打扮成一个漂亮而又时尚的女孩，奈吉尔给安德亚推荐了流行的品牌衣服和鞋子。（节选自《穿普拉达的女王》）

Andrea: Okay. So I'm screwing it [ɪt] up. Mmm. I don't [dəʊnt] want [wɒnt] to [tu:]. I just wish that [ðæt] I knew what [wɒt] I could do Nigel?

Nigel: Hmm?

Andrea: Nigel. Nigel.

Nigel: No. I don't [dəʊnt] know what [wɒt] you expect [ɪk'spekt] me to [tu:] do. There's nothing in the whole closet ['klɒzɪt] that [ðæt]'ll fit [fɪt] a size six. I can guarantee [ˌgærən'ti:] you. These are all sample size, two and four. All right [raɪt], we're doing this for you, and…

安德里亚：好吧，我表现很差劲。我并不想那样。我只希望知道我能做些什么。奈吉尔?

奈吉尔：嗯?

安德里亚：奈吉尔、奈吉尔。

奈吉尔：不，我不知道你期望我怎么做。这里根本没有M号的衣服。这些都是样衣尺寸，XS号和S号。好吧，这件给你，还有……

电影简介:

《驯龙高手》(*How to Train Your Dragon*)由梦工厂动画制作，于2010年3月26日上映。其故事内容改编自葛蕾熙达·柯维尔于2003年所写的同名童书。负责担任电影的配音演员有杰伊·巴鲁切尔、亚美莉卡·费雷拉、乔纳·希尔、克里斯托夫·梅兹-普莱瑟、克雷格·费格森以及杰拉德·巴特勒等人。

住在博克岛的维京居民正受到恶龙的袭击，少年希卡普和他的朋友戈伯也加入了战斗。(节选自《驯龙高手》)

—Nice of you to join the party! I thought you'**d** [juːd] been carried off.

—Who, me? No, come on. I'm way to muscular for their taste.

—They woul**d**n't ['wʊdnt] know what to **d**o [duː] with all this.

—Well, They nee**d** [niːd] toothpicks, **d**on't [dəʊnt] they?

—The meathea**d** ['miːthed] with attitu**d**e ['ætɪtjuːd] and interchangeable hands is Gobber.

—很高兴你也来参加这样的晚会，我还以为你被抓走了。

—谁？我？得了吧。我肌肉太多，它们不喜欢。

—它们不知道怎么吃所有的这些。

—好吧，它们需要牙签，是吧？

—那个脾气暴躁，还装着义肢的傻瓜叫Gobber。

Unit 3 [k] & [g]

[k]

发音要素

[k]是舌后软腭爆破音。发音时舌后部隆起紧贴软腭，憋住气，然后突然分开，气流送出口腔，形成爆破音。[k]是清辅音，声带不振动。

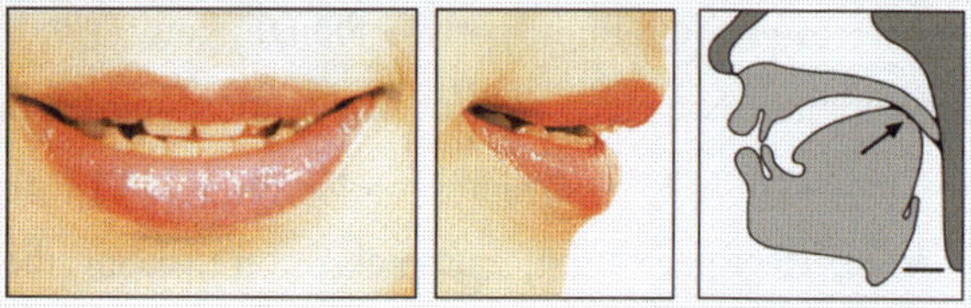

大话发音

口吃的人说话时易发出“嗑、嗑、嗑”的声音，由此大家俗称之为“磕巴”。

发“嗑”音，去掉声带振动，就是[k]的发音。

嗑

发音代言人

cake

[keɪk] 蛋糕

常见发音字母及字母组合

音标	对应字母	自然发音规则	单词示例
[k]	k	字母k在单词中发[k]音。	kite [kaɪt] 风筝
[k]	c	字母c在单词中可发[k]音。	cat [kæt] 猫

[k]	ck	字母组合ck在单词中发[k]音。	**back** [bæk] 后背
[k]	cc	字母组合cc在单词中可发[k]音。	**occupy** ['ɒkjupaɪ] 占据

[g]

发音要素

[g]是舌后软腭爆破音。发音时舌后部隆起紧贴软腭，憋住气，然后突然分开，气流送出口腔，形成爆破音。[g]是浊辅音，声带振动。

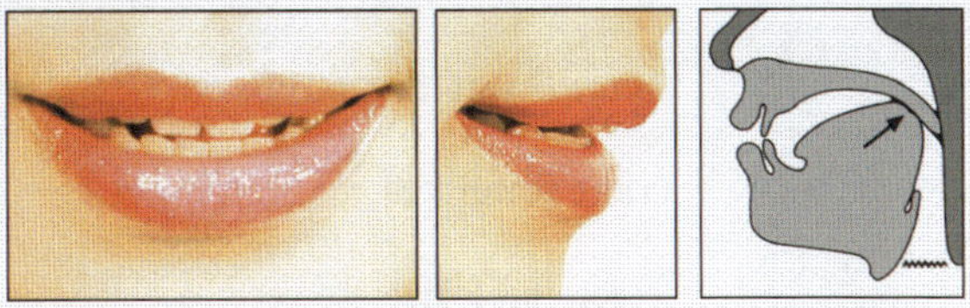

大话发音

大母鸡，咯、咯叫，快来看看我下的蛋。

母鸡一般在下蛋以后，就会“咯、咯”地叫，告诉主人来捡蛋啦。鸡叫时发出的“咯、咯”声就是[g]的发音。

咯

发音代言人

glove

[glʌv] 手套

常见发音字母及字母组合

音标	对应字母	自然发音规则	单词示例
[g]	g	字母g在单词中可发[g]音。	**gate** [geɪt] 门
[g]	gu	字母组合gu在单词中可发[g]音。	**guest** [gest] 客人

[g]	gue	字母组合gue在单词中可发[g]音。	vague [veɪg] 模糊的
[g]	gg	字母组合gg在单词中可发[g]音。	egg [eg] 鸡蛋

发音操练

[k]	[g]
class [klɑ:s] 班级	glass [glɑ:s] 玻璃
come [kʌm] 来	gum [gʌm] 口香糖
crane [kreɪn] 鹤	grain [greɪn] 粮食
kick [kɪk] 踢	tiger ['taɪgə] 老虎
lack [læk] 缺少	lag [læg] 落后
leak [li:k] 漏	league [li:g] 团
pick [pɪk] 挖，掘	pig [pɪg] 猪
take [teɪk] 拿	tag [tæg] 标签
pack [pæk] 背包	egg [eg] 鸡蛋
account [ə'kaʊnt] 账户	guide [gaɪd] 向导

基础短语

- catch [kætʃ] a cold [kəʊld] 感冒
- take [teɪk] a look [lʊk] 看一眼
- record ['rekɔ:d] breaker ['breɪkə] 打破纪录者
- a good [gʊd] guy [gaɪ] 一个好小伙
- grain [greɪn] like [laɪk] a Cheshire cat [kæt] 无缘无故地傻笑
- put all one's eggs [egz] in one basket ['bɑ:skɪt] 孤注一掷

以句识音

1. He gets up at six o'clock [klɒk].
   他六点钟起床。
2. The kids [kɪdz] often go [gəʊ] hiking ['haɪkɪŋ] at weekends [ˌwi:k'endz].
   孩子们常在周末远足。
3. The truck [trʌk] driver stops at the same cafe ['kæfeɪ] coming ['kʌmɪŋ] and going ['gəʊɪŋ].
   卡车司机往返都停在同一个饭店。
4. Care [kɛə] killed [kɪld] a cat [kæt].
   忧虑伤身。
5. A cat [kæt] may look [lʊk] at the king [kɪŋ].
   猫也可以看国王（小人物也该有些权利）。
6. A good [gʊd] beginning [bɪ'gɪnɪŋ] makes [meɪks] a good [gʊd] ending.
   善始方能善终。

经典绕口令（运动你的舌头）

1. Can [kæn] you can [kæn] a can [kæn] as a canner ['kænə] can [kæn] can [kæn] a can [kæn]?
   你能够像罐头工人一样装罐头吗？
2. How many cookies ['kʊkɪz] could [kʊd] a good [gʊd] cook [kʊk] cook [kʊk] if a good [gʊd] cook [kʊk] could [kʊd] cook [kʊk] cookies ['kʊkɪz]? A good cook [kʊk] could [kʊd] cook [kʊk] as much cookies ['kʊkɪz] as a good [gʊd] cook [kʊk] who could [kʊd] cook [kʊk] cookies ['kʊkɪz].
   如果一个好的厨师能做小甜饼，那么他能做多少小甜饼呢？一个好的厨师能做出和其他好厨师一样多的小甜饼。
3. If you're keen [ki:n] on stunning kites [kaɪts] and cunning ['kʌnɪŋ] stunts, buy a cunning ['kʌnɪŋ] stunning stunt kite [kaɪt].
   如果你非常想要好的风筝和精彩的表演，就去买一只漂亮的、灵巧的特技风筝吧。
4. A cricket ['krɪkɪt] critically ['krɪtɪkli] cricked [krɪkɪd] at a critical ['krɪtɪkl] cricket ['krɪkɪt] match, and so this cricket ['krɪkɪt] quitted the cricket ['krɪkɪt] match quickly ['kwɪkli].
   一只蟋蟀在一场关键性的斗蟋比赛中发生严重的痉挛，于是这只蟋蟀很快退出了比赛。

5. A big black [blæk] bug [bʌg] bit a big [bɪg] black [blæk] dog [dɒg] on his big [bɪg] black [blæk] nose!

一只大黑虫子咬了一只大黑狗的大黑鼻子。

影音荟萃

一 听音乐学音标

Take Me Home, Country Road
乡村路，带我回家

John Denver

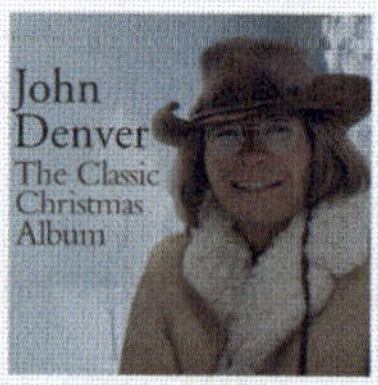

Almost heaven, West Virginia	西弗吉尼亚，简直像天堂
Blue Ridge Mountain, Shenandoah River	有蓝岭群山，谢南多厄河
Life is old there	那里生活久远
Older than the trees	比树木更悠久
Younger than the mountains	比群山更年轻
Growing like [laɪk] a breeze	像轻风般成长
Country ['kʌntri] roads, take [teɪk] me home	乡村路，带我回家
To the place I belong	去我属于的地方
West Virginia, Mountain Mama	西弗吉尼亚，大山妈妈
Take [teɪk] me home, country ['kʌntri] road	乡村路，带我回家
All my memories gather round her	我所有的记忆，全是关于她
Miner's Lady stranger to blue water	矿工的太太，连海也没见过
Dark [dɑːk] and dusty painted on the sky [skaɪ]	黑暗与灰尘，笼罩着天空
Misty taste of moonshine	似月有薄雾色
Tear drops in my eyes	眼泪涌上我眼窝
Country ['kʌntri] roads, take [teɪk] me home	乡村路，带我回家
To the place I belong	去我属于的地方

West Virginia, Mountain Mama	西弗吉尼亚，大山妈妈
Take [teɪk] me home, country roads	乡村路，带我回家
I hear her voice in the morning hours	清晨我听见她的声音
She calls me	是她在呼唤我
The radio reminds me of my home far away	收音机使我想起遥远的家
And driving down the road	驱车沿路而下
I'll get a feeling	我感觉到
That I should have been home	我昨天就该回家
Yesterday, yesterday	该回家
Country ['kʌntri] roads, take [teɪk] me home	乡村路，带我回家
To the place I belong	去我属于的地方
West Virginia, Mountain Mama	西弗吉尼亚，大山妈妈
Take [teɪk] me home, country roads	乡村路，带我回家
Take [teɪk] me home, country roads	乡村路，带我回家
Take [teɪk] me home, country roads	乡村路，带我回家

歌曲评论

《乡村路，带我回家》（*Take Me Home, Country Road*）是由约翰·丹佛(John Denver)创作并演唱的著名乡村歌曲。约翰·丹佛演唱的歌曲大部分都是自己创作的，并且成为乡村歌曲与摇滚相结合的典范。《乡村路，带我回家》一般人都会认为是一首思乡的歌，但其实是一首环保公益歌曲。这首歌创作于1971年，并使他一跃成为著名的乡村歌星。丹佛是在中国最有名的美国乡村歌手，他甚至超过了在美国比他名气大得多的乡村明星，就是因为这首脍炙人口的《乡村路，带我回家》，歌曲旋律轻快，给人描绘了一幅美丽的美国西部风光。

My Heart Will Go On

我心永恒

Celine Dion

Every night in my dreams	夜夜在我梦里
I see you, I feel you	我见到了你，感觉到了你
That is how I know you go [gəʊ] on	因而我到知道你心依旧
Far across the distance	跨越那遥远的
And spaces between us	空间和距离
You have come to show you go [gəʊ] on	向我展现你依旧未变的心

Near, far, wherever you are	无论远近，无论你在哪里
I believe that the heart does go [gəʊ] on	我坚信你的心不会改变
Once more you open the door	如果你再次打开我心门
And you're here in my heart	你会发现你在我心里
And my heart will go [gəʊ] on and on	我心将永恒不移
Love can touch us one time	我们被爱触动
And last for a lifetime	直到生命的最终
And never let go [gəʊ] till we're gone	都不会与我们离弃
Love was when I loved you	爱是当我爱你
One true time I hold to	真正地拥有你
In my life we'll always go [gəʊ] on	我们就会永远相依

Near, far, wherever you are	无论远近，无论你在哪里
I believe that the heart does go [gəʊ] on	我坚信你的心不会改变
Once more you open the door	如果你再次打开我心门
And you're here in my heart	你会发现你在我心里
And my heart will go [gəʊ] on and on	我心将永恒不移

You're here, there's nothing I fear	有你我无所畏惧
And I know that my heart will go [gəʊ] on	我知道我心将永恒不移
We'll stay forever this way	我们将永远在一起
You are safe in my heart	你平安地住我心里
And my heart will go [gəʊ] on and on	我的心将永远与你相依

歌曲评论

席琳·迪翁（Celine Dion）1968年3月30日生于加拿大魁北克，是一位著名的法语和英语女流行歌手，有流行天后之称。作为全球最畅销的女歌手之一，席琳·迪翁在全球的专辑销量已经超过了2亿张。

《我心永恒》，泰坦尼克号主题曲，由好莱坞主流电影著名作曲家詹姆斯·霍纳（James Horner）一手制作，具有浓烈民族韵味的爱尔兰锡哨在他的精巧编排下，尽显悠扬婉转而又凄美动人。歌曲的旋律从最初的平缓到激昂，再到缠绵悱恻的高潮，一直到最后荡气回肠的悲剧尾声，短短四分钟的歌曲实际上是整部影片的浓缩版本。歌曲由韦尔·杰宁斯（Will Jennings）作词，加拿大女歌手席琳·迪翁（Celine Dion）演唱。《我心永恒》也是世界上最为人所熟知的歌曲之一。它在美国、英国、法国、比利时、澳大利亚、丹麦和瑞士等多个国家都曾登上单曲榜首位，是世界上最畅销的单曲之一。

二 看电影学音标

电影简介：

电影《一个购物狂的自白》（*Confession of a Shopaholic*）根据英国畅销书作家索菲·金塞拉的“购物狂”系列改编而成。索菲被誉为“女性都会小说”的代表人物，通过她幽默又深刻的笔触，活泼可爱的购物狂丽贝卡跃然纸上，成为无数女性读者喜爱的角色。

丽贝卡为了换零钱买丝巾，来到热狗摊前和老板协商，打算用支票买下所有的热狗，最后发生了什么呢？（节选自《一个购物狂的自白》）

—Excuse [ɪk'skju:z] me. It's an emergency.

—Back [bæk] of the line!

—Excuse [ɪk'skju:z] me, this is an emergency. Excuse [ɪk'skju:z] you, excuse [ɪk'skju:z] me! Do you do cash back [bæk]?

—让一下，紧急情况!

—到后面排队!

—不好意思，这是紧急情况。你让一下，不好意思。你能兑现吗?

电影简介：

《朱莉与朱莉娅》（*Julie & Julia*）由诺拉·艾芙隆执导，梅丽尔·斯特里普、艾米·亚当斯主演。讲述了曾在法国生活过的美国人朱莉·查尔德写了一本美食书，而隔代的美国女孩朱莉娅·鲍威尔根据她的书来逐一实践，并发表在博客上，结果开始拥有大批粉丝，也因此懂得人生意义的故事。该电影根据朱莉·鲍威尔著《美味关系：朱莉与朱莉娅》与朱莉亚·查尔德著《我的法兰西岁月》改编而成的。

朱莉娅在向朋友讲述自己对鸡蛋的感受。（节选自《朱莉与朱莉娅》）

—Yesterday I poached an egg [eg]. It seemed like the perfect thing to do on perhaps the second worst workday in recorded history.

—Explain to me how you've never eaten an egg [eg] in your whole life.

—I've had eggs [egz] in, like, cakes. Never had an "egg" [eg] egg [eg]. I was a very willful child. It's simmering.

—昨天，我做了个荷包蛋。在度过史上第二个糟糕工作日之后，那貌似是很好的放松方式。

—跟我说说，你为啥从来不吃鸡蛋。

—我吃含有鸡蛋的食物，比如蛋糕。从没吃过“蛋形的”蛋，我是个很任性的小孩。水开了。

Unit 4 [f] & [v]

[f]

发音要素

[f]是唇齿摩擦辅音。发音时下唇轻触上齿，气流由唇齿间通过，形成摩擦音。[f]是清辅音，声带不振动。

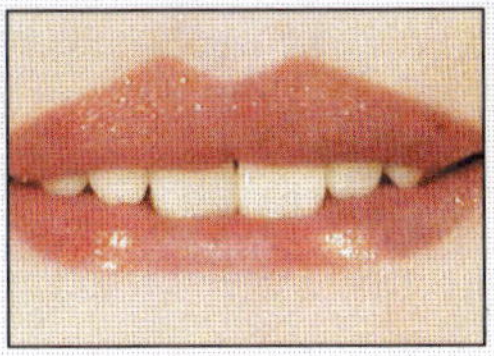

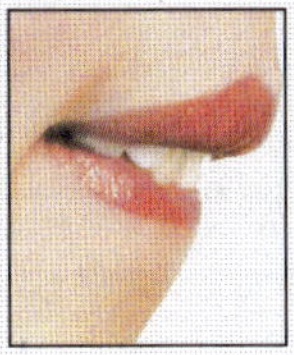

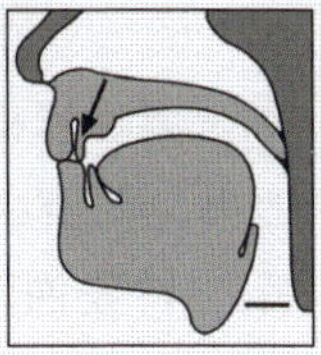

大话发音

水开了，要冒出来了，就会发出“咈、咈”声。

沸腾的水或开锅的粥，当要从锅里冒出来时，就会有“咈、咈”的声音，就是[f]的发音。

咈

发音代言人

fish

[fɪʃ] 鱼

常见发音字母及字母组合

音标	对应字母	自然发音规则	单词示例
[f]	f	字母f在单词中可发[f]音。	face [feɪs] 脸

[f]	ff	字母ff在单词中发[f]音。	**cliff** [klɪf] 悬崖
[f]	fe	字母组合fe在单词中可发[f]音。	**life** [laɪf] 生活
[f]	ph	字母组合ph在单词中发[f]音。	**phone** [fəʊn] 电话

[v]

发音要素

[v]是唇齿摩擦辅音。发音时下唇轻触上齿，气流由唇齿间通过，形成摩擦音。[v] 是浊辅音，声带振动。

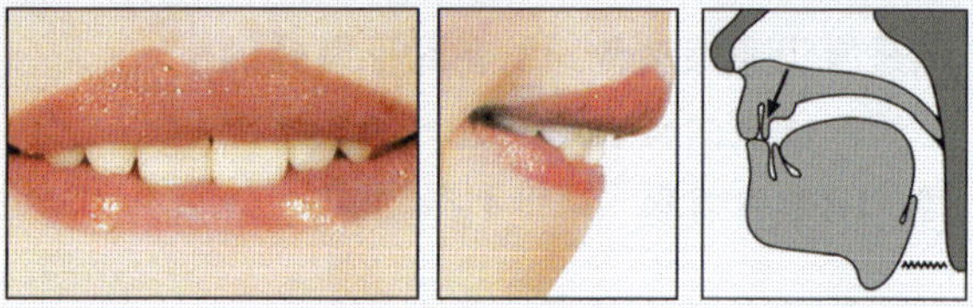

大话发音

[v] 这个在汉语中没有对应的汉字，类似于小朋友生气时会把牙齿咬住下嘴唇，在发出“唔”的声音。

生气咬住嘴唇发出的“唔”音与[v]的发音相似。

唔

发音代言人

vase

[vɑːz] 花瓶

常见发音字母及字母组合

音标	对应字母	自然发音规则	单词示例
[v]	v	字母在v单词中发[v]音。	**vote** [vəʊt] 投票

[v]	ve	字母组合ve在单词中发[v]音。	five [faiv] 五

发音操练

[f]	[v]
fast [fɑːst] 快	vast [vɑːst] 巨大的
fan [fæn] 扇子	van [væn] 大篷车
few [fjuː] 很少	view [vjuː] 观点
fowl [faʊl] 家禽	vowel ['vaʊəl] 元音
leaf [liːf] 树叶	leave [liːv] 离开
proof [pruːf] 证明	prove [pruːv] 证明
safe [seɪf] 安全	save [seɪv] 拯救
surf [sɜːf] 冲浪	serve [sɜːv] 服务
photo ['fəʊtəʊ] 照片	slave [sleɪv] 奴隶
knife [naɪf] 刀子	live [lɪv] 生存

基础短语

- very [veri] fast [fɑːst]　非常快
- beautiful ['bjuːtɪfl] flowers ['flaʊəz]　美丽的花
- find [faɪnd] a new life [laɪf]　找到一种新生活
- a very ['veri] vicious ['vɪʃəs] fellow ['feləʊ]　一个非常阴险的家伙
- a fine [faɪn] view [vjuː] of the mountain　山的优美景色
- as far[fɑː] back as 1955 (nineteen fifty ['fɪfti]-five [faɪv])　早在 1955 年

以句识音

1. Fortune ['fɔ:tʃu:n] favors ['feɪvəz] the brave [breɪv].
天佑勇者。

2. It is one of [əv] my favorite ['feɪvərɪt] novels ['nɒvəlz].
这是我最喜爱的小说之一。

3. I felt [felt] as if [ɪf] he'd never know fatigue [fə'ti:g].
我觉得他好像永远也不会疲倦。

4. Feed [fi:d] a cold and starve [stɑ:v] a fever ['fi:və].
伤风时宜吃，发热时宜饿。

5. It is very ['veri] difficult ['dɪfɪkəlt] for [fɔ:] us to finish ['fɪnɪʃ] it before five [faɪv].
五点钟以前我们很难完成。

6. Turning around, he found [faʊnd] himself [hɪm'self] face [feɪs]-to-face [feɪs] with his father ['fɑ:ðə].
一转身，他发现他的父亲就在他面前。

经典绕口令（运动你的舌头）

1. A Finnish ['fɪnɪʃ] fisher ['fɪʃə] named Fisher ['fɪʃə] failed [feɪld] to fish [fɪʃ] any fish [fɪʃ] one Friday ['fraɪdeɪ] afternoon [ˌɑ:ftə'nu:n] and finally ['faɪnəli] he found [faʊnd] out a big fissure ['fɪʃə] in his fishing ['fɪʃɪŋ] net.
一个名叫费希尔的芬兰渔民在一个星期五的下午未能捕捉到任何鱼，结果他发现他的渔网上有一个大裂口。

2. Franc's [fræŋk] father ['fɑ:ðə] is frying ['fraɪɪŋ] French [frentʃ] fries [fraɪz] for his five [faɪv] fire-fighter [faɪə'faɪtə] friends [frendz] after they finished ['fɪnɪʃt] a fire-fighting [faɪə'faɪtɪŋ] in a factory ['fæktəri].
在结束对一家工厂的灭火战斗以后，弗兰克的父亲在为他的五个消防队员朋友炸薯条。

3. A flea [fli:] and a fly [flaɪ] flew [flu:] up in a flue [flu:]. Said the flea [fli:], "Let us fly [flaɪ]!" "Let us flee [fli:]!" Said the fly [flaɪ]. So they flew [flu:] through a flaw [flɔ:] in the flue [flu:].
一只跳蚤和一只苍蝇飞进烟道里。跳蚤说："让我们飞吧！"苍蝇说："让我们逃跑吧！"就这样，它们就飞越了烟道里的一条裂纹。

4. Vincent ['vɪnsnt] vowed [vaʊd] vengeance ['vendʒəns] very ['veri] vehemently ['vi:əməntli].
文森特发誓要实施强烈的报复。

5. Vivian ['vɪvɪən] believes [bɪ'li:vs] violet ['vaɪələt] bugs have [hæv] very ['veri] big value ['vælju:].
薇薇安相信蓝紫色的窃听器有很大的价值。

影音荟萃

一 听音乐学音标

I Just Fall in Love Again
重浴爱河

Anne Murray

Dreaming, I must be dreaming	做梦，我一定是做梦
Or am I really lying here with you	否则是真的与你同眠
Baby, you take me in your arms	宝贝，你将我拥入怀中
And though I'm wide awake	虽然我十分清醒
I know my dream is coming true	我知道此刻美梦成真
And though I just fall [fɔ:l] in love again	尽管我再次坠入爱河
Just one touch and then it happens every time	偶然便成习惯
And there I go	就这样
I just fall [fɔ:l] in love again	我再入爱河
And when I do	在此刻
I can't help myself	我情不自禁地
I fall [fɔ:l] in love with you	爱上了你
Magic, it must be magic	魔法，这一定是魔法
The way I hold you and the night just seem to	我就这样拥抱着你
fly	夜晚如风飞逝
Easy, for [fɔ:] you to take me to a star	你带我登星易如反掌
Heaven is that moment when I look in your	我看着你的眼睛便是天堂
eyes	

And though I just fall [fɔːl] in love again	尽管我再次坠入爱河
Just one touch and then it happens every time	偶然便成习惯
And there I go	就这样
I just fall [fɔːl] in love again	我再入爱河
And when I do	在此刻
I can't help myself	我情不自禁地
I fall [fɔːl] in love with you	爱上了你
Can't help myself	我情不自禁地
I fall in love with you	爱上了你

And though I just fall [fɔːl] in love again	尽管我再次坠入爱河
Just one touch an then it happens every time	偶然便成习惯
And there I go	就这样
I just fall [fɔːl] in love again	我再入爱河
And when I do	在此刻
Can't help myself	我情不自禁地
I fall [fɔːl] in love with you	爱上了你
Can't help myself	我情不自禁地
I fall [fɔːl] in love with you	爱上了你

歌曲评论

Anne Murray（安妮·莫莉，全名：Morna Anne Murray，1945年6月20日出生）是加拿大著名乡村女歌手，从1968年至今已发行32张录音室专辑、1张现场专辑、15张精选集，全球唱片销量超过5400万张。迄今获得1座全美音乐奖、4座格莱美奖、24座朱诺奖，是入驻加拿大音乐名人堂（1993年）、好莱坞星光大道（1980年）的著名歌手。她个人最爱的歌曲却一直排在Billboard's Country Singles Chart的第四名、Billboard's U.S. Adult Contemporary Chart的第三名之外：歌曲 *I Just Fall In Love Again*、*Shadows in the Moonlight* 和 *Broken Hearted Me*（都是1979的作品）。

When You Believe

只要你相信

Mariah Carey & Whitney Houston

Many nights we've [wiːv] prayed	许多夜晚我们曾恳切祈祷

With no proof anyone could hear　不能证明任何人可以听到
In our hearts a hopeful song　我们的心如一阕希望之歌
We barely understood　自己难以参透
Now we are not afraid　如今我们不再害怕
Although we know there's much to fear　尽管我们知道仍有许多事情令人畏惧
We were moving ['mu:vɪŋ] the mountains long　翻山越岭后
Before we knew we could　才知晓自己能够做到

There can be miracles when you believe [bɪ'li:v]　只要你相信，奇迹就会实现
Though hope is frail, it's hard to kill　尽管希望渺茫，却难以抹杀
Who knows what miracles you can achieve [ə'tʃi:v]　谁能知晓，你可以实现什么奇迹
When you believe [bɪ'li:v], somehow you will　只要你相信，你或许就会
You will when you believe [bɪ'li:v]　只要你相信，奇迹就会实现

And this time of fear　在这恐惧之时
When prayer so often proves [pru:vz] in vain　当祈祷屡次落空时
Hope is like the summer birds　希望像是夏日的鸟儿
To swiftly flown away　太早飞离
Now I'm standing here　此刻我却站在这里
My heart so full I can't explain　觉得心塞，难以言表
Seeking faith and speaking words　寻觅着信念
I never thought I'd say　说着未曾想过要说的话

There can be miracles when you believe [bɪ'li:v]　只要你相信，奇迹就会实现
Though hope is frail, it's hard to kill　尽管希望渺茫，却难以抹杀
Who knows what miracles you can achieve [ə'tʃi:v]　谁能知晓，你可以实现什么奇迹
When you believe [bɪ'li:v], somehow you will　只要你相信，你或许就会
You will when you believe [bɪ'li:v]　只要你相信，奇迹就会实现

They don't always happen when you ask　它们不总在你祈求的时候发生
And it's easy to give in to your fear　也很容易屈服于你的畏惧
But when you are blinded by your pain　但当你被痛苦蒙蔽时
Can't see your way safe through the rain　在风雨中看不见出路
Thought of a still resilient voice　希望仍然是一个坚定有力的声音
Says love is very near　告诉你爱已临近

There can be miracles when you believe [bɪ'li:v]	只要你相信，奇迹就会实现
Though hope is frail, it's hard to kill	尽管希望渺茫，却难以抹杀
Who knows what miracles you can achieve [ə'tʃi:v]	谁能知晓，你可以实现什么奇迹
When you believe [bɪ'li:v] somehow you will	只要你相信，你或许就会
Now you will	你现在就会
You will when you believe [bɪ'li:v]	只要你相信，你就会
You will when you believe [bɪ'li:v]	只要你相信，你就会
Just believe [bɪ'li:v]	只要相信
Just believe [bɪ'li:v]	我坚信
You will when you believe [bɪ'li:v]	只要你相信，奇迹就会实现

歌曲评论

玛丽亚·凯莉（Mariah Carey）是美国著名歌星，和惠特妮·休斯顿等五位歌手并称为“跨世纪天后”，有着辉煌的音乐史记录。她以2亿多张的唱片销量和无数的音乐榜单记录，5个八度的高亢音域和洛可可式的演唱技巧以及标志性的海豚音闻名于世。她是音乐史上拥有最多Billboard冠军单曲的女歌手，同时也是拥有最多Billboard冠军单曲的独唱歌手。

惠特妮·休斯顿（Whitney Elizabeth Houston）是位曾多次获得格莱美奖的超级流行天后，她以强而有力的嗓音、一字多转音的感染力与宽广的音域为世人所熟知，誉为“美利坚之声”。惠特妮在全世界有超过一亿七千万的销售纪录。她也是首张专辑销量最高的女歌手和单张专辑销量最高的女歌手。根据吉尼斯世界纪录，惠特妮也是获奖最多的女歌手。（美国时间2012年2月11日，惠特尼在比弗利希尔顿酒店被宣布死亡，死因系心脏病发滑入浴缸溺水而亡，终年48岁。）

*When you believe*由玛丽亚·凯莉和惠特妮·休斯顿演唱，史蒂芬施华兹作曲，娃娃脸（美国著名艺人，歌手，监制，艺名：Babyface）监制。这首歌曲是1998年上映的动画片《埃及王子》的主题曲，在当时流传度极广，深受人们喜爱。

二 看电影学音标

电影简介：

美国情景喜剧《老友记》（*Friends*）第一季，于1994年9月22日在美国NBC首播，该季共24集，于1995年5月18日结束。平均收视率居年度第九，收视人口约1488万人。整部戏由三男三女共六位俊男美女担纲演出，不时请到明星与设计师等各界名流客串参与，播出以来一直为NBC电视网的招牌戏之一。

爱玛过一周岁生日，罗斯和瑞秋为爱玛准备了生日晚会。远在新泽西订的蛋糕送错了，瑞秋正在打电话要求退换。（节选自《老友记》）

Rachel: No, no, this is not what I ordered, okay? I went all the way to New Jersey so that I could have the perfect ['pɜːfɪkt] cake for [fɔː] my daughter's birthday. And I need a bunny cake right now!

Ross: Ask them if [ɪf] it would be faster ['fɑːstə] if [ɪf] we cut the baby's face [feɪs] off [ɒf] the penis, so we could put it on the bunny. That is a weird sentence.

瑞秋：不是，不是，这不是我要订的。我特地去新泽西州，只为了我女儿有完美的生日蛋糕，还有，我需要兔子蛋糕，现在!

罗斯：如果要快点的话，我们可以从……上取下她的照片，再贴到兔子蛋糕上。这样说真奇怪。

电影简介：

《美丽心灵》（*A Beautiful Mind*），是一部改编自同名传记而获得奥斯卡金像奖的电影，影片讲述了患有精神分裂症但却在博弈论和微分几何学领域潜心研究而最终获得诺贝尔经济学奖的数学家约翰·福布斯·纳什的故事。传记是由西尔维雅·娜萨儿所撰写，于1998年出版，电影则于2001年上映。

在普林斯顿大学，约翰·福布斯·纳什第一次见到自己的浪子室友查尔斯。（节选自《美丽心灵》）

Charles: Oh, Christ! The prodigal roommate arrives [ə'raɪvz].

Nash: Roommate?

Charles: Oh, God, no. Did you know that having ['hævɪŋ] a hangover ['hæŋəʊvə] is not having ['hævɪŋ] enough water in your body to run your Krebs cycles? Which is exactly what happens to you when you're dying of thirst. So, dying of thirst would probably feel pretty much like the hangover ['hæŋəʊvə] that finally bloody kills you.

查尔斯：噢，天啊，你的浪子室友抵达了。

纳什：室友?

查尔斯：噢，天啊，不要。你知不知道酒喝多了，就会使你的身体里缺乏足够的水去进行克雷布斯循环？这就和你快要渴死时所发生的情况是一样的。所以，渴死也就很可能和醉酒后血腥而死的感觉差不多。

Unit 5 [θ] & [ð]

[θ]

发音要素

[θ]是舌齿摩擦辅音。发音时舌尖轻触上齿背，气流由舌齿间送出，形成摩擦音。[θ] 是清辅音，声带不振动。

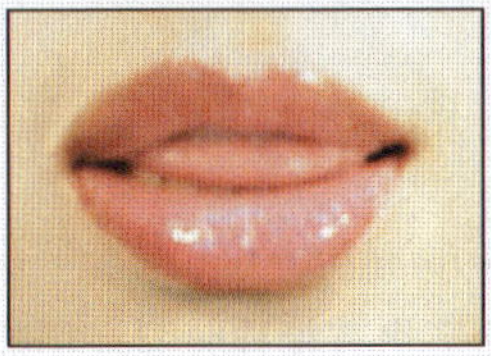

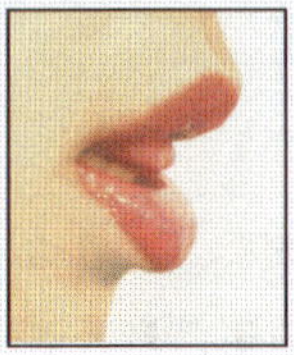

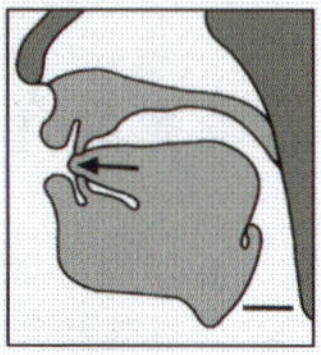

大话发音

舌尖在两齿之间，气流穿过阻碍送出。

当气流穿过舌齿间，通过阻碍形成摩擦，气流自己产生的声音就是就是[θ]的发音。

撕

发音代言人

mouth

[maʊθ] 嘴

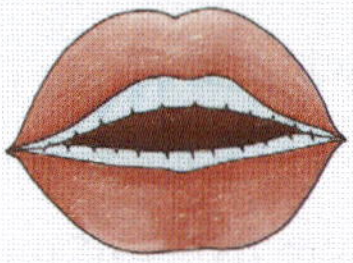

常见发音字母及字母组合

音标	对应字母	自然发音规则	单词示例
[θ]	th	字母th在单词中可发[θ]音。	earth [ɜːθ] 土地

[ð]

发音要素

[ð]是舌齿摩擦辅音。发音时舌尖轻触上齿背，气流由舌齿间送出，形成摩擦音。[ð] 是浊辅音，声带振动。

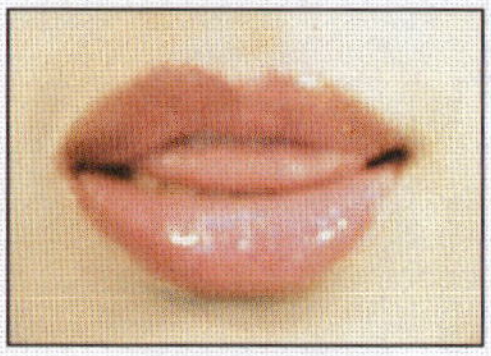

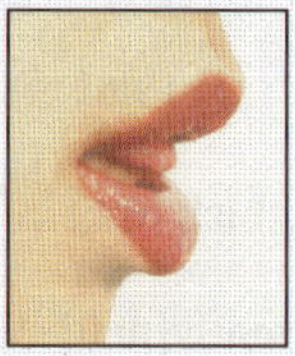

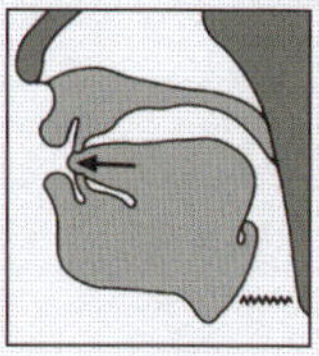

大话发音

这是一个很难的音标，发音时舌尖在两齿之间，然后气流穿过，就像睡觉时发出的 zz 声，与汉字中“资”发音方式相似。

当气流在舌齿间穿过时，振动声带，就发出 [ð] 的发音。

资

发音代言人

feather

['feðə] 羽毛

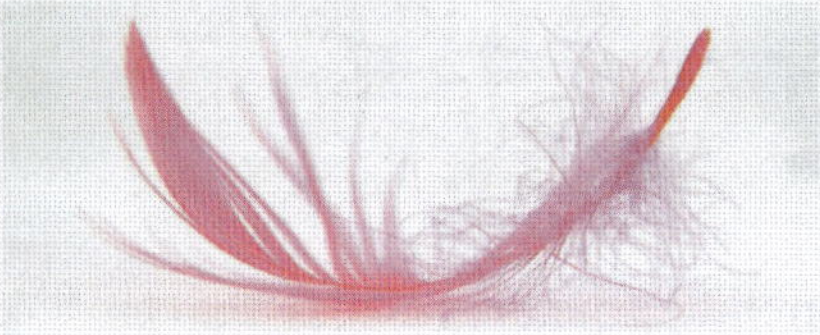

常见发音字母及字母组合

音标	对应字母	自然发音规则	单词示例
[ð]	th	字母th在单词中可发[ð]音。	this [ðɪs] 这个
[ð]	the	字母the在单词中可发[ð]音。	breathe [bri:ð] 呼吸

发音操练

[θ]	[ð]
thief [θi:f] 小偷；贼	**that** [ðæt] 那个
thin [θɪn] 薄的	**these** [ði:z] 这些
thick [θɪk] 厚的	**those** [ðəuz] 那些
tooth [tu:θ] 牙齿	**father** ['fɑ:ðə] 爸爸
cloth [klɔθ] 布	**clothe** [kləuð] 穿衣
bath [bɑ:θ] 沐浴	**bathe** [beɪð] 沐浴；洗澡
theme [θi:m] 主题	**they** [ðeɪ] 他们
thank [θæŋk] 感谢	**there** [ðɛə] 那里
thing [θɪŋ] 物；东西	**thus** [ðʌs] 这样
faith [feɪθ] 信任；信仰	**whether** ['weðə] 天气

基础短语

- through [θru:] these [ði:z] examples 通过这些实例
- with [wɪð] thick [θɪk] feather ['feðə] 有厚厚的羽毛
- a mother ['mʌðə] in her sixth [sɪksθ] month [mʌnθ] 一个怀孕六个月的母亲
- a thousand ['θauznd] thanks [θæŋks] 多谢
- a healthy ['helθi] father ['fɑ:ðə] 一个健康的父亲
- through [θru:] thick [θɪk] and thin [θɪn] 不畏艰险

以句识音

1. They [ðeɪ] may thank [θæŋk] themselves [ðəm'selvz] for that [ðæt].
他们自作自受。

2. Mr. Smith [smɪθ] talked about this [ðɪs], that [ðæt], and the [ði:] other ['ʌðə].
史密斯先生谈了各种各样的事情。

3. They [ðeɪ] will stick together [tə'geðə] through [θru:] thick [θɪk] and thin [θɪn].
不管有什么艰难险阻他们都会团结在一起。

4. The [ðə] sea covers almost three [θri:]-fourths [fɔ:θs] of the [ði:] earth [ɜ:θ]'s surface.
海洋几乎占地球表面的四分之三。

5. The [ðə] teacher pointed out that [ðæt] that [ðæt] "that" [ðæt] that [ðæt] that [ðæt] student had written was in the wrong place.
老师指出那个学生写的那个"that"用错了地方。

6. May the [ðə] fourth [fɔ:θ] is China's Youth [ju:θ] Day.
五月四日是中国的青年节。

经典绕口令（运动你的舌头）

1. I thought [θɔ:t] a thought [θɔ:t]. But the [ðə] thought [θɔ:t] I thought [θɔ:t] wasn't the [ðə] thought [θɔ:t] I thought [θɔ:t] I thought [θɔ:t]. If the thought [θɔ:t] I thought [θɔ:t] I thought [θɔ:t] had been the [ðə] thought [θɔ:t] I thought [θɔ:t], I wouldn't have thought [θɔ:t] so much.
我有一种想法，但是我的这种想法不是我曾经想到的那种想法。如果这种想法是我曾经想到的想法，我就不会想那么多了。

2. Nothing ['nʌθɪŋ] is worth [wɜ:θ] thousands ['θaʊzndz] of deaths [deθs].
没有什么值得数千人死亡。

3. There [ðeə] those [ðəʊz] thousand ['θaʊznd] thinkers ['θɪŋkəz] were thinking ['θɪŋkɪŋ] how the [ði:] other ['ʌðə] three [θri:] thieves [θi:vz] went through [θru:].
成千上万的人在思考其他三个小偷是怎么通过的。

4. Elizabeth's [ɪ'lɪzəbəθs] birthday ['bɜ:θdeɪ] is on the [ðə] third [θɜ:d] Thursday ['θɜ:zdeɪ] of this [ðɪs] month [mʌnθ].
伊丽莎白的生日是这个月的第三个星期四。

5. Thank [θæŋk] the [ði:] other ['ʌðə] three [θri:] brothers ['brʌðəz] of their [ðeə] father's ['fɑ:ðəz] mother's ['mʌðəz] brother's ['brʌðəz] side.
谢谢舅公的另外三个兄弟。

影音荟萃

一 听音乐学音标

I Need to Be in Love

我要恋爱

Carpenters

The hardest thing [θɪŋ] I've ever done is keep believing
There's someone in this crazy world for me
The way that people come and go through [θruː] temporary lives
My chance could come and I might never know
I used to say, "No promises, let's keep it simple."
But freedom only helps you say goodbye
It took a while for me to learn that nothing ['nʌθɪŋ] comes for free
The price I paid is high enough for me
I know I need to be in love
I know I've wasted too much time
I know I ask perfection of a quite imperfect world
And fool enough to think [θɪŋk] that's what I'll find

So here I am with pockets full of good intentions
But none of them will comfort me tonight
I'm wide awake at 4 a.m. without a friend in sight

我所经历的最困难的事情就是
坚信
在这个疯狂的世界总有一个人为我而活
人们在这短暂的生命中
来去匆匆
缘分很可能就这样跟我错身而过
过去我常说:
"不要承诺，简单最好"
但是自由只会让人离别
后来我才知道
获得总要付出代价
我已付出得太多
我要恋爱
我浪费的时间已经很多
在这不完美的世界
寻找着完美
只有像我这样的愚人才会相信
我可以找到

纵使今晚
我满怀希望
但还是无法开怀
半夜四点，我辗转难眠
身边无人陪伴

I'm hanging on a hope but I'm all right
I know I need to be in love
I know I've wasted too much time
I know I ask perfection of a quite imperfect world
And fool enough to **th**ink [θɪŋk] that's what I'll find
I know I need to be in love
I know I've wasted too much time
I know I ask perfection of a quite imperfect world
And fool enough to **th**ink [θɪŋk] that's what I'll find

一切只能寄托希望，但是我真的还好
我要恋爱
我浪费的时间已经很多
在这不完美的世界
寻找着完美
只有像我这样的愚人才会相信
我可以找到
我要恋爱
我浪费的时间已经很多
在这不完美的世界
寻找着完美
只有像我这样的愚人才会相信
我可以找到

歌曲评论

卡朋特乐队（Carpenters）是美国 70 年代商业上最成功的柔情音乐团体之一，来自康涅狄格州黑文市的一支兄妹二重唱组合——哥哥 Richard（生于 1946 年 10 月 15 日，键盘手兼歌手）和妹妹 Karen（生于 1950 年 3 月 2 日，歌手兼鼓手）。卡朋特兄妹于1965年开始组织乐队，其单曲*Close to You*（靠近你）于1969年11月15日一举走红，其后，他们在整个70年代大获成功。*Yesterday Once More*（昨日重现）、*Top of the World*（世界之巅）、*Please Mr. Postman*（请等一下，邮差先生）等歌曲广为人知。1983年2月4日，卡伦 · 卡朋特因长期严重的神经性厌食症而突然去世，卡朋特乐队随之告终。

I Need to Be in Love 是卡朋特组合1976年出的专辑《*A Kind of Hush*》中的一首歌曲。

Breathe
呼吸

Taylor Swift

I see your face in my mind as I drive away
Cause none of us thought it was gonna end that way
People are people and sometimes we change our minds

我驾车离开时，我的脑海出现了你的面容
我们谁也没想过
是这样的结局
但我们毕竟是人
有时我们会改变自己的想法

But it's killing me to see you go after all this time

但是这害得我要看你离去

Music starts playing like the end of a sad movie
It's the kinda ending you don't really wanna see
Cause it's tragedy and it'll only bring you down
Now I don't know what to be without [wɪ'ðaʊt] you around

音乐响起，就像一个悲伤的电影落幕
这是你最不希望看到的结局
因为这样的悲剧只会让你失望
我不知道没有你在身边会是怎样

And we know it's never simple, never easy
Never a clean break, no one here to save me
You're the [ðə] only thing I know like the back of my hand
And I can't breathe [bri:ð] without you, but I have to
Breathe without [wɪ'ðaʊt] you, but I have to

我们知道这并不简单，这并不容易
从来没有划清界限，没有人能够救我
你是唯一一个
我能了如指掌的人
离开你我不能呼吸
不过我必须如此
没有你继续呼吸，不过我必须如此

Never wanted this, never want to see you hurt
Every little bump in the road, I tried to swerve
People are people and sometimes it doesn't work out
And nothing we say is gonna save us from the fallout

从来不想这样，从来不想看你受伤
在小路上的每个颠簸，我都尝试着转弯
但我们毕竟是人
有时候这是行不通的
没什么可以解救我们

And we know it's never simple, never easy
Never a clean break, no one here to save me
You're the only thing I know like the back of my hand
And I can't breathe [bri:ð] without [wɪ'ðaʊt] you, but I have to
Breathe [bri:ð] without [wɪ'ðaʊt] you, but I have to
Breathe [bri:ð] without [wɪ'ðaʊt] you, but I have to
It's 2 a.m., feeling like I just lost a friend
Hope you know it's not easy, easy for me
It's 2 a.m., feeling like I just lost a friend
Hope you know this isn't easy, easy for me
And we know it's never simple, never easy

我们知道这并不简单，并不容易
永远无法一刀两断，没有人能拯救我
你是唯一一个
我能了如指掌的人
离开你我不能呼吸

不过我必须如此
没有你继续呼吸，不过必须这样做
没有你继续呼吸，不过我必须如此
2点钟了，感觉就像我失去了一个好友
希望你明白这对我来说并不容易
2点钟了，感觉就像我失去了一个好友
希望你明白这对我来说并不简单
我们都知道它并不简单，并不容易

Never a clean break, no one here to save me | 永远无法一刀两断，没有人能拯救我
Oh, I can't breathe [bri:ð] without [wɪ'ðaʊt] you but I have to | 噢……没有你我不能呼吸 不过我必须如此
Breathe [bri:ð] without [wɪ'ðaʊt] you, but I have to | 没有你继续呼吸，不过我必须如此
Breathe [bri:ð] without [wɪ'ðaʊt] you, but I have to | 没有你继续呼吸，不过我必须如此
I'm sorry, I'm sorry ... | 对不起，对不起……

歌曲评论

*Breathe*是Taylor Swift 在专辑*Fearless*中的一首与Colbie Caillat合唱的美国抒情风格的歌曲，讲述的是一段友谊的结束。*Breathe*于 2008年10月21日作为*Fearless*的宣传单曲发行，是Taylor三张专辑里唯一一首和别人合唱的歌曲。这首歌获得了2010年第52届格莱美"Best Pop Collaboration with Vocals"的提名，最终输给了Colbie和Jason Mraz合唱的*Lucky*。

二 看电影学音标

电影简介：

《麻雀变凤凰》（*Pretty Woman*）（又称《漂亮女人》）是朱莉娅·罗伯茨的成名作，是一部典型的讲述出身经历低俗的女子如何与身份悬殊的男人相遇相爱并结婚的现代灰姑娘故事。

爱德华要带维维安去参加一个晚会，所以他要维维安打扮得体且高贵。（节选自《麻雀变凤凰》）

Edward: We may be going at evening, need something ['sʌmθɪŋ] to wear. | 爱德华：我们晚上要出去，需要穿合适的衣服。
Vivian: Like what? | 维维安：怎样的？
Edward: Nothing ['nʌθɪŋ] too flashy or too sexy. Conservative, understand? | 爱德华：不要太花哨，也不要太性感。保守点的，知道吗？
Vivian: Boring! | 维维安：没意思！

Edward: Elegant! Any questions?

Vivian: Can I call you Eddie?

Edward: I will expect the answer.

Vivian: I would stay for two **th**ousand ['θaʊznd].

Edward: I would pay four, I'll see you tonight.

Vivian: Baby, I'm going to treat you so nice, you never get to wanna let me go!

Edward: Three **th**ousand ['θaʊznd] six days and Vivian, I will let you go.

Vivian: But I'm here now. Ha-ha-three **th**ousand ['θaʊznd] dollars!!

爱德华：要高贵！还有问题吗？

维维安：我可以叫你爱迪吗？

爱德华：我会期待的。

维维安：给我两千美元，我会留下的。

爱德华：我会付你四千，今晚见。

维维安：亲爱的，我会好好伺候你的，你可能会不想让我走了！

爱德华：六天三千美元，维维安，到时候我会让你走的。

维维安：但我已经在这里了。哈哈——三千美元！

电影简介：

《面纱》（*The Painted Veil*）是一部美国电影。电影讲述男女主角为爱流离，由伦敦至上海再到瘟疫蔓延的荒僻农乡，远走千里，情欲迷失，最终在陌生的国度、动荡的乱世，却找到了心之所在的故事。

母亲和吉蒂之间的对话。（节选自《面纱》）

—The point is whe**th**er ['weðə] I'm in love with him, and I'm not.

—You'd better be careful, young lady. Time can run out, you know.

—Oh, stop it, mother ['mʌðə]. Honestly. The very idea that a woman should marry any Tom, Dick, or Harry regardless of her own feelings is simply prehistoric.

—How much longer do you expect your fa**th**er ['fɑːðə] to go on supporting you?

—关键是我爱不爱他，而我不爱他。

—孩子，你还是小心点。岁月不饶人的。

—哦，母亲别说了。真的。不顾自己的感情，随便就嫁个人，这种想法简直太落伍了。

—你指望你父亲把你养到什么时候？

Unit 6 [ʃ] & [ʒ]

[ʃ]

发音要素

[ʃ]是舌端齿龈后部摩擦辅音。发音时舌端是靠近齿龈后部，舌身抬起靠近上腭，双唇稍收圆并略突出。气流通过时形成摩擦音。[ʃ] 是清辅音，声带不振动。

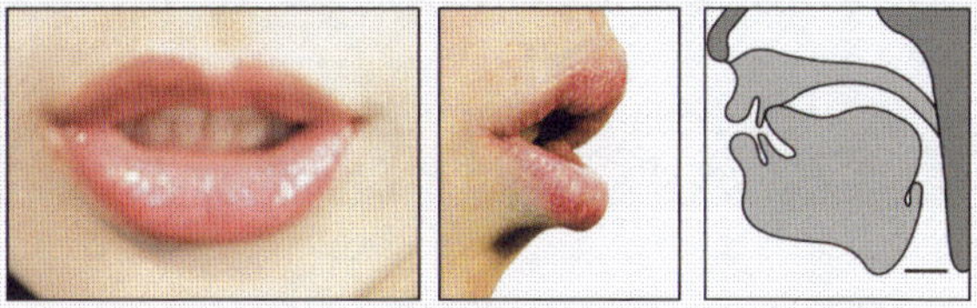

大话发音

动物界中最威风凛凛的要数狮子了，“狮”与 [ʃ] 同音。

当说“狮”字时，就会发出[ʃ]音，不过声带不振动。

狮

发音代言人

cash

[kæʃ] 现金

常见发音字母及字母组合

音标	对应字母	自然发音规则	单词示例
[ʃ]	sh	字母组合sh在单词中发[ʃ]音。	fish [fɪʃ] 鱼

[ʃ]	s	字母s可发[ʃ]音。	sugar ['ʃʊgə] 糖
[ʃ]	ss	字母组合ss可发[ʃ]音。	pressure ['preʃə] 压力
[ʃ]	c	字母c可发[ʃ]音。	ocean ['əʊʃn] 海洋
[ʃ]	ch	字母组合ch可发[ʃ]音。	chef [ʃef] 主厨
[ʃ]	t	字母t可发[ʃ]音。	station ['steɪʃn] 车站

[ʒ]

发音要素

[ʒ]是舌端齿龈后部摩擦辅音。发音时舌端是靠近齿龈后部，舌身抬起靠近上腭，双唇稍收圆并略突出。[ʒ]是浊辅音，声带振动。

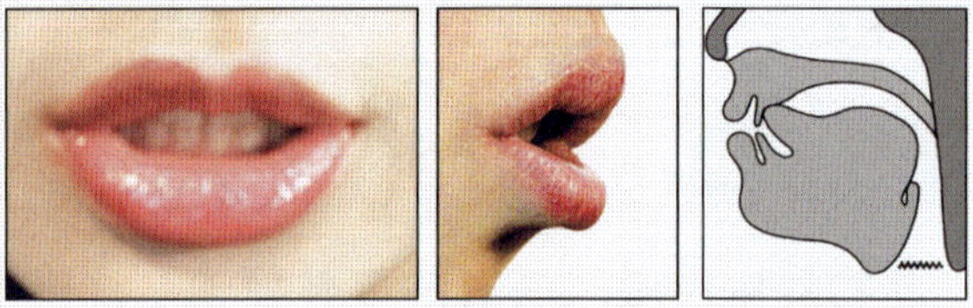

大话发音

“日”在汉语拼音中是发仄声，把它发成平声，就和[ʒ]的发音相似。

和汉语中表示太阳的“日”字发音相似，发平音，就发出[ʒ]的音了。

日

发音代言人

television

['telɪvɪʒn] 电视

常见发音字母及字母组合

音标	对应字母	自然发音规则	单词示例
[ʒ]	s	字母s在单词中可发[ʒ]音。	**pleasure** ['pleʒə] 快乐；娱乐
[ʒ]	g	字母g在单词中可发[ʒ]音。	**garage** ['gærɑːʒ] 车库
[ʒ]	z	字母z在单词中可发[ʒ]音。	**seizure** ['siːʒə] 捉住；查封

发音操练

[ʃ]	[ʒ]
ship [ʃɪp] 船	**leisure** ['leʒə] 闲暇
shoe [ʃuː] 鞋	**measure** ['meʒə] 测量
shop [ʃɒp] 商店	**vision** ['vɪʒn] 视力；视觉
wash [wɒʃ] 洗	**massage** ['mæsɑːʒ] 按摩
dish [dɪʃ] 盘子	**treasure** ['treʒə] 财宝
push [pʊʃ] 推	**usual** ['juːʒuəl] 通常的
sure [ʃʊə] 确信的	**revision** [rɪ'vɪʒn] 修订；修改
Asia ['eɪʃə] 亚洲	**closure** ['kləʊʒə] 停业；关闭
mission ['mɪʃn] 任务	**provision** [prə'vɪʒn] 供应
machine [mə'ʃiːn] 机器	**prestige** [pre'stiːʒ] 威望

基础短语

- push [pʊʃ] the sheep [ʃiːp] 赶羊
- feel flushed [flʌʃt] with shame [ʃeɪm] 因惭愧而感到脸红

- in good financial [faɪ'nænʃl] shape [ʃeɪp] 经济情况良好
- the treasure ['treʒə] house of art 艺术的宝库
- the closure ['kləʊʒə] of information [ˌɪnfə'meɪʃn] 消息的封锁
- the vision ['vɪʒn] of a poet 诗人的想象力

以句识音

1. Don't mention ['menʃn] it.
不客气。

2. Is she studying English ['ɪŋglɪʃ]?
她正在学英语吗？

3. She showed [ʃəʊd] her appreciation [əˌpri:ʃi'eɪʃn] for my help.
她对我的帮助表示感谢。

4. Measure ['meʒə] for measure ['meʒə].
以牙还牙。

5. She takes pleasure ['pleʒə] in window-shopping ['ʃɒpɪŋ].
她喜欢只看不买。

6. The shopkeeper ['ʃɒpˌki:pə] gave me short measure ['meʒə].
店家给我的分量不足。

经典绕口令（运动你的舌头）

1. "Shall [ʃæl] I show you the shop [ʃɒp] for shoes [ʃu:z] and shirts [ʃɜ:ts]?" Shirley ['ʃɜ:lɪ] said to Shelly ['ʃeli].
雪莉对谢利说：“要我带你去买衣服和鞋子的店吗？”

2. She [ʃi:] sells seashells ['si:ʃelz] by the seashore ['si:ʃɔ:]. The shells ['ʃelz] she sells are surely seashells ['si:ʃelz]. So if she sells shells [ʃelz] on the seashore ['si:ʃɔ:], I'm sure she sells seashore ['si:ʃɔ:] shells [ʃelz].
她在海岸卖贝壳，她卖的贝壳是真正的贝壳。因此，若她在海岸上卖贝壳，我肯定她卖的是海岸贝壳。

3. Sheep [ʃi:p] shouldn't ['ʃʊdnt] sleep in a shack [ʃæk]. Sheep [ʃi:p] should [ʃʊd] sleep in a shed [ʃed].

羊儿不应住简棚，羊儿应住好羊棚。

4. In his garage ['gærɑ:ʒ] there have been three broken televisions ['telɪvɪʒnz].

在他的车库里已经有三台坏电视了。

5. Dr. Johnson and Mr. Johnson, after great consideration [kənˌsɪdə'reɪʃn], came to the conclusion [kən'klu:ʒn].

约翰逊博士和约翰逊先生经过仔细的考虑后，得出了一个结论。

影音荟萃

一 听音乐学音标

She
她

Groove Coverage

She [ʃi:] hangs out every day nearby the beach	她每天在海边漫步
Havin' a Heineken fallin' asleep	喝杯喜力啤酒便入睡
She [ʃi:] looks so sexy when she [ʃi:]'s walking the sand	漫步在沙滩上的她 看上去如此性感
Nobody ever put a ring on her hand	还从未有人给她戴上戒指
Swim to the ocean['əʊʃn] shore [ʃɔ:] fishing[fiʃɪŋ] in the sea	海边游泳，海里捕鱼
She [ʃi:] is the story, the story is she	她就是传说，传说就是她
She [ʃi:] sings to the moon and the stars in the sky	她向天上的月亮和星星唱歌
Shining ['ʃaɪnɪŋ] from high above, you shouldn't ['ʃʊdnt] ask why	它们在一闪一闪 不要问为什么
She [ʃi:] is the one that you never forget	她就是那个你忘不了的人

She [ʃi:] is the heaven-sent angel you met	她是天堂派来的天使
Oh, she [ʃi:] must be the reason why God made	噢，她就是
a girl	上帝制造女孩的原因
She [ʃi:] is so pretty all over the world	她是世界上最美丽的女孩
She [ʃi:] puts the rhythm, the beat in the drum	她让鼓点变得更加铿锵
She [ʃi:] comes in the morning and the evening	她早上出现
she [ʃi:] 's gone	晚上就不见
Every little hour every second you live	你活着的每分每秒
Trust in eternity that's what she [ʃi:] gives	永远相信那是她赋予你的
She [ʃi:] looks like Marilyn, walks like Suzanne	她长得像玛丽莲，走路又像苏珊妮
She [ʃi:] talks like Monica and Marianne	她说话像莫妮卡和玛丽安
She [ʃi:] wins in everything that she [ʃi:] might	只要她愿意
do	她可以得到一切
And she [ʃi:] will respect you， forever just you	但她永远都尊重你，只是因为是你
She [ʃi:] is the one that you never forget	她就是那个你忘不了的人
She [ʃi:] is the heaven-sent angel you met	她是天堂派来的天使
Oh, she [ʃi:] must be the reason why God made	噢，她就是上帝制造女孩
a girl	的原因
She [ʃi:] is so pretty all over the world	她是世界上最美丽的女孩
She [ʃi:] is so pretty all over the world	她是世界上最美丽的女孩
She [ʃi:] is so pretty	她如此的美丽
She [ʃi:] is like you and me, like them like we	她就像你和我，像他们像我们
She [ʃi:] is in you and me	她就在你我中间
She [ʃi:] is the one that you never forget	她就是那个你忘不了的人
She [ʃi:] is the heaven-sent angel you met	她是天堂派来的天使
She [ʃi:] must be the reason why God made a	噢，她就是上帝制造女孩
girl	的原因
She [ʃi:] is so pretty all over the world (oh...)	她是世界上最美丽的女孩
Na na na na na ...	呐，呐，呐，呐，呐……

歌曲评论

Groove Coverage（舞动精灵王族）是德国2001年的新晋乐队，以其混合多种元素的舞曲风格迅速走红，驰名全欧。乐队曾有12首单曲进入德国前50强，其中更是有3首单曲进入前10。4张独立专辑发行量超过500万张（仅在中国发行量就超过200万张）。G.C.立志成为德国最成功的舞曲音乐家。*God Is A Girl*（上帝是个女孩）就是Groove Coverage的经典作品之一。另外，在中国颇为受欢迎的歌曲还有：*Far away from Home*、*7 Years and 50 Days*、*She*、*On the Radio*等。近年来的代表作品有：*Innocent*，*Angeline*等。

She 是乐队2004年出品的专辑*7 Years and 50 Days*中的一首歌，轻松愉快的节奏深受歌迷喜欢。

Rise to the Occasion
我能应付

BWO

I take you one step further	我带你前进一步
I take you one step further	我带你前进一步
I will rise to the occasion [ə'keɪʒn]	我能应付
I will always be there by your side	我会永远守在你身边
I will rise to the occasion [ə'keɪʒn]	我能应付
You can count on my pride ah ah ah ah	你可以相信我
The words are on your lips	有些话就在你嘴边
And I can hear you recite	我能听到你在默念
You're going through the motions	通过这些动作
And I know how you fight	我知道你是如何抗争的
But you don't need to worry	但你无须担心
About thieves in the night	夜晚的强盗
Cause I will be there by your side	因为我会守在你身边
Your life has been a struggle	你的生活一直都是在抗争
Now come see about me	现在来看我
I've got my graduation	我已经毕业了
You're my final degree	你就是我拿到的最终学位
I will ignore the warnings	当我给你自由时
While I'm setting you free	我会忽略所有的警告
Cause I will be there by your side	因为我会守在你身边
I will rise to the occasion [ə'keɪʒn]	我能应付
I will always be there by your side	我会永远守在你身边
I will rise to the occasion [ə'keɪʒn]	我能应付

You can count on my pride ah ah ah ah	你可以相信我
Who said life should be easy	谁说生活很容易
That was not my refrain	那不是我的状态
My life has been preparing	我的生活一直都在
For the storm and the rain	为狂风暴雨做准备
So when the winds are blowing	因此，当狂风来临时
I'll be your hurricane	我会是你的飓风
Cause I will be there by your side	因为我会守在你身边
I will rise to the occasion [ə'keɪʒn]	我能应付
I will always be there by your side	我会永远守在你身边
I will rise to the occasion [ə'keɪʒn]	我能应付
You can count on my pride ah ah ah ah	你可以相信我
The words are on my lips	有些话就在我嘴边
And you can hear me recite	你能听到我在默念
I'm going through the motions	通过这些动作
And you know how much I fight	你知道我是如何抗争的
But I don't need to worry	但是我无须担心
About thieves in the night	夜晚的强盗
Cause you will be there by my side	因为你会守在我身边
And when you feel it's over	当你感觉一切都结束时
I take you one step further	我会带你前进一步
And when you feel it's over	当你感觉一切都结束时
I take you one step further	我会带你前进一步
And when you feel it's over	当你感觉一切都结束时
I take you one step further	我会带你前进一步
You know you can count on my pride ah ah ah ah	你知道你可以相信我
I will rise to the occasion [ə'keɪʒn]	我能应付
I will always be there by your side	我会永远守在你身边
I will rise to the occasion [ə'keɪʒn]	我能应付
You can count on my pride ah ah ah ah	你可以相信我
I will rise to the occasion [ə'keɪʒn]	我能应付
I will always be there by your side	我会永远守在你身边
I will rise to the occasion [ə'keɪʒn]	我能应付
You can count on my pride ah ah ah ah	你可以相信我

歌曲评论

空壳乐队（Bodies Without Organs，BWO，2003～2010）曾经是瑞典的一个电子流行音乐组合，共有三名成员：马丁·罗林斯基（Martin Rolinski，主唱）、亚历山大·巴德（Alexander Bard，键盘/伴唱/编曲）和玛丽娜·斯西普仁科（Marina Schiptjenko，键盘/伴唱/编曲）。乐队的名字“Bodies Without Organs”取自法国哲学家吉尔·德勒兹提出的哲学概念。这个三人小组，糅合了动感的欧陆舞曲、动人的抒情曲风及畅快的八十年代风格，横扫九十年代的瑞典怪趣流行舞曲团Army Of Lovers的主脑亚历山大·巴德领军的欧陆超级流行团体。2010年初，在经历了不到六年发五张专辑的紧张职业生涯后，BWO宣布暂时解散。三位BWO的成员都认为这是友好的解散，并不会妨碍他们未来和BWO或其他组织的合作。

BWO于2009年4月1号发行他们的第四张录音专辑，包括12首新歌和两首remix。其中第五首歌曲 *Rise to the Occasion*，感觉回到了八十年代的流行乐坛，马丁不再用力咬着字眼，不再用尖厉的声音吟唱，采用了比较平和淡定的发音方式，偶尔会有八十年代美国流行乐坛的感觉，编曲虽然不是特别出彩，倒也一气呵成，不容大脑多作思考，是一首比较容易让人放松心情的歌。

二 看电影学音标

电影简介：

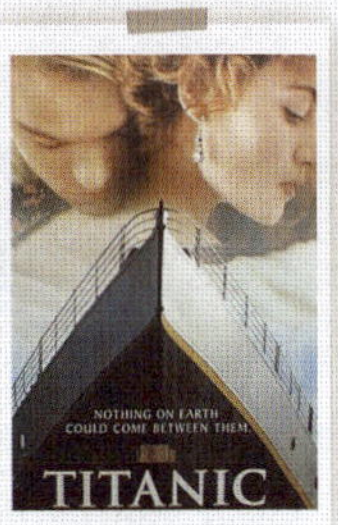

《泰坦尼克号》（*Titanic*）是美国福克斯公司于1994年拍摄的一部浪漫史诗式的灾难电影，由詹姆斯·卡梅隆创作、编辑、制作、导演及监制，好莱坞著名影星莱昂纳多·迪卡普里奥、凯特·温斯莱特出演。影片以1912年泰坦尼克号邮轮在其处女航行中触礁冰山而沉没的事件为背景，描述了处于不同阶层的两个人——穷画家杰克和贵族女罗丝抛弃世俗的偏见坠入爱河，最终杰克把生存的机会让给了罗丝的感人故事。影片于1997年11月1日在东京首映。

泰坦尼克号正要起航，乘客们纷纷登船。（节选自《泰坦尼克号》）

Man:	Look at the boat.	男士：看这船！
Boy:	Dad, it's a **sh**ip [ʃɪp].	男孩：爸爸，是大轮船。
Man:	You are right.	男士：你说得对。
Rose:	I don't see what all the fuss is about. It doesn't look any bigger than the Mauritania.	罗丝：没什么大不了的嘛！不会大过毛里塔尼亚号。

Cal: You can be blase about some things, Rose, but not about Titanic. It's over a hundred feet longer than Mauritania, and far more luxurious. Your daughter is much too hard to impress, Ruth.

卡尔：有些东西你可以小瞧，罗丝，但绝对不能小看泰坦尼克号。它比毛里塔尼亚号长一百多尺，而且要豪华得多。你女儿真是挑剔啊，露丝。

Ruth: So this is the **sh**ip [ʃɪp] they say is unsinkable.

露丝：这就是他们说的不沉之船？

Cal: It is unsinkable. God himself couldn't sink this **sh**ip [ʃɪp].

卡尔：没错，绝对不会沉，上帝也不能让这艘船沉。

电影简介：

《地心历险记2：神秘岛》（*Journey2: The Mysterious Island*）由布拉德·佩顿执导，道恩·强森、乔什·哈切森等联袂主演。在这一部中乔什·哈切森饰演的男主角肖恩接收到来自神秘岛屿的求救信号，这个信号与他失踪的祖父息息相关。肖恩决定去神秘岛一探究竟，但母亲的男友（强森饰演）竭力阻止他，因为传说神秘岛有许多未知的危险。肖恩一意孤行，为了保证他的安全，母亲的男友只好陪同他前往，与他们一起去的还有飞行员父女。

肖恩一行人在神秘岛上发现了埋藏的金子宝藏，肖恩想起了史蒂文森的《金银岛》

（节选自《地心历险记2：神秘岛》）

—Wait, what's that?

—Volcanic ash?

—It looks like…

—Gold. Pure gold.

—The trea**s**ure ['treʒə] Stevenson talked about in *Trea**s**ure* ['treʒə] *Island*. Volcanoes are made of what they erupt. So if the thing's erupting gold, then it's…

—A mountain of gold.

—等等，那是什么？

—火山灰？

—它看上去像……

—金子，纯金。

—这是个宝藏，史蒂文森在《金银岛》中谈到过，火山是由火山喷发的东西构成的。因此，如果这个东西能喷发出金子，那么它就是……

—金山。

Unit 7 [tʃ] & [dʒ]

[tʃ]

发音要素

[tʃ]是舌端齿龈破擦辅音。发音时舌身抬高，舌端抵上齿龈后部，气流通过时发出破擦音。[tʃ] 是清辅音，声带不振动。

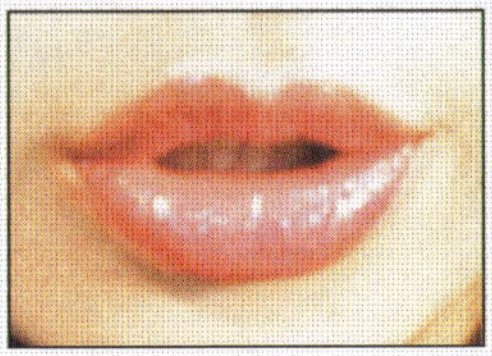

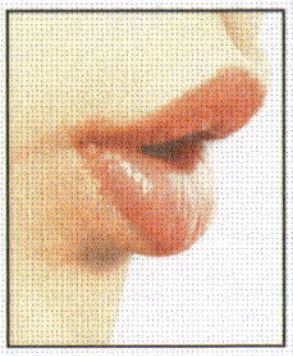

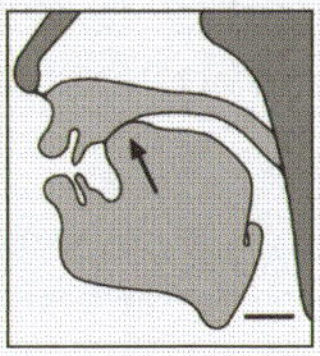

大话发音

小女孩，脸皮薄，哧哧地笑的时候，发出“嗤”的声音，就与 [tʃ] 的发音相似。

声带不动，嘴巴撅起，发出[tʃ]音。

嗤

发音代言人

chair

[tʃeə] 椅子

常见发音字母及字母组合

音标	对应字母	自然发音规则	单词示例
[tʃ]	ch	字母组合ch在单词中可发[tʃ]音。	church [tʃɜːtʃ] 教堂

[tʃ]	tch	字母组合tch可发[tʃ]音。	watch [wɒtʃ] 手表

[dʒ]

发音要素

[dʒ]是舌端齿龈破擦辅音。发音时舌身抬高，舌端抵上齿龈后部，气流通过时发出破擦音。[dʒ]是浊辅音，声带振动。

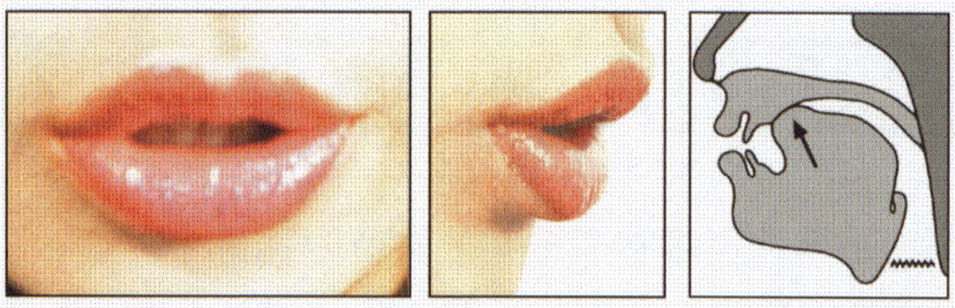

大话发音

那个人太胖了，椅子被他压得“吱吱”响。

椅子被压得“吱吱”响的声音就类似于[dʒ]的发音。

吱

发音代言人

jam [dʒæm]

果酱

常见发音字母及字母组合

音标	对应字母	自然发音规则	单词示例
[dʒ]	j	字母j在单词中可发[dʒ]音。	job [dʒɒb] 工作
[dʒ]	g	字母g在单词中可发[dʒ]音。	general ['dʒenrəl] 将军
[dʒ]	ge	字母组合ge在单词中可发[dʒ]音。	large [lɑːdʒ] 大的

[dʒ]	dge	字母组合dge在单词中发[dʒ]音。	bridge [brɪdʒ] 桥

发音操练

[tʃ]	[dʒ]
chain [tʃeɪn] 锁链	jeep [dʒi:p] 吉普车
cheap [tʃi:p] 便宜的	Jane [dʒeɪn] 简（人名）
cheer [tʃɪə] 欢呼	joke [dʒəʊk] 玩笑
china ['tʃaɪnə] 瓷器	change [tʃeɪndʒ] 改变
chat [tʃæt] 闲谈	cage [keɪdʒ] 笼子
lunch [lʌntʃ] 午饭	joy [dʒɔɪ] 欢乐
much [mʌtʃ] 许多	June [dʒu:n] 六月
touch [tʌtʃ] 触摸	germ [dʒɜ:m] 细菌
catch [kætʃ] 抓住	badge [bædʒ] 徽章
ditch [dɪtʃ] 沟；渠	judge [dʒʌdʒ] 法官

基础短语

- watch [wɒtʃ] TV 看电视
- come to China ['tʃaɪnə] 来到中国
- just a child [tʃaɪld] 只是个孩子
- turn over the page [peɪdʒ] 翻过这一页
- orange ['ɒrɪndʒ] juice [dʒu:s] 橘子汁
- made in Japan [dʒə'pæn] 日本制造

以句识音

1. The match [mætʃ] won't catch [kætʃ].
   火柴点不着。
2. Charles [tʃɑ:lz] wears a digital ['dɪdʒɪtl] watch [wɒtʃ].
   查尔斯戴了一只数字手表。
3. Would you like some orange ['ɒrɪndʒ] juice [dʒu:s]?
   来点儿橘汁吗？
4. There was just a suggestion [sə'dʒestʃən] of a smile on her face.
   她脸上只流露出稍许微笑。
5. After lunch [lʌntʃ] he challenged ['tʃælɪndʒd] me to a game of chess [tʃes].
   饭后他向我发起挑战，让我和他下象棋。
6. Teaching ['ti:tʃɪŋ] young children ['tʃɪldrən] is a challenging ['tʃælɪndʒɪŋ] and rewarding job [dʒɒb].
   教幼儿是一项既挑战性又值得做的工作。

经典绕口令（运动你的舌头）

1. Chopshop [ˈtʃɒpʃɒp] shops stock chops [tʃɒps].
   印章店备有印章。
2. If two witches ['wɪtʃɪz] would watch [wɒtʃ] two watches ['wɒtʃɪz], which witch [wɪtʃ] would watch [wɒtʃ] which watch [wɒtʃ]?
   如果两个女巫看两个手表，那么哪个女巫会看哪个手表？
3. Cheerful ['tʃɪəfl] Charlie ['tʃɑ:li] chose [tʃəuz] cheesy ['tʃi:zi] chowder ['tʃaudə].
   快乐的查理选择了干酪海鲜汤。
4. The judge [dʒʌdʒ] in his jeans can't jump [dʒʌmp] into his jeep [dʒi:p].
   那位身穿牛仔裤的法官无法跳上他的吉普车。
5. There is a kitten in the kitchen ['kɪtʃɪn]. In the kitchen ['kɪtʃɪn] I fry the chicken ['tʃɪkɪn]. A fly flies into the kitchen ['kɪtʃɪn] while I fry the chicken ['tʃɪkɪn].
   厨房里有一只小猫，我在厨房做炸鸡，当我在做炸鸡时，一只苍蝇飞进厨房。

影音荟萃

一 听音乐学音标

Chasing the Sun
追逐太阳

The Wanted

I'm better	我很好
So much [mʌtʃ] better now	已经好多了
I see the light, touch the light	我看见光亮，触摸光亮
We're together now	我们终于站在一起了
I'm better	我很好
So much [mʌtʃ] better now	已经好多了
Look to the skies, gives me life	看着天空，给我生命
We're together now	我们终于站在一起了
We've only just begun	我们才开始
Hypnotized by drums	沉迷于鼓点的节奏中
Until forever comes	直到永恒来临之际
You'll find us chasing ['tʃeɪsɪŋ] the sun	你会发现我们正在追逐太阳
They said this day wouldn't come	他们说这一天不会到来
We refused to run	我们拒绝奔忙
We've only just begun	这只是开始
You'll find us chasing ['tʃeɪsɪŋ] the sun	你会发现我们正在追逐太阳
Oh oh oh oh oh oh	哦……
Oh oh oh oh oh oh	哦……
Oh oh oh oh oh oh	哦……
You'll find us chasing ['tʃeɪsɪŋ] the sun	你会发现我们正在追逐太阳
Oh oh oh oh oh oh	哦……
Oh oh oh oh oh oh	哦……

Oh oh oh oh oh oh	哦……
You'll find us **ch**asing ['tʃeɪsɪŋ] the sun	你会发现我们正在追逐太阳
When daylight's fading	当阳光渐逝
We're gonna play in the dark	我们将会在黑暗中起舞
Till it's golden again	直到旭日东升
And now it feels so amazing	一切都如此美好
Can see you coming	只因你的到来
And we'll never grow old again	我们永远都不会老去
You'll find us **ch**asing ['tʃeɪsɪŋ] the sun	你会发现我们正在追逐太阳
I'm never	我从不
I'm never down	我从不放弃
Lying here, staring up	我躺在这里，凝视前方
And you're looking down	你睥睨一切
I'm never	我从不
I'm never down	我从不放弃
Live forever, forever	我一直坚持
With you around	只为和你在一起
We've only just begun	我们才开始
Hypnotized by drums	沉迷于鼓点的节奏中
Until forever comes	直到永恒来临之际
You'll find us **ch**asing ['tʃeɪsɪŋ] the sun	你会发现我们正在追逐太阳
They said this day wouldn't come	他们说这一天不会到来
We refused to run	我们拒绝奔忙
We've only just begun	这只是开始
You'll find us **ch**asing ['tʃeɪsɪŋ] the sun	你会发现我们正在追逐太阳
The sun, the sun, the sun	太阳，太阳，太阳
You'll find us **ch**asing ['tʃeɪsɪŋ] the sun	你会发现我们正在追逐太阳
Oh oh oh oh oh oh	哦……
Oh oh oh oh oh oh	哦……

Oh oh oh oh oh oh	哦……
You'll find us chasing ['tʃeɪsɪŋ] the sun	你会发现我们正在追逐太阳
Oh oh oh oh oh oh	哦……
Oh oh oh oh oh oh	哦……
Oh oh oh oh oh oh	哦……
You'll find us chasing ['tʃeɪsɪŋ] the sun	你会发现我们正在追逐太阳
When the daylight's fading	当阳光渐逝
We're gonna play in the dark	我们将会在黑暗中起舞
Till it's golden again	直到旭日东升

And now it feels so amazing	一切都如此美好
Can see you coming	只因你的到来
And we'll never grow old again	我们永远都不会老去
You'll find us chasing ['tʃeɪsɪŋ] the sun	你会发现我们正在追逐太阳

You'll find us chasing ['tʃeɪsɪŋ] the sun	你会发现我们正在追逐太阳
When the daylight's fading	当阳光渐逝
We're gonna play in the dark	我们将会在黑暗中起舞
Till it's golden again	直到旭日东升

And now it feels so amazing	一切都如此美好
Can see you coming	只因你的到来
And we'll never grow old again	我们永远都不会老去
You'll find us chasing ['tʃeɪsɪŋ] the sun	你会发现我们正在追逐太阳
Oh oh oh oh oh oh	哦……
Oh oh oh oh oh oh	哦……
Oh oh oh oh oh oh	哦……
You'll find us chasing ['tʃeɪsɪŋ] the sun	你会发现我们正在追逐太阳
Oh oh oh oh oh oh	哦……
Oh oh oh oh oh oh	哦……
Oh oh oh oh oh oh	哦……
You'll find us chasing ['tʃeɪsɪŋ] the sun	你会发现我们正在追逐太阳

歌曲评论

《追逐太阳》（*Chasing The Sun*）这首歌曲是由英国偶像男子团体The Wanted演唱的，是二十世纪福克斯和蓝天工作室合作的卖座3D动画系列《冰川时代4》（另译《冰河世纪4》）发布的第二支主题曲。

The Wanted（Tom，Max，Nathan，Jay 和 Siva），希望把自己标榜成特立独行的乐队，即在通常的流行乐中加入摇滚和独立乐队的音乐元素。该团体签约环球音乐旗下，于2014年宣布解散。出道单曲*All Time Low*，发行日期为2010年7月5日。这支单曲第一周就一举拿下了英国单曲榜的冠军。乐队于2011年7月10日发行*Glad You Came*专辑，并凭借同名歌曲登上英国UK单曲榜首位，成为冠军。

Imagine
想象

John Lennon

Imagine [ɪ'mædʒɪn] there's no heaven	试着想象根本就没有天堂
It's easy if you try	做这样的想象很简单
No hell below us	我们的脚下没有地狱
Above us only sky	我们的头上只有天空
Imagine [ɪ'mædʒɪn] all the people	想象所有的人们
living for today...	每天踏实地活着……
Imagine [ɪ'mædʒɪn] there's no countries	试着想象这世上不再有国别
It isn't hard to do	做这样的想象并不难
Nothing to kill or die for	没有杀戮或牺牲的借口
And no religion [rɪ'lɪdʒən] too	也没有任何宗教的束缚
Imagine [ɪ'mædʒɪn] all the people	想象所有的人们
living life in peace...	都能过着平静的生活
You may say I'm a dreamer	你可以说我在做梦
But I'm not the only one	但并非只有我这样
I hope some day you'll join [dʒɔɪn] us	我希望未来你会和我们一起

And the world will be as one	这样全世界将合而为一
Imagine [ɪ'mædʒɪn] no possessions	试着想象没有物质财富的生活
I wonder if you can	我不知道你是否向往着这种生活方式
No need for greed or hunger	富人无须贪得无厌，而穷人亦无须挨饿受冻
A brotherhood of man	人们像兄弟姐妹般住在一起
Imagine [ɪ'mædʒɪn] all the people	想象所有的人们
sharing all the world...	分享着同一个世界
You may say I'm a dreamer	你可以说我在做梦
But I'm not the only one	但并非只有我这样
I hope some day you'll join [dʒɔɪn] us	我希望未来你会和我们一起
And the world will live as one	这样全世界将合而为一

歌曲评论

约翰·列侬是全世界最成功的摇滚乐队“甲壳虫”的灵魂人物，在认识来自日本的艺术家小野洋子后，他不但与前妻离婚而娶了她，而且还眼看着乐队在辉煌的巅峰时刻解散。作为一个歌手兼思想领袖，列侬在同时代人乃至后人心中的分量远远超过了任何娱乐界人士。他在六十年代吸毒，目无宗教和政府，但远不及别人干得过火，他在七十年代致力于研究东方宗教和宣扬童话般的爱，但远不如以前热烈，可他改变了成千上万人的思想，并有一颗小行星以他的名字命名，这却是真的。

《想象》是一首看似严肃，实则来自倾听者自身的歌。对于并不打算了解它的背景的人来说，这首歌有足够的空间感和神圣气息，可以引人肃静，在呼吸之间，不经意获取了梦想的许可证——那就像生活在压力之中的人突然被解放出来，随着钢琴漫步，舞动胆怯的手，听来自高处的歌声怎样回响。列侬的演唱已经不再充满小伙子的热情放肆，而是有着超脱、宽容而不容辩驳的散漫。这声音听起来像预言者的祈祷，而歌词却依然是固执的理想。或许列侬所要求的都太绝对、太过纯洁，但作为梦，难道你我就不曾有过吗？大同世界、友爱和平的蓝图或许永不能实现，但听他毫无顾忌地唱来，实在有太多感慨和感动。如果我们这些俗人已经不敢自称是梦想者，那么听听梦想者的歌，也算得上一点慰藉，梦想有千差万别，对梦想的坚持却只有一种。

二 看电影学音标

电影简介:

《朱莉与朱莉娅》（*Julie & Julia*）由诺拉·艾芙隆执导，梅丽尔·斯特里普、艾米·亚当斯主演。讲述了曾在法国生活过的美国人朱莉·查尔德写了一本美食书，而隔代的美国女孩朱莉娅·鲍威尔根据她的书来逐一实践，并发表在博客上，结果开始拥有大批粉丝，也因此懂得人生意义的故事。

朱莉认为做荷包蛋很容易，可事实并非如此。不过，最终朱莉还是成功地做出了荷包蛋，并且在晚饭时吃了她平生第一个鸡蛋。（节选自《朱莉与朱莉娅》）

Julie: I thought eggs were going to be greasy and slimy, but it tastes like **ch**eese [tʃi:z] sauce. Yum. Julia **Ch**ild [tʃaɪld], you are so good.

Friend: **Ch**eers [tʃɪəz].

Husband: **Ch**eers [tʃɪəz]. And, may I say, excellent wine?

朱莉：我本以为鸡蛋会又腻又滑，可是它吃起来就像奶酪酱汁般美味。朱莉·查尔德，你真棒!

朋友：干杯!

丈夫：干杯！而且，我得说，美酒啊!

电影简介:

《暮光之城4：破晓（下）》（*The Twilight Saga*：*Breaking Dawn—Part 2*）由美国演员克里斯汀·斯图尔特、英国演员罗伯特·帕丁森、美国演员泰勒·洛特纳主演，是《暮光之城》系列的最后一部，影片于2012年11月16日在美国上映。

雅各布为了让贝拉的父亲不再为贝拉担心，回家后立即找到贝拉的父亲，将自己的狼形态展现给查理看，查理吓了一大跳。（节选自《暮光之城4：破晓（下）》）

—Look, in order for Bella to get better, she had to chan**ge** [tʃeɪndʒ].

—What do you mean "chan**ge** [tʃeɪndʒ]"?

—Here goes nothing.

—What the hell are you doing?

—You don't live in the world you think you do.

—Jacob, put your clothes on.

—Now, this may seem strange [streɪndʒ], really strange [streɪndʒ]. But stranger ['streɪndʒə] things happen every day. Trust me.

—听着，为了让贝拉身体感觉好点，她必须有所改变。

—你指的改变是什么？

—你真是什么也不懂。

—你在搞什么鬼？

—你并不生活在你想的世界里。

—雅各布，把衣服穿上。

—这看起来很奇怪，是吧？不过更奇怪的事情每天都发生，相信我。

Unit 8 [ts] & [dz]

[ts]

发音要素

[ts]是舌端齿龈破擦辅音。舌端先贴住齿龈，堵住气流，然后下降，气流送出口腔。[ts] 是清辅音，声带不振动。

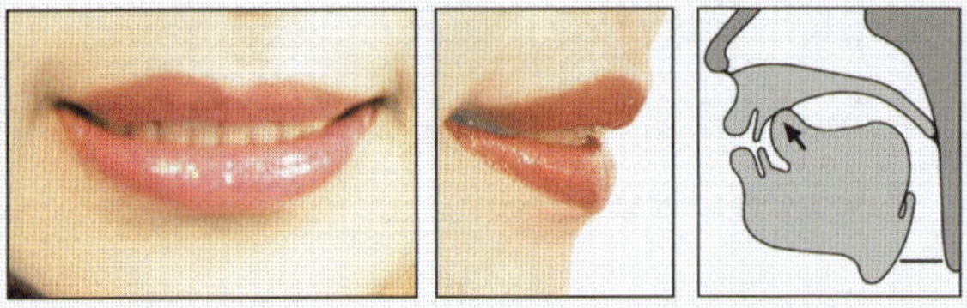

大话发音

旧时的蒸汽火车发动时，一边冒着白烟，一边发出“呲、呲”的声音。

蒸汽火车发动时发出的“呲、呲”声就是[ts]的发音。

呲

发音代言人

boots

[bu:ts] 靴子（复数）

常见发音字母及字母组合

音标	对应字母	自然发音规则	单词示例
[ts]	ts	字母组合ts发[ts]音。	cats [kæts] 猫（复数）
[ts]	tes	字母组合tes可发[ts]音。	rates [reɪts] 比率（复数）

[dz]

发音要素

[dz]是舌端齿龈破擦辅音。舌端先贴住齿龈，堵住气流，然后下降，气流送出口腔。[dz] 是浊辅音，声带振动。

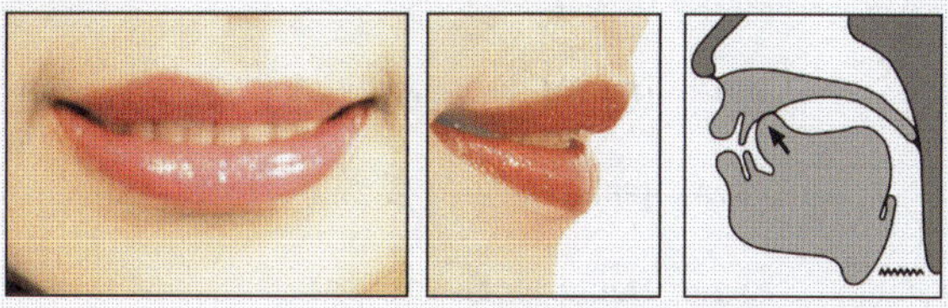

大话发音

在热锅里煎肉时，肉会发出"嗞、嗞"的声音。
把肉放在很烫的煎锅里，肉里的水分遇热油挥发时发出的"嗞、嗞"声就是[dz]的发音。

嗞

发音代言人

hands

[hændz] 手（复数）

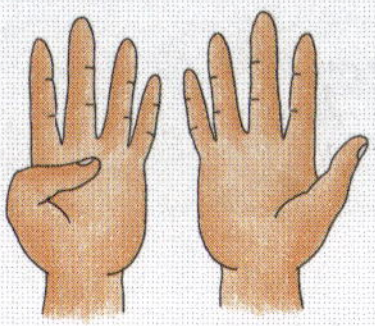

常见发音字母及字母组合

音标	对应字母	自然发音规则	单词示例
[dz]	ds	字母组合ds在单词中可发[dz]音。	beds ['bedz] 床（复数）

发音操练

[ts]	[dz]
carts [kɑːts] 大车（复数）	cards [kɑːdz] 卡片（复数）
mates [meɪts] 伙伴（复数）	maids [meɪdz] 少女（复数）
seats [siːts] 座位（复数）	seeds [siːdz] 种子（复数）
rates [reɪts] 比率（复数）	raids [reɪdz] 空袭（复数）
bats [bæts] 球拍（复数）	bids [bɪdz] 命令（第三人称单数）
coats [kəʊts] 外套（复数）	roads [rəʊdz] 路（复数）
pats [pæts] 轻拍（第三人称单数）	pads [pædz] 便签本（复数）
heats [hiːts] 加热（第三人称单数）	heeds [hiːdz] 听从（第三人称单数）
shirts [ʃɜːts] 衬衫（复数）	feeds [fiːdz] 喂养（第三人称单数）
cuts [kʌts] 切；割（第三人称单数）	needs [niːdz] 需要（第三人称单数）

基础短语

- lots [lɒts] and lots [lɒts] 许许多多
- arts [ɑːts] and crafts [krɑːfts] 工艺品
- odds [ɒdz] and ends [endz] 零碎的东西
- hundreds ['hʌndrədz] of peasants ['pezənts] 几百个农民
- thousands ['θaʊzndz] of birds [bɜːdz] 数千只鸟
- rain cats [kæts] and dogs 下倾盆大雨

以句识音

1. That sounds [saʊndz] better.
这听起来还好点儿。

2. Now let's [lets] go and meet our guests [gests].

我们现在去迎一下客人吧。

3. The students ['stju:dnts] were in high spirits ['spɪrɪts] all through the sports [spɔ:ts] meet.

学生们在整个运动会期间都情绪高昂。

4. He holds [həʊldz] two spades [speɪdz] in his hands [hændz].

他手里拿着两把铁锹。

5. He often puts [pʊts] his hands [hændz] in his pockets ['pɒkɪts].

他常把手放在口袋里。

6. He sometimes sends [sendz] postcards ['pəʊstkɑ:dz] to his friends [frendz].

他有时给朋友们寄明信片。

经典绕口令（运动你的舌头）

1. Lots [lɒts] of little London Lamplighters light London's lots [lɒts] of little lights [laɪts].

许多矮小的伦敦灯夫点燃了伦敦的许多小灯。

2. His shirts [ʃɜ:ts] soon shrank in the suds [sʌdz].

他的衬衫在肥皂水中很快就收缩了。

3. A box of biscuits ['bɪskɪts], a box of mixed biscuits ['bɪskɪts].

一盒饼干，一盒混合饼干。

4. Two toads [təʊdz] have heavy loads [ləʊdz] on their backs.

两只蟾蜍背上背着沉重的货物。

5. There were lots [lɒts] of fights [faɪts] in the streets [stri:ts].

街道上有很多打斗事件。

影音荟萃

一 听音乐学音标

Drama, Love & 'Lationships

戏剧、爱情和关系

Babyface

It's [ɪts] not about who's right or who's wrong	不论我们谁是对的，谁是错的
It's [ɪts] not about who's weaker or who's strong	不论我们谁坚强，谁又软弱
It's [ɪts] not about who's innocent or who's fault	不论我们谁犯了错，谁又无辜
It ain't really about that kinda thing at all	这跟我上面说的一点关系都没有
It's [ɪts] not about who does it or done it or did it to who	不论谁对谁 做了什么样的事情
Don't matter if the both of you lose	你失去什么都无所谓
It's [ɪts] really not about nothing except for me and you	除了对你和我而言 这些真的都没什么
It's [ɪts] about drama and love and 'lationships	这是关于戏剧，爱情和关系
And when the going gets [gets] tough you deal with it	当事情变得糟糕的时候 你尝试着去解决
And you don't ever you never walk away from it	并且你从来未曾想到过逃避
You hold on, you be strong	你坚持着并且变得坚强
It's [ɪts] about drama and drugs and making it	这是关于戏剧，毒品和成功
If your somebody messed up you dig it in	如果有人使你心绪迷乱
Don't let nobody come between you you just stay with it	不要让任何人打开你的心扉 你只是观望着（他们）
You hold on and be strong	你坚持着并且变得坚强
And hold on, yes you do*	坚持着，是的，你这样做了*
*（repeat）	*（重复）
It's [ɪts] not about the stupid things that we say	这和我们之前说的愚蠢的话题无关

We're always saying stupid things anyway	人们总是会不时地说些愚蠢的话
It's [ɪts] not about the secrecy of the lines	这和那些潜藏心底的秘密无关
Girl everybody's got a secret to hide	亲爱的，每个人心中都会有自己的小秘密
It's [ɪts] not about who was it who was she	无论谁是谁
who's creeping on who	谁又爱上谁
Won't matter if the both of us lose	我们两个人失去什么都无所谓
It's really not 'bout nothing, 'cept for me and	除了对你和我而言
you	这些真的都没什么
Ain't 'bout your pride	与你的娇蛮无关
Ain't 'bout yourself	与你的自我无关
It's [ɪts] 'bout you do it to and no one else	只在于唯有你可以这样对我
Ain't 'bout the her	与那个她无关
Ain't 'bout the lies	与那些谎言无关
Ain't 'bout the crazy things that's running	与你心中闪现过的
through your mind	那些疯狂的事情无关
It's [ɪts] 'bout the love that's supposed to last	只是关于那些
and never dies	注定不朽的爱情

歌曲评论

肯尼思·布赖恩·埃德蒙（Kenneth Brian Edmonds），1959年4月10日出生于美国印第安纳波利斯，艺名娃娃脸（Babyface），是一位集超级金曲词曲作者、唱片制作人、电影监制、歌手、键盘手、吉他手和企业家等七种身份于一身的巨星。他曾是节奏布鲁斯组合“The Deele”的成员之一。埃德蒙家族音乐人才辈出，他的弟弟Kevon和哥哥Melvin是另一个节奏布鲁斯组合“After 7”的成员。在2014年，他和Toni Braxton合作推出了最新的抒情单曲《*Roller Coaster*》。*Drama, Love & 'Lationships* 是其深情款款的一首热门歌曲。

Fields of Gold
金色的麦田

Sting

You'll remember me when the west wind moves	你会记得我
Upon the fields [fi:ldz] of barley	每当西风拂过那片麦田
You'll forget the sun in his jealous sky	你会忘记天空中妒忌的骄阳
As we walk in fields [fi:ldz] of gold	每当我们漫步于金色的麦田

So she took her love	她带着爱意
For to gaze awhile	凝望着
Upon the fields [fi:ldz] of barley	那无垠的麦田
In his arms she fell as her hair came down	垂下丝丝秀发，她躺进了他的臂弯
Among the fields [fi:ldz] of gold	在那金色的麦田里
Will you stay with me, will you be my love	你可愿留下？可愿成为我的爱人？
Among the fields [fi:ldz] of barley	在那无垠的麦田里
We'll forget the sun in his jealous sky	我们会忘记天空中妒忌的骄阳
As we lie in fields [fi:ldz] of gold	躺在这金色的麦田里
See the west wind move like a lover so	瞧西风吹来，如恋人般拂过
Upon the fields [fi:ldz] of barley	那无垠的麦田
Feel her body rise when you kiss her mouth	亲吻她的唇，感受她身体的悸动
Among the fields [fi:ldz] of gold	在那金色的麦田里
I never made promises lightly	我从不轻易许下承诺
And there have been some that I've broken	尽管我也曾失言
But I swear in the days still left	但我发誓，在今后的日子里
We'll walk in fields [fi:ldz] of gold	我们会漫步在这金色的麦田间
We'll walk in fields [fi:ldz] of gold	我们会漫步在这金色的麦田间
Many years have passed since those summer days	多少年已悄然流过 自从那些夏天
Among the fields [fi:ldz] of barley	我们共同走过金色的麦田
See the children run as the sun goes down	看着孩子们夕阳下追逐嬉戏
Among the fields [fi:ldz] of gold	在那片金色的麦田间
You'll remember me	你会记得我
When the west wind moves upon the fields [fi:ldz] of barley	每当西风拂过那片麦田
You can tell the sun in his jealous sky	你可以告诉天空中妒忌的骄阳
When we walked in fields [fi:ldz] of gold	我们曾徜徉于这片金色的麦田
When we walked in fields [fi:ldz] of gold	我们曾徜徉于这片金色的麦田
When we walked in fields [fi:ldz] of gold	我们曾徜徉于这片金色的麦田

歌曲评论

斯汀（Sting）是英国著名歌星，也曾是一名出色的摇滚乐手，无论作为Police乐队主唱还是后来的个人发展生涯，他都留下了很多经典歌曲。

歌曲*Fields of Gold*为斯汀所作，犹如他本人一样的简单质朴，在悠扬的风笛中倾诉着纯洁的爱情：纵使有一天你我各奔东西，这金色的麦田也会如影随形。美丽的爱情与美丽的大自然交织在一起所迸发出的力量是任何人都无法抗拒的，也是不愿抗拒的。在这歌声中，连离别似乎都显得那么的淡，那么的真。

二 看电影学音标

电影简介：

《街角的商店》（*The Shop around the Corner*）是著名电影喜剧大师刘别谦1940年执导的一部经典喜剧片，由詹姆斯 · 斯图尔特与玛格丽特 · 苏利文等主演。讲述一个商店里发生的种种故事。影片刻画了小人物的寂寞心灵，有十分温馨动人的戏剧效果。

一位太太对香烟盒产生了兴趣，诺瓦克小姐充分发挥自己的口才，最终说服太太买了一个香烟盒。（节选自《街角的商店》）

Miss Novak: Good morning, madam. **It's** [ɪts] a lovely box, isn't it?

Lady: Oh, yes. **It's** [ɪts] a candy box, isn't it?

Owner: Well, we...

Miss Novak: Yes, madam, a candy box, and I should say, a very unusual one. May I open it for you?

Owner: Yes, madam. Tha**t's** [ðæts] *Ochi Tchornya*. **It's** [ɪts] a very popular classic.

诺瓦克小姐：早安，太太。这个盒子很美吧？

太太：是的，这是个糖果盒吧？

店主：噢，我们……

诺瓦克小姐：太太，这是糖果盒，没错，而且是非常特殊的糖果盒。要我替您打开吗？

店主：太太，正是“欧奇恰尼亚”，一首耳熟能详的古典乐。

电影简介：

美国电影《诺丁山》（*Notting Hill*）拍摄于1998年，由朱莉娅·罗伯茨、休·格兰特、瑞斯·伊凡斯、迪兰·莫兰、约翰·斯拉普内尔、米莎·巴顿主演。它讲述了小人物威廉与明星安娜的爱情故事。

威廉在伦敦的诺丁山经营着一家书店，这天大明星安娜·斯科特来光顾他的书店了。所以他心情很好。现在正在帮自己的店员买橙汁，可是不幸又幸运的是，他把橙汁洒到了安娜的衣服上。他们是怎么解决这件事情的呢？（节选自《诺丁山》）

William: I'm so sorry. I'm so sorry. Here. Let me…

Anna: Get your han**ds** [hændz] off!

William: I'm really sorry. I… I live just over the street. I have, um, water and soap. You can get cleaned up.

Anna: No, thank you. I just need to get my car back.

William: I also have a phone. I'm confident that in five minutes… we could have you spick-and-span and back on the street again. In the non-prostitute sense, obviously.

Anna: All right. Well, what do you mean, "Just over the street"? Give it to me in yar**ds** [jɑːdz].

William: Uh, 18 yar**ds** [jɑːdz]. That's my house there with the blue front door.

威廉：对不起，我非常抱歉。来，让我……

安娜：把手拿开！

威廉：我真的很抱歉，我……我就住在街对面，那有水和肥皂，可以让你弄干净。

安娜：不，谢谢，我只想找到我的车。

威廉：我还有个电话，我想只要五分钟，就能让你弄干净回到街上了，绝对没有不尊重你的意思。

安娜：好吧，你说"就在街对面"是多远？具体是多少？

威廉：大概18码。那扇蓝色的门就是我的家。

Unit 9 [tr] & [dr]

[tr]

发音要素

[tr]是齿龈后部破擦辅音。发音时舌身与[r]相似，舌尖贴在齿龈后部，气流冲破阻碍发出短促的[t]后立即发[r]音。[tr]是清辅音，声带不振动。

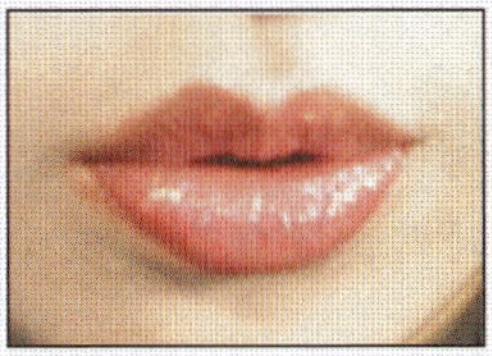

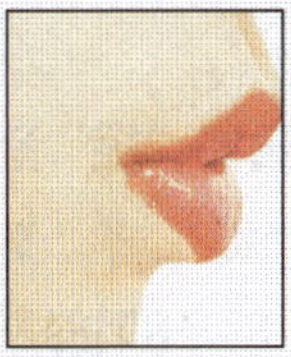

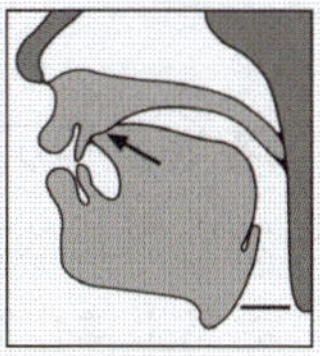

大话发音

嘴巴撅起来，做出发“戳”音的口型，让气流冲出。

车的轮胎被戳破，做出“戳”音的口型，气流穿出，声带不动，就是[tr]的发音。

戳

发音代言人

tree

[tri:] 树

常见发音字母及字母组合

音标	对应字母	自然发音规则	单词示例
[tr]	tr	字母组合tr在单词中发[tr]音。	**truck** [trʌk] 卡车

[dr]

发音要素

[dr]是齿龈后部破擦辅音。发音时舌身与[r]相似，舌尖贴齿龈后部，气流冲破阻碍发出短促的[d]后立即发[r]音。[dr]是浊辅音，声带振动。

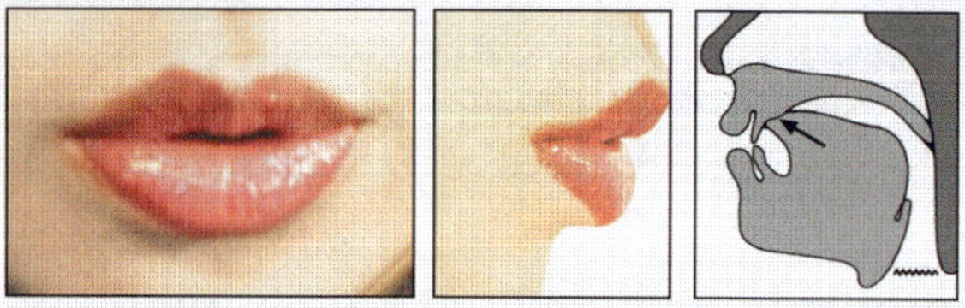

大话发音

这个音和汉语的“捉”音相似。
发出汉语的“捉”音，更轻些，更急促，发出后马上停止，就是[dr]的发音。

捉

发音代言人

dragon

['drægən] 龙

常见发音字母及字母组合

音标	对应字母	自然发音规则	单词示例
[dr]	dr	字母组合dr在单词中发[dr]音。	**dream** [dri:m] 梦

发音操练

[tr]	[dr]
trap [træp] 陷阱	**drag** [dræg] 拖拽

train [treɪn] 火车	drain [dreɪn] 排水沟
trip [trɪp] 旅行	drug [drʌg] 药物；毒品
try [traɪ] 试图	drop [drɒp] 落下
trim [trɪm] 修剪	drought [draʊt] 干旱
track [træk] 踪迹	drink [drɪŋk] 喝
trade [treɪd] 交易	drift [drɪft] 漂流
travel ['trævl] 旅行	drive [draɪv] 驾驶
trick [trɪk] 诡计	dress [dres] 连衣裙
trial [traɪəl] 试验	drama ['drɑːmə] 戏剧

基础短语

- try [traɪ] again 再试一次
- foreign trade [treɪd] 对外贸易
- a brief introduction [ˌɪntrə'dʌkʃn] 简介
- the drop-outs ['drɒpˌaʊts] 退出者
- dream [driːm] a dream [driːm] 做梦
- dress [dres] up 打扮

以句识音

1. George has dreadful ['dredfl] manners.
   乔治的举止令人厌恶。
2. He dressed [drest] up as a drummer ['drʌmə].
   他打扮成一个鼓手。
3. Hundreds ['hʌndrədz] of drivers ['draɪvəz] gathered here.
   这里聚集了数百名司机。
4. I dreamed [driːmd] of playing the drum [drʌm].

我梦见打鼓了。

5. He is trying ['traɪɪŋ] to treat [tri:t] the man better.
他试着对这个男人好一点。

6. There are lots of trees [tri:z] in the country ['kʌntri].
农村地区有很多树木。

经典绕口令（运动你的舌头）

1. The tacky tractor ['træktə] trailers ['treɪləz] trucks [trʌks].
破烂的拖拉机是用来拖卡车的。

2. The druggers ['drʌgəz] hate the drummers ['drʌməz]' drums [drʌmz].
吸毒者讨厌鼓手的鼓。

3. The driver ['draɪvə] was drunk [drʌŋk] and drove [drəʊv] the doctor's car directly into the deep ditch.
这个司机喝醉了，他把医生的车开进了一条深沟里。

4. How much dew would a dewdrop ['dju:drɒp] drop [drɒp] if a dewdrop ['dju:drɒp] could drop dew?
如果一颗露珠会掉下露水，那么一颗露珠会掉下多少露水呢？

5. Do drop [drɒp] in at the Dewdrop ['dju:drɒp] Inn.
一定要到露珠旅馆里坐一下。

影音荟萃

一 听音乐学音标

Vincent
文森特

Don McLean

Starry starry night 星星闪烁的夜晚

Paint your palette blue and grey
Look out on a summer's day
With eyes that know the darkness in my soul
Shadows on the hills
Sketch the trees [tri:z] and the daffodils
Catch the breeze and the winter chills
In colors on the snowy linen land

让调色板描绘出你深深的忧郁和晦暗
让那双洞察我灵魂深处的眼睛
面朝着夏日的白昼
山脉的影子
勾勒出树和水仙的轮廓
捕捉微风和冬季的寒意
在这如雪般的大地画布上

*Now I understand what you try [traɪ] to say to me
And how you suffered for your sanity
And how you tried [traɪd] to set them free
They would not listen
They did not know how
Perhaps they' ll listen now*

*现在我才理解你要对我诉说的那些事
你在清醒的时候是怎样受着折磨
你又怎样地想带给他们解脱
那些人不会听到
因为他们无法体会
又或许，他们现在才知道*

Starry starry night
Flaming flowers that brightly blaze
Swirling clouds in violet haze
Reflect in Vincent eyes of china blue
Colors changing hue
Morning fields of amber grain
Weathered faces lined in pain
Are soothed beneath the artist's loving hand
*(Repeat)

星星闪烁的夜晚
鲜花怒放 争奇斗艳
那些在紫罗兰的薄雾中旋转的云朵
都在文森特瓷器一样湛蓝的眸子里
变幻着色彩
清晨琥珀色的原野
饱经风霜的痛楚的脸
画家用深情的手抚慰那些忧伤
*（重复）

For they could not love you
But still your love was true [tru:]
And when no hope was left inside
On that starry starry night
You took your life as lovers often do
But I could have told you Vincent
This world was never meant for one
as beautiful as you

尽管他们无法爱你
但你的爱千真万确
星星闪烁的夜晚
没有一线希望留下
你带走了自己的生命，就像殉情的爱人一样
但我要告诉你 文森特
这个世界将不会有什么
如你一般地美好

Starry starry night
Portraits ['pɔ:treɪts] hung in empty halls

星星闪烁的夜晚
让调色板描绘出你深深的忧郁和晦暗

Frameless heads on nameless walls
With eyes that watch the world
and can't forget
Like the strangers ['streɪndʒə(r)z] that you've met
The ragged man in ragged clothes
A silver thorn in a bloody rose
Lie crushed and broken on the virgin snow

没有名字的墙上 没有镶边的头像
观望世界的深邃目光
让人难以忘怀
就像你曾遇到的
衣衫褴褛的陌生人
就像是躺在圣洁的雪地里
血红的玫瑰中银白的荆棘

Now I think I know what you try to say to me
That how you suffered for your sanity
And how you try [traɪ] to set them free
They would not listen
they're not listening still
Perhaps they never will

现在我才知道你要对我说的那些事
你在清醒的时候是怎样受着折磨
你又怎样地想带给他们解脱
那些人不会听到
他们依旧不会听到
又或许他们永远不会知道

歌曲评论

什么样的歌是杀人的歌？人们都在唱《轻歌销魂》，却不知道，这销魂的歌者就是唐·麦克莱恩。1971年，26岁的唐演唱了著名的“American Pie”（《美国馅饼》），这首歌证明了他作为一个民谣歌手的无可争议的敏感性和现实性。在这张“馅饼”中，他描述了自己——一个经历过动荡生活和社会剧变的青年对“美国梦”的眷恋和失落。这首长达8分多钟的叙事曲讲述了1959年以来的社会演进和个人体验，充满怀旧的哀伤与自由主义的抒怀。

唐·麦克莱恩1945年10月2日生于纽约。60年代中期，唐·麦克莱恩在纽约民歌俱乐部开始了他的音乐生涯。70年代他虽然演唱了许多中小学校园歌曲，但一直被音乐界拒之门外。后来他以一首《我是如此爱她》走红，艺术家联合会这才和麦克莱恩签约。

Dreams Will Never Die
梦将长存

Isgaard

As long as people try to find a peaceful way
As long as springtime melts the frozen sea
As long as we can see the glow in children

只要我们能找到更妥善的方式
只要春天能融化冰冻的海洋
只要我们还能看到

['tʃildrən]'s eyes	孩子眼中闪烁神光
As long as we go on singing our songs	只要我们还能一直歌唱
Hope will be the source of the river of life	希望将是生命之源
Love will break the spell of inner strife	爱将粉碎内心彷徨
Dreams [dri:mz] will never die	梦将长存
As long as we live	只要我们还活着
As long as the clouds pass by	只要天空还飘过云彩
Dreams [dri:mz] can learn to fly	梦想将学会飞翔
As long as we still believe in God	只要我们仍然相信真理
High in the sky	在那天空之上
As long as God is visible in you and me	只要真理还活在心上
As long as people fight for better days	只要人们还在为美好奋战
Patience is the street that we have to walk on	坚韧是我们必须跋涉的路
Eden is the place where we come from	伊甸园是我们走来的地方
Dreams [dri:mz] will never die	梦将长存
As long as we live	只要我们还活着
As long as the clouds pass by	只要天空还飘过云彩
Dreams [dri:mz] can learn to fly	梦想将学会飞翔
As long as we still believe in God	只要我们仍然相信真理
High in the sky	在那天空之上
Dreams [dri:mz] will never die	梦将长存
As long as we live	只要我们还活着
As long as the clouds pass by	只要天空还飘过云彩
Dreams [dri:mz] can learn to fly	梦想将学会飞翔
As long as we still believe in God	只要我们仍然相信真理
High in the sky	在那天空之上
Mai arrendersi mai l'odoi non vincerà	坚持就是胜利
La mia fede oramai è verità	信仰就是力量
Dreams [dri:mz] will never die	梦将长存
As long as we live	只要我们还活着
As long as the clouds pass by	只要天空还飘过云彩
Dreams [dri:mz] can learn to fly	梦想将学会飞翔
As long as we still believe in God	只要我们仍然相信真理
High in the sky	在那天空之上
Still believe high in the sky	坚信，在那天空之上

歌曲评论

与莎拉·布莱曼、夏绿蒂可媲美的天籁女声——伊思嘉（Isgaard），来自德国。她的名字具有诗意，也透露出不凡的气质。她的歌声像夏绿蒂一样有一尘不染的气质，音色听起来很纯真，同时也如莎拉·布莱曼般充满致命的魅惑力。伊思嘉受过正统歌剧训练，同时以透彻、完美的高音而渐受注目。

在乐迷期盼下，这位从未现身的神秘女高音——伊思嘉，在2003年推出个人的第一张概念专辑《金钥匙》。这位享有“新世纪绝妙唯美梦幻天籁”称号的德国新美声唱将，用她纯金的美声化成的一把金钥(Golden Key)，打开了乐迷禁锢已久的心房。*Dreams Will Never Die*收录于其中。

二 看电影学音标

电影简介:

作为意大利新现实主义旗手的德·西卡在1952年的《温别尔托·D》（*UMBERTO D.*）之后便开始了他的意大利通俗剧阶段。《终站》(*Your Final Destination*)就是在此情况下的转型之作，辛辣幽默的讽刺成为他的主要表达方式。本片讲述的是，来到罗马车站的美国妇人玛丽·霍布斯，坐上前往巴黎的火车，但她一直坐立不安，此时乔班尼走了过来，劝她不要走，她有所心动，决定乘下一班车走。

玛丽匆忙地来到火车站，要买一张去米兰的车票。（节选自《终站》）

Mary: Please, when the next train [treɪn] leave for Milan?
Conductor: Milan? There is one in 20 minutes, at 7.
Mary: Could you tell me what train [treɪn] I could take from Milan to Paris?
Conductor: Why not take the 8:30 that goes straight through to Paris?
Mary: No. No. I'll take one at 7. Where do I buy the ticket?
Conductor: Window 5.
Mary: Thank you.

玛丽：请问一下，下一趟去米兰的火车是几点？
售票员：米兰吗？20分钟后有一趟，7点。
玛丽：你能告诉我从米兰到巴黎，我应该乘哪趟车吗？
售票员：为什么不乘8:30直达巴黎的那趟呢？
玛丽：不，不，我还是坐7点的那趟，请问在哪买票？
售票员：第五窗口。

玛丽：　谢谢。

电影简介：

《盗梦空间》（*Inception*）讲述由莱昂纳多扮演的造梦师，带领约瑟夫·高登-莱维特、艾伦·佩吉扮演的特工团队，进入他人梦境，从他人的潜意识中盗取机密，并重塑他人梦境的故事。影片剧情游走于梦境与现实之间，被定义为“发生在意识结构内的当代动作科幻片”。影片由克里斯托弗·诺兰执导，莱昂纳多·迪卡普里奥、玛丽昂·歌迪亚等主演。

柯布在训练筑梦师阿丽瑞德妮，在她的梦中向她讲述造梦的可能性。（节选自《盗梦空间》）

—Now, in a **dr**eam [dri:m], our mind continuously does this. We create and perceive our world simultaneously. Our mind does this so well that we don't even know what's happening. That allows us to get right in the middle of that process.

—How?

—By taking over the creating part. Now, this is where I need you. You create the world of the **dr**eam [dri:m]. We bring the subject into that **dr**eam [dri:m], and they fill it with their subconscious.

—How could I ever acquire enough details to make them think that it's reality?

—Well, **dr**eams [dri:mz], they feel real while we're in them, right? It's only when we wake up that we realize something was actually strange. Let me ask you a question. You never really remember the beginning of a **dr**eam [dri:m], do you? You always wind up right in the middle of what's going on.

—如果是在梦里，我们的头脑连续不断地做着这样的事：我们一边创造，同时一边感知我们的世界。我们的头脑做得如此出色，以至于我们甚至都不明白怎么回事。那使得我们能够直接介入这一过程之中。

—怎么介入？

—通过担当起创造者的角色。这里就是我需要你的地方：你创造出梦中的世界，我们把主体带入那个梦，他们用自己的潜意识充满梦境。

—我怎么可能获得足够的细节，好让他们认为是真的？

—我们做的梦，感觉都很真实，只要我们是在梦里，不是么？只有当我们醒了之后，才会意识到有些不对劲。我来问你个问题：你从来回忆不起某个梦的开头，对吗？你只记得梦做到一半，然后就断了的那一部分。

Unit 10 [s] & [z]

[s]

发音要素

[s]是舌齿摩擦辅音。发音时舌端靠近齿龈，气流由舌端齿龈间送出，形成摩擦音。[s] 是清辅音，声带不振动。

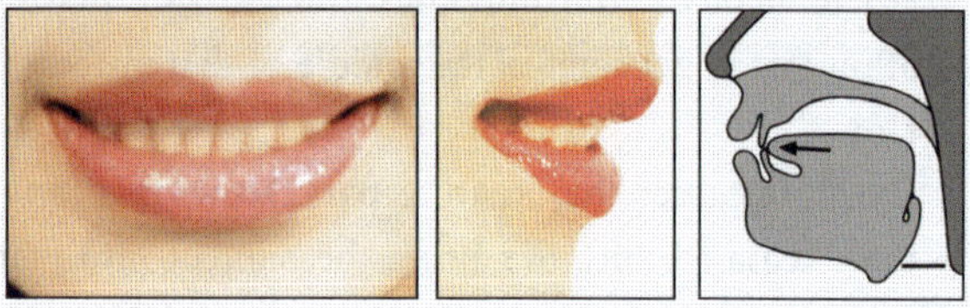

大话发音

汽车熄火了，发出“嘶、嘶”的声音。

汽车熄火了，发出“嘶、嘶”的声音，就类似于[s]的发音。

嘶

发音代言人

gas

[gæs] 汽油

常见发音字母及字母组合

音标	对应字母	自然发音规则	单词示例
[s]	s	字母s在单词中可发[s]音。	**star** [stɑː] 星星
[s]	se	字母组合se在单词中可发[s]音。	**house** [haʊs] 房子

[s]	ss	字母组合ss在单词中发[s]音。	kiss [kɪs] 亲吻
[s]	sc	字母组合sc在单词中可发[s]音。	science ['saɪəns] 科学
[s]	ce	字母组合ce在单词中可发[s]音。	rice [raɪs] 大米

[z]

发音要素

[z]是舌齿摩擦辅音。发音时舌端靠近齿龈，气流由舌端齿龈间送出，形成摩擦音。[z]是浊辅音，声带振动。

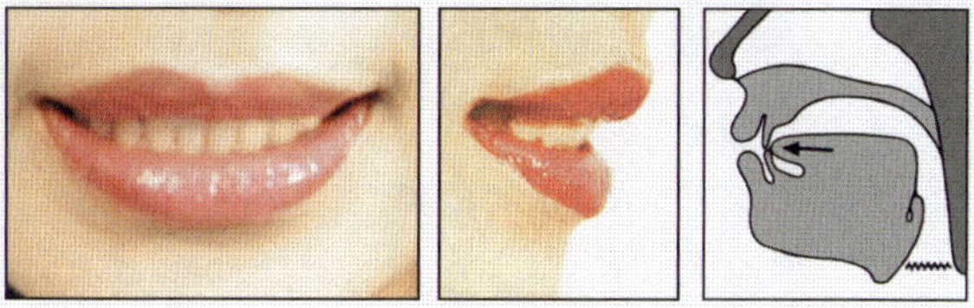

大话发音

爱情是美滋滋的。“滋”与这个发音就很相似。使舌尖前部先顶住上齿背，然后慢慢离开，气流从窄缝中挤出。

[z]的发音主要是舌尖与上齿背之间缝隙里流过的气流产生的噪音，好像是吹口哨的声音。

滋

发音代言人

zebra

['zi:brə] 斑马

常见发音字母及字母组合

音标	对应字母	自然发音规则	单词示例
[z]	z	字母z在单词中发[z]音。	zero ['zɪərəʊ] 零

[z]	s	字母s在单词结尾时可发[z]音。	**boxes** ['bɒksɪz] 盒子（复数）
[z]	se	字母组合se在单词中可发[z]音。	**lose** [lu:z] 丢失
[z]	ze	字母组合ze在单词中可发[z]音。	**doze** [dəʊz] 打瞌睡
[z]	zz	字母组合zz在单词中发[z]音。	**buzz** [bʌz] 蜂音

发音操练

[s]	[z]
seal [si:l] 图章	**zeal** [zi:l] 热情
sow [səʊ] 播种	**zone** [zəʊn] 地带
sue [sju:] 控告	**zoo** [zu:] 动物园
bus [bʌs] 公共汽车	**buzz** [bʌz] 蜂音
ice [aɪs] 冰	**eyes** [aɪz] 眼睛（复数）
loose [lu:s] 松的	**lose** [lu:z] 丢失
race [reɪs] 赛跑	**raise** [reɪz] 举起
science ['saɪəns] 科学	**used** [ju:zd] 旧的
horse [hɔ:s] 马	**zipper** ['zɪpə] 拉链
fuss [fʌs] 大惊小怪	**doze** [dəʊz] 打瞌睡

基础短语

- easy ['i:zi] for use [ju:z] 便于使用
- a lazy ['leɪzi] husband ['hʌzbənd] 懒惰的丈夫
- brothers ['brʌðəz] and sisters ['sɪstəz] 兄弟姐妹
- sing [sɪŋ] and dance [dɑ:ns] 唱歌跳舞

- sum [sʌm] up experience [ɪks'pɪərɪəns] 总结经验
- six [sɪks] pairs of scissors ['sɪzəz] 六把剪刀

以句识音

1. I used [ju:zd] to smoke.
   我过去吸烟。
2. Sing [sɪŋ] us a song [sɒŋ], please [pli:z].
   请给我们唱支歌吧。
3. Speak [spi:k] less [les] and listen ['lɪsn] more.
   少说多听。
4. A still [stɪl] tongue makes [meɪks] a wise [waɪz] head.
   智者寡言。
5. Man proposes [prə'pəʊzɪz], God disposes [dɪs'pəʊzɪz].
   谋事在人，成事在天。
6. The sun [sʌn] rises ['raɪzɪz] in the east [i:st] and sets [sets] in the west [west].
   太阳从东方升起，在西方落下。

经典绕口令（运动你的舌头）

1. Susan ['su:zn] shines shoes [ʃu:z], shoes [ʃu:z] shine Susan ['su:zn]. She ceased [si:st] shining shoes [ʃu:z], for shoes [ʃu:z] shock Susan ['su:zn].
   苏珊把鞋子擦亮，鞋子把苏珊照亮。她停止了将鞋子擦亮，因为鞋子把苏珊吓坏了。
2. The sixth [sɪksθ] sick [sɪk] sheik's [ʃi:ks] sixth [sɪksθ] sheep's [ʃi:ps] sick [sɪk].
   第六个患病的酋长的第六只羊患病了。
3. Sam's [sæmz] shop stocks [stɒks] short spotted ['spɒtɪd] socks [sɒks].
   萨姆的店备有圆点短袜。
4. This [ðɪs] is [ɪz] a zither ['zɪðə]. Is [ɪz] this [ðɪs] a zither ['zɪðə]?
   这是一把古筝，这是古筝吗？
5. Fuzzy ['fʌzi] wuzzy ['wʌzi] was a bear. Fuzzy ['fʌzi] wuzzy ['wʌzi] had no hair. Fuzzy ['fʌzi] wuzzy ['wʌzi] wasn't fuzzy ['fʌzi], was he?
   毛茸茸、软绵绵的是玩具熊。毛茸茸、软绵绵，一根头发也没有。毛茸茸、软绵绵的玩具熊并不毛茸茸，是吗？

影音荟萃

一 听音乐学音标

Seasons in the Sun
阳光下的季节

Westlife

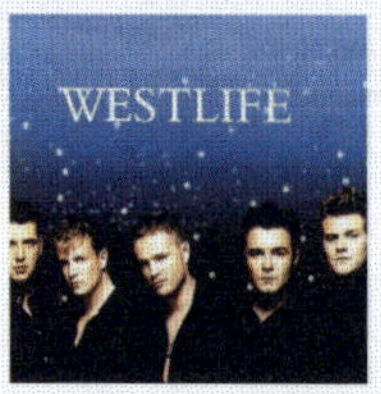

Goodbye to you, my trusted ['trʌstɪd] friend	再见了，我的挚友
We've known each other since [sɪns] we were nine or ten	我们九岁十岁时 就相识
Together we've climbed hills and trees	曾经一起爬山爬树
Learned of love and ABCs	学习过爱和ABC
Skinned [skɪnd] our hearts and skinned [skɪnd] our knees	我们心意相同 情同手足
Goodbye my friend, it's hard to die	再见了我的挚友，友情是不死的
When all the birds are singing in the sky	当所有的鸟儿都在天空歌唱时
Now that spring [sprɪŋ] is in the air	春天就弥漫在那空气中
Pretty girls are everywhere	到处都会有可爱的女孩
Think of me and I'll be there	想起我，我就会出现在那里
We had joy, we had fun	我们曾拥有幸福快乐
We had seasons ['sɪznz] in the sun [sʌn]	也曾拥有阳光下的季节
But the hills that we climbed	但我们爬过的那些山
Were just seasons ['sɪznz] out of time	只是时光外的季节罢了
Goodbye papa, please pray for me	再见了，爸爸，请为我祈祷吧
I was the black sheep of the family	我曾是家里的害群之马
You tried to teach me right from wrong	你曾试图教我改邪归正
Too much wine and too much song [sɒŋ]	而我却沉迷于歌酒狂欢
Wonder how I got along	真不知我是如何过来的
Goodbye papa, it's hard to die	再见了，爸爸，亲情是不死的
When all the birds are singing ['sɪŋɪŋ] in the sky [skaɪ]	当所有的鸟儿都在天空歌唱时
Now that the spring [sprɪŋ] is in the air	春天就弥漫在那空气中
Little children are everywhere	到处都会有淘气的孩子

When you see [si:] them I'll be there	当你看见他们时，我就会出现在那里
We had joy, we had fun	我们曾拥有幸福快乐
We had seasons in the sun [sʌn]	也曾拥有阳光下的季节
But the wine and the song [sɒŋ]	但那酒与歌
Like the seasons ['si:znz] have all gone	就像那些季节，早已逝去
We had joy, we had fun	我们曾拥有幸福快乐
We had seasons ['si:znz] in the sun [sʌn]	也曾拥有阳光下的季节
But the wine and the song [sɒŋ]	但那酒与歌
Like the seasons ['si:znz] have all gone	就像那些季节，早已逝去
Goodbye Michelle, my little one	再见了，米歇尔，我的小宝贝
You gave me love and helped me find the sun	你给了我爱，帮我找到阳光
[sʌn]And every time that I was down	每当我消沉的时候
You would always come around	你总是会来到我身边
And get my feet back on the ground	让我重新脚踏实地
Goodbye Michelle, it's hard to die	再见了，米歇尔，爱情是不死的
When all the birds are singing ['sɪŋɪŋ] in the sky	当所有的鸟儿
[skaɪ]	都在天空歌唱时
Now that the spring [sprɪŋ] is in the air	春天就弥漫在那空气中
With the flowers everywhere	到处都会有美丽的花儿
I wish that we could both be there	我希望我们能一起徜徉在那春天里
We had joy, we had fun	我们曾拥有幸福快乐
We had seasons ['si:znz] in the sun [sʌn]	也曾拥有阳光下的季节
But the hills that we climbed	但我们爬过的那些山
Were just seasons ['si:znz] out of time	只是时光外的季节罢了
We had joy, we had fun	我们曾拥有幸福快乐
We had seasons ['si:znz] in the sun [sʌn]	也曾拥有阳光下的季节
But the wine and the song	但那酒与歌
Like the seasons ['si:znz] have all gone	就像那些季节，早已逝去
We had joy, we had fun	我们曾拥有幸福快乐
We had seasons ['si:znz] in the sun [sʌn]	也曾拥有阳光下的季节
But the wine and the song	但那酒与歌
Like the seasons ['si:znz] have all gone	就像那些季节，早已逝去
We had joy, we had fun	我们曾拥有幸福快乐
We had seasons ['si:znz] in the sun [sʌn]	也曾拥有阳光下的季节
But the wine and the song [sɒŋ]	但那酒与歌
Like the seasons ['si:znz] have all gone	就像那些季节，早已逝去

歌曲评论

*Seasons in the Sun*是西城男孩翻唱的经典曲目，家喻户晓。

事实上，*Seasons in the Sun*绝对不是一首愉快的曲子，甚至还十分地伤感。这是一位法国歌手Jacques Brel的作品，原名叫作*Le Moribond*（将死的人），发表于1961年。歌曲的内容大致描述一个罹患癌症、不久于人世的男子，在面临死亡的时候，对父亲、妻子以及挚友的依依难舍。

Desperado
亡命之徒

Carpenters

Desperado, why don't you come to your senses ['sensɪz]
You been out ridin' fences ['fensɪz] for so long now
Oh, you're a hard one
But I know that you got your reasons ['ri:znz]
These [ði:z] things [θɪŋz] that are pleasin' you
Can hurt you somehow

Don't you draw the queen of diamonds, boy
She'll beat you if she's [ʃi:z] able
You know the queen of hearts is [ɪz] always ['ɔ:lweɪz] your best bet
Now it seems [si:mz] to me, some fine things [θɪŋz]
Have been laid upon your table
But you only want the ones [wʌnz] that you can't get
Desperado, oh, you ain't gettin' no younger
Your pain and your hunger, they're drivin' you home
And freedom, oh freedom well,
that's just some people talkin'
Your prison is [ɪz] walking through this world all alone

亡命之徒啊
为何你还不清醒
你筑起心墙
已如此之久
哎，你这个固执的家伙
但是我知道你有你的理由
那些令人开心的事情
也能伤害到你

孩子，别抽那张方块Q
她会带给你的只有伤痛
你知道红心Q是你最好的选择（喻指爱你的女生）
在我看来
你的面前
有着很好的选择
但是你只想要
你得不到的那些
亡命之徒啊，你已不再年轻
你的痛苦和饥饿
正在逼你回头
自由，噢自由
那只是有些人说的
你是孤独闯世界的囚犯

Don't your feet get cold in the winter time	难道冬天时，你的双脚不冷吗
The sky won't snow and the sun won't shine	天空不会下雪，太阳也不会照耀
It's hard to tell the night time from the day	无法分清白天和黑夜
You're losin' all your highs [haɪz] and lows [ləʊz]	无法感知开心和悲伤
Ain't it funny how the feeling goes [gəʊz] away	毫无知觉难道不可笑吗
Desperado, why don't you come to your senses ['sensɪz]	亡命之徒啊 你为什么还不清醒
Come down from your fences ['fensɪz], open the gate	推翻心墙 打开心门吧
It may be rainin', but there's [ðeəz] a rainbow above you	也许会有风雨， 但是雨后必有彩虹在你之上
You better let somebody love you	你最好让某人来爱你
(let somebody love you)	（让某人来爱你）
You better let somebody love you	你最好让某人来爱你
before it's too late	在一切都太迟之前

歌曲评论

《亡命之徒》（*Desperado*）是美国摇滚乐队——老鹰乐队的第二张录音室专辑，在英国伦敦的Island Studios录音棚录制，并于1973年发行。它是一张以*Dalton Gang*（道尔顿帮/道尔顿兄弟）和美国旧时西部为灵感的概念专辑。虽然标题曲（歌曲 *Desperado*）是老鹰乐队的代表曲目之一，但是它从来没有作为单曲发布。后来卡朋特乐队翻唱了这首歌，并把它收录在*Horizon*专辑中。

二 看电影学音标

电影简介：

《一夜风流》（*It Happened One Night*）是美国导演法兰克·卡普拉所执导的一部电影，由克拉克·盖博与克劳黛·考尔白所主演。《一夜风流》是卡普拉生涯的代表作之一，也被认为是美国电影史上相当重要的一部电影。荣获第7届奥斯卡包括最佳影片在内的五项大奖。

富家女艾莉·安德鲁小姐搭乘长途巴士离家出走，在巴士上偶遇落魄记者彼得·华恩。在长途汽车站，艾莉要乘的车子开走了，只有彼得在那等候她。（节选自《一夜风流》）

Ellen: Where's the bus [bʌs] to New York?

Clerk: Well, it left about 20 minutes ago.

Ellen: Oh, that's ridiculous [rɪ'dɪkjʊləs]. I was on that bus [bʌs]. I told them to wait.

Clerk: I'm sorry ['sɒri], Miss [mɪs], but it's gone.

Peter: Good morning. Remember me? I'm the fellow you slept [slept] on last [lɑ:st] night.

Ellen: Seems [si:mz] to me, I've already thanked you for that. What time's the next bus [bʌs]?

Clerk: 8:00 tonight.

Ellen: 8:00? That's 12 hours.

艾莉：到纽约的巴士呢？

职员：哦，20分钟前就开走了。

艾莉：噢，这太荒谬了，我也坐那辆巴士，我有叫他们等我。

职员：抱歉，小姐。但是车已经开走了。

彼得：早安，记得我吗？你昨晚睡在我身上。

艾莉：我已经谢过你了。下一班什么时候开？

职员：今晚八点钟。

艾莉：八点钟？还有12个小时呢！

电影简介：

《敢死队2》（*The Expendables 2*）是由西蒙·韦斯特执导，西尔维斯特·史泰龙、布鲁斯·威利斯主演的动作电影，主要讲述的是比利（利亚姆·海莫斯沃斯饰演）在执行一项任务时被残忍杀害，以史泰龙为首的“敢死队”发誓为他报仇的故事。该电影于2012年9月4日在中国大陆上映。

敢死队队长巴尼和最年轻的队员比利在出发前的对话。比利向巴尼介绍自己的女朋友。（节选自《敢死队2》）

—Where's [weəz] she from?

—She's [ʃi:z], uh, she's French. Believe it or not, I met her at Afghanistan, she was a nurse.

—That comes [kʌmz] in handy.

—Yeah. And you'd like her. You know, she's [ʃi:z] the kind of person you'd wanna do things [θɪŋz] for.

—她是哪里人？

—她是法国人。信不信由你，我们是在阿富汗认识的。她是个护士。

——定很会照顾人吧。

—对，她是个好女孩。我愿意为她做任何事。

Unit 11 [h]

[h]

发音要素

[h]是声门摩擦辅音。发音时气流送出口腔，在通过声门时发出轻微摩擦；口形随其后的元音而变化；[h]是清辅音，声带不振动。

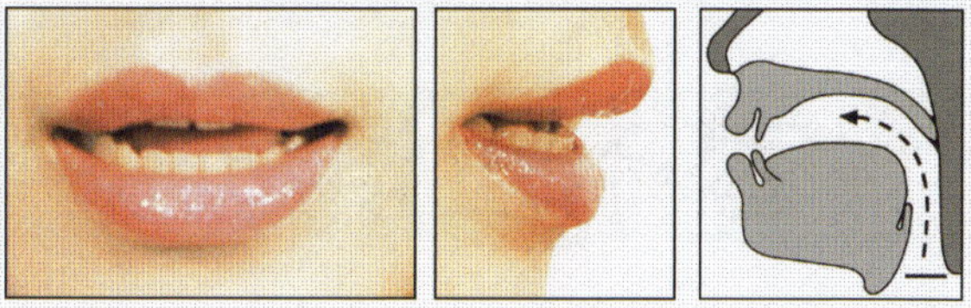

大话发音

汉语中喝水的“喝”与 [h] 发音相似。

当气流从声门处穿出，声音放平，就是[h]的发音。

喝

发音代言人

hand

[hænd] 手

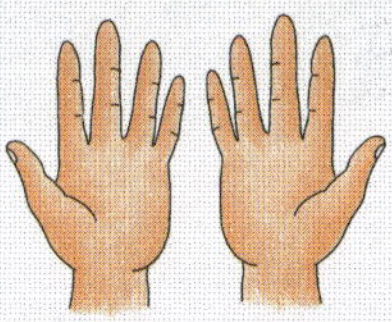

常见发音字母及字母组合

音标	对应字母	自然发音规则	单词示例
[h]	h	字母h在单词中可发[h]音。	**ham** [hæm] 火腿
[h]	wh	字母组合wh可发[h]音。	**who** [hu:] 谁

发音操练

[h]	
he [hiː] 他	hot [hɒt] 热的
hard [hɑːd] 硬的	help [help] 帮助
hurry ['hʌri] 急忙	happy ['hæpi] 高兴的
behind [bɪ'haɪnd] 在……后面	behave [bɪ'heɪv] 表现
whose [huːz] 谁的	whole [həʊl] 整体的

基础短语

- in a hurry ['hʌri] 匆忙地
- have a healthy ['helθi] habit 有个健康的习惯
- live in harmony ['hɑːməni] 和睦相处
- ahead [ə'hed] of time 提前
- do a great harm [hɑːm] to 对……很有害
- whatever happens ['hæpənz] 无论发生什么事

以句识音

1. Help [help]!

救命!

2. Stop him [hɪm]!

抓住他!

3. It can't be helped [helpt].

实在没办法。

4. Health [helθ] is happiness ['hæpinəs].

健康是福。

5. She hasn't ['hæznt] heard [hɜːd] from her husband ['hʌzbənd] for half [hɑːf] a month.
她有半个月没收到她丈夫的信了。

6. The hunter ['hʌntə] held [held] a gun in his hand [hænd] and hid [hɪd] himself ['hɪmself] behind [bɪ'haɪnd] the house [haʊs].
猎人手里拿着枪躲在房子后面。

经典绕口令（运动你的舌头）

1. The wise hunt [hʌnt] hit [hɪt] himself [hɪm'self] behind [bɪ'haɪnd] the high [haɪ].
那个聪明的猎人由于兴奋而打到了自己

2. His [hɪz] elder brother often helps [helps] him [hɪm] with his homework ['həʊmwɜːk].
他的哥哥经常帮他做作业。

3. Each one has [hæz] his [hɪz] or her own habit ['hæbɪt].
每个人都有他/她自己的习惯。

4. He [hiː] only has [hæz] a handful ['hændfʊl] of hard [hɑːd] food.
他只有很少的硬硬的食物。

5. Henry ['henri] is a helping ['helpɪŋ] hand [hænd].
亨利是个乐于助人的人。

影音荟萃

一 听音乐学音标

Tears in Heaven

泪洒天堂

Eric Clapton

Would you know my name	如果我能在天堂见到你
If I saw you in heaven ['hevn]	你会知道我的名字吗
Would you be the same	如果我能在天堂见到你

If I saw you in heaven ['hevn]	你是否依然如昔
I must be strong and carry on	我必须坚强和坚持
Because I know I don't belong here in heaven	因为我知道天堂
['hevn]	不是现在我要去的地方
Would you hold [həuld] my hand	如果我能在天堂遇见你
If I saw you in heaven ['hevn]	你会握住我的手吗
Would you help [help] me stand	如果我能在天堂遇见你
If I saw you in heaven ['hevn]	你会帮我站立起来吗
I'll find my way through night and day	我会找到自己继续过日子的方法
Because I know I just can't stand here [hiə] in	因为我知道
heaven ['hevn]	我不能待在天堂
Time can bring you down	时间可以打击你
Time can bend your knees	时间可以使你屈服
Time can break your heart [hɑːt]	时间也可以使你心碎
Have [hæv] you begging please	你只要祈祷
Begging please	请你衷心地祈祷
Beyond the door there's peace I'm sure	在这扇门后即可见到平和
And I know there'll be no more tears in heaven	而且我知道
['hevn]	我不再泪洒天堂
Would you know my name	如果我能在天堂见到你
If I saw you in heaven ['hevn]	你会知道我的名字吗
Would you be the same	如果我能在天堂见到你
If I saw you in heaven ['hevn]	你是否依然如昔
I must be strong and carry on	我必须坚强和坚持
Because I know I don't belong here [hiə] in	因为我知道
heaven ['hevn]	天堂不是现在我要去的地方

歌曲评论

埃里克·帕特里克·克莱普顿（Eric Patrick Clapton，1945年3月30日～），英国音乐人、歌手及作曲人。他曾经获得过格莱美奖，是20世纪最成功的音乐家之一，在摇滚名人堂里有三项成就。他还是有史以来最伟大的吉他手之一，2003年在滚石杂志评选的“一百大吉他手”中位列第四，在“百大摇滚艺术家”里面排名第53位。

20世纪60年代末，在伦敦和纽约街头墙壁上最显眼的涂鸦就是“克莱普顿（Clapton）”了。他在42岁时“老来得子”。然而，1991年3月，四岁的儿子从纽约数十层高的公寓阳台意外坠亡。这首《泪洒天堂》是克莱普顿用他已经被悲痛碾得粉碎的心为纪念他的儿子所作，其不仅使他在1992年独得五项格莱美大奖，更成为埃里克·克莱普顿享誉国际的代表作。

二 看电影学音标

电影简介：

《断背山》（*Brokenback Mountain*）是一部2005年的美国爱情、剧情片，改编自安妮·普露所著的同名短篇小说《断背山》，由华人导演李安执导，好莱坞著名影星杰克·吉伦哈尔、希斯·莱杰、米歇尔·威廉姆斯和安妮·海瑟薇倾情出演。影片讲述了1963年至1981年的美国怀俄明州，两个男人之间情爱与性爱的复杂关系。该片在威尼斯电影节夺得金狮奖，在第78届奥斯卡金像奖中获得八项提名，并夺得了最佳导演、最佳改编剧本与最佳电影配乐三项大奖。

恩尼斯给杰克的妻子打电话，才知道杰克出了意外，已经死了。（节选自《断背山》）

—**H**ello [hə'ləʊ].

—**H**ello [hə'ləʊ], this is Ennis Del Mar.

—**Wh**o [huː]? **Wh**o [huː] is this?

—Ennis Del Mar. I’m an old buddy of Jack’s.

—Jack used to mention you. You’re the fishing buddy or the **h**unting ['hʌntɪŋ] buddy, I know that. Would have let you know what **h**appened ['hæpənd]··· but I wasn’t sure about your name or address. Jack kept **h**is [hɪz] friends’ addresses in **h**is [hɪz] **h**ead [hed].

—喂？

—喂，我是恩尼斯·戴尔·玛。

—谁？你是谁？

—恩尼斯·戴尔·玛，杰克的老朋友。

—杰克曾提起过你。你是他钓鱼还是打猎的朋友，不过我不确定你的姓名或地址。我该让你知道发生了什么事。杰克把朋友的地址都存在脑子里。

Unit 12 [n]

[n]

发音要素

[n]是舌尖齿龈鼻辅音。发音时双唇微张开，舌尖抵上齿龈，软腭下垂，气流从鼻腔送出。

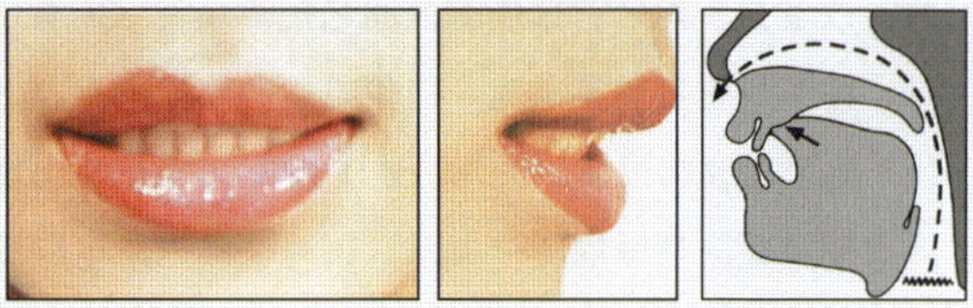

大话发音

如果那个女孩拒绝我该怎么办呢？汉语中的“呢”与 [n] 的发音相似。

发[n]的音时，气流要由鼻腔流出，气振声带。

呢

发音代言人

nose

[nəʊz] 鼻子

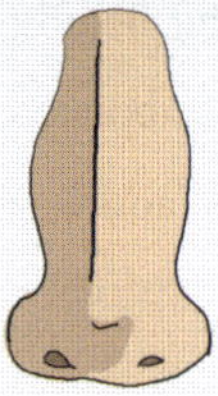

常见发音字母及字母组合

音标	对应字母	自然发音规则	单词示例
[n]	n	字母n在单词中可发[n]音。	**noodle** ['nu:dl] 面条
[n]	nn	字母组合nn可发[n]音。	**funny** ['fʌni] 滑稽可笑的

[n]	kn	字母组合kn在单词开头可发[n]音。	knee [ni:] 膝盖

发音操练

[n]	
woman ['wʊmən] 妇女	needle ['ni:dl] 针
night [naɪt] 夜晚	now [naʊ] 现在
rain [reɪn] 雨	learn [lɜ:n] 学习
turn [tɜ:n] 翻，转	sunny ['sʌni] 晴朗的
knight [naɪt] 骑士	knock [nɒk] 敲，击

基础短语

- human ['hju:mən] nature ['neɪtʃə] 人的天性
- no [nəʊ] need [ni:d] to know [nəʊ] 没必要知道
- a green [gri:n] hand [hænd] 新手
- a narrow-minded ['nærəʊ'maɪndɪd] man [mæn] 一个心胸狭窄的人
- a nasty ['nɑ:sti] illness ['ɪlnəs] 很讨厌的病症
- on [ɒn] pins [pɪnz] and needles ['ni:dlz] 坐立不安

以句识音

1. The man [mæn] is rotten ['rɒtən] and mean [mi:n].
   那个人又坏又吝啬。
2. I need [ni:d] another [ə'nʌðə] nice [naɪs] name [neɪm].
   我需要另一个好名字。

3. Don't [dəʊnt] spend [spend] more money ['mʌni] than [ðən] you earn [ɜːn].
不要入不敷出。

4. He is a thin-skinned ['θɪn'skɪnd] person ['pɜːsn].
他是个神经过敏的人。

5. He never ['nevə] does things in reason ['riːzn].
他做事从来没有道理。

6. Can [kæn] you mention ['menʃn] the new [njuː] novels ['nɒvəlz]?
你能谈谈那本新小说吗？

经典绕口令（运动你的舌头）

1. A noisy ['nɔɪzi] noise [nɔɪz] annoys [ə'nɔɪz] an [ən] oyster.
嘈吵的噪音惹恼牡蛎。

2. Nine [naɪn] nice [naɪs] night [naɪt] nurses ['nɜːsɪz] nursing ['nɜːsɪŋ] nicely ['naɪsli].
九位友善的夜班护士愉快地照料病人。

3. Ann [æn] sent [sent] Andy ['ændi] ten [ten] hens [henz] and [ænd] Andy ['ændi] sent [sent] Ann [æn] ten [ten] pens [penz].
安给安迪送了10只母鸡，安迪给安送了10支钢笔。

4. Canners ['kænəz] can [kæn] can [kæn] what they can [kæn] can [kæn] but can [kæn] not can [kæn] things that can't [kænt] be canned [kænd].
罐头工人能够把他们能制成罐头的东西制成罐头，但是不能把无法制成罐头的东西制成罐头。

5. Ned [ned] Nott [nɒt] was shot and [ænd] Nick [nɪk] Nam [nɑːm] was not [nɒt]. So it is better to be Nam [nɑːm] than Nott [nɒt]. Some say Nott [nɒt] was not [nɒt] shot. But Nam [nɑːm] says he shot Nott [nɒt]. Either the shot Nam [nɑːm] shot at Nott [nɒt] was not [nɒt] shot or Nott [nɒt] was shot. If the shot Nam [nɑːm] shot shot Nott [nɒt], Nott [nɒt] was shot. But if the shot Nam [nɑːm] shot shot Nam [nɑːm], then Nam [nɑːm] was shot, not Nott [nɒt]. However, the shot Nam [nɑːm] shot shot not Nam [nɑːm] but Nott [nɒt].
内德诺特被射杀而尼克纳姆则没有被射杀。那么，做纳姆先生比做诺特先生好。有些人说诺特并没有被射杀，但纳姆说他射杀了诺特。要不是纳姆向诺特开的枪并没有将他射杀，便是诺特被射杀。假如纳姆开的枪射杀了诺特，诺特是被射杀了。但是，如果纳姆开的枪将纳姆射杀了，那么被射杀的是纳姆，不是诺特。可是，纳姆开的枪并没有将纳姆射死，反而射死的是诺特。

影音荟萃

一 听音乐学音标

Greenfields
绿草地

The Brothers Four

O**n**ce [wʌns] there were gree**n** [gri:n] fields	曾经，阳光妩媚
Kissed by the su**n** [sʌn]	绿草盈盈
O**n**ce [wʌns] there were valleys	曾经
Where rivers used to ru**n** [rʌn]	河流在山谷川流不息
O**n**ce [wʌns] there were blue skies	曾经
With white clouds high above	蓝蓝的天上
O**n**ce [wʌns] there were part of	白云飘飘
A**n** [æn] everlasting love	我们是
We were the lovers who strolled	漫步在绿草地的恋人
Through gree**n** [gri:n] fields	这些都是我们永恒爱情
Gree**n** [gri:n] fields are go**n**e [gɒn] now	的一部分
Parched by the su**n** [sʌn]	太阳烘烤着大地
Go**n**e [gɒn] from the valleys	绿草地已经消逝
Where rivers used to ru**n** [rʌn]	山谷中的河流
Go**n**e [gɒn] with the cold wi**n**d [wɪnd]	已经不再奔腾
That swept into my heart	我的心感觉到阵阵寒流
Go**n**e [gɒn] with the lovers	抛开山盟海誓的恋人
Who let their dreams depart	已经离去
Where are the gree**n** [gri:n] fields	我们曾经
That we used to roam	漫步的绿草地
I'll **n**ever ['nevə] k**n**ow [nəʊ]	我永远不知道
What made you ru**n** [rʌn] away	你为什么要离开
How ca**n** [kæn] I keep searching	直到乌云满天

When [wen] dark clouds hide the day	我依然在找寻
I only ['əʊnli] know ['nəʊ]	我知道这里
There's nothing ['nʌθɪŋ] here for me	已经没有任何东西留给我
Nothing ['nʌθɪŋ] in [ɪn] this wide world	在这宽广的世界
Left for me to see	我已经找不到任何属于我的东西
But I'll keep on [ɒn] waiting	但我依然在等待
Till you return [rɪ'tɜːn]	直到你回来
I'll keep on [ɒn] waiting	我会一直等到
Until the day you learn [lɜːn]	你得知的那一天
You can't [kænt] be happy	当你的心依然在流浪
While your hearts on [ɒn] the roam	你不会快乐
You can't [kænt] be happy	你不会快乐
Until [ən'tɪl] you bring it home	直到你把心带回家
Home to the green [griːn] fields and me	带回到绿草地和我身边
Once [wʌns] again [ə'geɪn]	我会再次等在那里

歌曲评论

The Brothers Four（四兄弟合唱团）是美国老牌民谣乐队之一，成立于五十年代末，比 The Beatles出名还要早。这个乐队由四个华盛顿大学的学生Bob Flick、 John Paine 、Mike Kirkand和Dick Foley组成。乐队一组就是四十多年，唱的一直都是传统的通俗民谣。“四兄弟合唱团”的音乐大多以原声木吉他、木贝斯、班卓琴、曼驼林伴奏，并配以完美的四个声部和音。

《绿草地》（*Greenfields*）是The Brothers Four（四兄弟合唱团）的专辑*Greatest Hits*中的一首歌曲。

二 看电影学音标

电影简介:

《为戴茜小姐开车》（*Driving Miss Daisy*）最初是美国剧作家阿尔弗雷德·尤里的话剧作品，1989年首演。1990年由布鲁斯·贝尔斯福德改编成电影，获得次年奥斯卡最佳影片奖。影片通过一个老年寡妇与忠实黑人之间的主仆关系，再现了美国南部25年来种族关系转变的时代特点。在1990年第62届奥斯卡奖角逐中，《为戴茜小姐开车》一举夺得了最佳影片、最佳女主角、最佳改编剧本、最佳化妆四项奖。

戴茜小姐的儿子伍森先生来看他的妈妈，正在和女仆艾戴拉谈论关于吸尘器的事情。（节选自《为戴茜小姐开车》）

Mr. Werthan: How are you, Idella?

Idella: Living.

Mr. Werthan: Where's the new [nju:] vacuum cleaner ['kli:nə]?

Idella: In [ɪn] the closet.

Mr. Werthan: She won't [wɒnt] touch it.

Idella: It gives me a shock every time I'm near [nɪə] it.

Mr. Werthan: It works for me.

Idella: Good! Then [ðen] you clean [kli:n] and I'll go down [daʊn] and run [rʌn] your office.

伍森先生: 你好吗？艾戴拉？

艾戴拉: 还活着。

伍森先生: 我拿来的新吸尘器在哪里？

艾戴拉: 在柜子里。

伍森先生: 她不肯碰它了。

艾戴拉: 我每次靠近它都会被电到。

伍森先生: 我用得好好的。

艾戴拉: 那好！那你打扫，我去替你管理公司。

Unit 13 [ŋ]

[ŋ]

发音要素

[ŋ]是舌后软腭鼻辅音。发音时软腭下垂，堵住口腔通道，气流从鼻腔送出。声带振动。

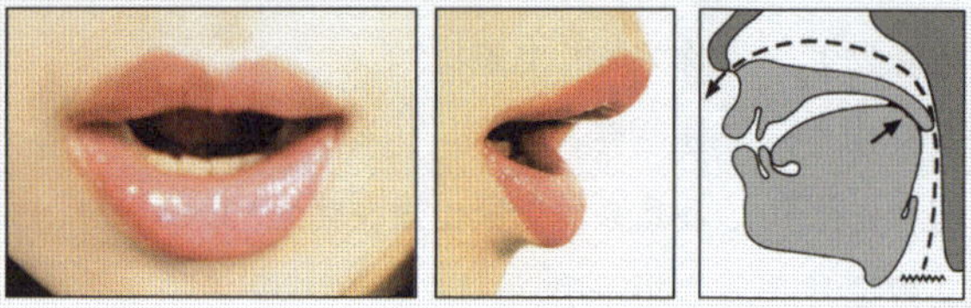

大话发音

同意别人的意见，大家会说，“嗯、嗯”。

对别人的意见、看法表示赞同时，会说“嗯、嗯”，就与[ŋ]的发音相似。

嗯

发音代言人

king

[kɪŋ] 国王

常见发音字母及字母组合

音标	对应字母	自然发音规则	单词示例
[ŋ]	n	字母n在单词中可发[ŋ]音。	**ink** [ɪŋk] 墨水
[ŋ]	ng	字母组合ng可发[ŋ]音。	**sing** [sɪŋ] 唱歌

发音操练

[ŋ]	
thank [θæŋk] 感谢	**drink** [drɪŋk] 喝
uncle ['ʌŋkl] 叔叔	**bang** [bæŋ] 猛击
bring [brɪŋ] 带来	**spring** [sprɪŋ] 春天
song [sɒŋ] 歌曲	**link** [lɪŋk] 连接
meaning ['miːnɪŋ] 意思	**morning** ['mɔːnɪŋ] 早晨

基础短语

- anything ['enɪθɪŋ] important 任何重要的事情
- singing ['sɪŋɪŋ] a song [sɒŋ] 唱一首歌
- knowing ['nəʊɪŋ] nothing ['nʌθɪŋ] 一无所知
- in the pink [pɪŋk] 身体很棒的
- fearing ['fɪərɪŋ] nothing ['nʌθɪŋ] 无所畏惧
- well-linked ['wel'lɪŋkt] 连接很好的

以句识音

1. Bring the ring [rɪŋ] to the wedding ['wedɪŋ].
   把戒指带到婚礼上。
2. The monkey ['mʌŋki] is hiding ['haɪdɪŋ] in the king [kɪŋ]'s garden.
   猴子藏在国王的花园里。
3. This morning ['mɔːnɪŋ] we saw a very boring ['bɔːrɪŋ] film.
   今天上午我们看了一场很乏味的电影。
4. It is a very warming ['wɔːmɪŋ] and heart-touching ['hɑːt'tʌtʃɪŋ] moment.
   这是一个非常温暖人心、扣人心弦的时刻。

5. Do you know the meaning ['miːnɪŋ] of the song [sɒŋ]?
你知道这首歌的意思吗？

6. They are doing ['duɪŋ] nothing ['nʌθɪŋ] now.
他们现在什么也没做。

经典绕口令（运动你的舌头）

1. Just think [θɪŋk], that sphinx ['sfɪŋks] has a sphincter ['sfɪŋktə] that stinks ['stɪŋks]!
试想想，那个狮身人面像的括约肌发臭了！

2. It is a fine thing [θɪŋ] to sing [sɪŋ] in the spring [sprɪŋ], I think [θɪŋk].
我觉得，在喷泉里唱歌是一件很好的事。

3. The king [kɪŋ] would sing [sɪŋ], after a ring [rɪŋ] that would go ding [dɪŋ].
铃响之后，国王将会唱歌。

4. Ding-dong ['dɪŋˌdɒŋ], ting-a-ling ['tɪŋəˌlɪŋ], what do you bring [brɪŋ]?
叮咚，叮铃，你拿来了什么？

5. Songs [sɒŋz] for singing ['sɪŋɪŋ], bells for ringing ['rɪŋɪŋ], these things [θɪŋz] I bring [brɪŋ].
歌声美妙，摇铃动听，这些都是我带来的。

影音荟萃

一 听音乐学音标

The Dock of the Bay
坐在港口码头

Otis Redding

Sittin' ['sɪtɪŋ] in the mornin' ['mɔːnɪŋ] sun	坐在早晨的阳光中
I'll be sittin' ['sɪtɪŋ] when the evenin' ['iːvnɪŋ] come	我将要一直等到夜晚的来临

Watching ['wɒtʃɪŋ] the ships roll in
And then I watch 'em roll away again, yeah

看着渔船拥进港口
再看着它们一个个离开

I'm sittin' ['sɪtɪŋ] on the dock of the bay
Watching ['wɒtʃɪŋ] the tide roll away
Ooo, I'm just sittin' ['sɪtɪŋ] on the dock of the bay
Wastin' ['weɪstɪŋ] time

坐在港口的码头
看着潮水退去
坐在港口的码头
消磨着我的时光

I left my home in Georgia
Headed for the 'Frisco bay
'Cause I've had nothing ['nʌθɪŋ] to live for
And look like nothin's ['nʌθɪŋ] gonna come my way

我离开在佐治亚洲的家
动身去了旧金山的港口
我什么都没留下
就像什么都没拥有过

So I'm just gonna sit on the dock of the bay
Watching ['wɒtʃɪŋ] the tide roll away
Ooo, I'm sittin' [sɪtɪŋ] on the dock of the bay
Wastin' [weɪstɪŋ] time

坐在港口的码头
看着潮水退去
坐在港口的码头
消磨着时光

Well, look like nothing's ['nʌθɪŋ] gonna change
Everything ['evrɪθɪŋ] remains the same
I can't do what people tell me to do
So I guess I'll just remain the same

就像没有事情改变过
就像他们当初一样
他们要求的——我不能做到
所以我想我仍然会和以前一样

Sittin' ['sɪtɪŋ] here resting ['restɪŋ] my bones
And this loneliness won't leave me alone
Oh, two thousand miles I roamed
Just to make this dock my home

静静地坐在这儿
这份孤独会一直陪在我身边
离开家2000英里
只想把这个港口作为我的家

Now, I'm just gonna sit at the dock of the bay
Watching ['wɒtʃɪŋ] the tide roll away
Oooo-wee, sittin' ['sɪtɪŋ] on the dock of the bay
Wastin' ['weɪstɪŋ] time, wastin' ['weɪstɪŋ] time

坐在港口码头
看着潮水退去
坐在港口的码头
消磨着我的时光

歌曲评论

小奥蒂斯·雷丁（Otis Ray Redding, Jr；1941年9月9日～1967年12月10日）是一位知名的美国灵魂乐歌手，以唱腔中的热情和单曲《坐在港口码头》广为人知。年仅26岁就死于飞机失事。

在他过世之后，唱片公司发行了《坐在港口码头》(*Sittin' on*) *the Dock of the Bay*（又译：坐在湾边的港口），该曲很快就直冲榜首，成为他一生之中唯一的冠军曲，可惜他自己却享受不到那些荣誉。1980年，他的两个儿子跟一个表弟组成了“The Reddings”合唱团，翻唱了(*Sittin' on*) *the Dock of the Bay*，并且得到第五十五名，成为有史以来第一首由原唱者的后人重新唱红的冠军曲。

二 看电影学音标

电影简介：

《大开眼戒》（*Eyes Wide Shut*）是汤姆·克鲁斯与妮可·基德曼继1992年的《大地雄心》后第2部夫妻档作品，也是大导演斯坦利·库布里克最后一部作品。电影讲述了内科医生威廉·比尔和妻子画廊经理爱丽丝凭借着事业的成功活跃在上流社会圈，之后威廉·比尔和爱丽丝开始厌恶本来平静的生活，开始背着对方偷腥，寻找刺激，之后威廉·比尔和爱丽丝认识到自己的错误，重归于好。

比尔来找多米诺，但却遇见了多米诺的朋友萨莉。（节选自《大开眼戒》）

—I'm Sally.

—Hello, Sally.

—So do you have any idea when you expect Domino back?

—I have no idea.

—You have no idea.

—To be perfectly honest, she may not even be coming ['kʌmɪŋ] back.

—She may not even be coming ['kʌmɪŋ] back?

—Well, I…

—You…

—I think [θɪŋk] there's something ['sʌmθɪŋ] that I should tell you.

—Really?

—Yeah. But I just don't know. I don't know.

—You don't know? Well, what is it?

—I don't know whether to tell you this.

—我是萨莉。

—你好，萨莉。

—你觉得多米诺什么时候会回来？

—我不知道。

—你不知道？

—坦白说，她也许不会回来了。

—她可能不会回来？

—呃，我……

—你……

—我想有些事情我应该告诉你。

—什么事？

—嗯。但是我不知道，我真的不知道。

—你不知道？呃，是什么事？

—我不知道是否应该告诉你这件事。

Unit 14 [w]

[w]

发音要素

[w]是舌后软腭半元音。发音时舌后部向软腭抬起，舌位高。双唇收小并向前突出，声带振动。发音短促，立刻滑向其后的元音。

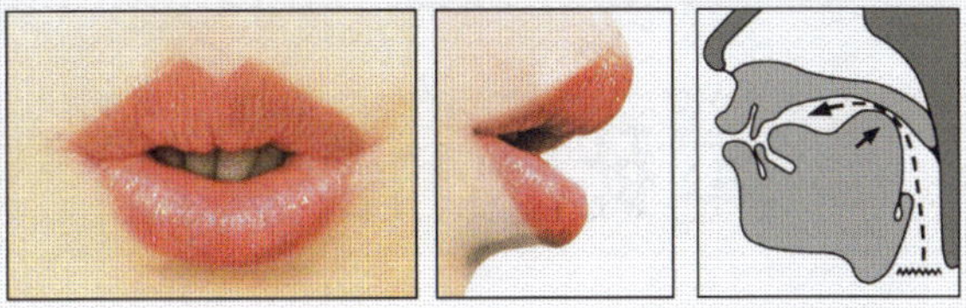

大话发音

[w] 音和公鸡打鸣时的叫声"喔、喔、喔"相似。

清晨，公鸡开始打鸣，"喔、喔、喔"，再轻些，就是[w]的发音。

喔

发音代言人

watch

[wɒtʃ] 表

常见发音字母及字母组合

音标	对应字母	自然发音规则	单词示例
[w]	w	字母w在单词中可发[w]音。	wet [wet] 湿的
[w]	wh	字母组合wh可发[w]音。	when [wen] 什么时候

发音操练

[w]	
west [west] 西方	**warm** [wɔːm] 温暖的
weather ['weðə] 天气	**wave** [weɪv] 波浪
reward [rɪ'wɔːd] 报酬	**wash** [wɒʃ] 洗
wide [waɪd] 宽的	**winter** ['wɪntə] 冬天
what [wɒt] 什么	**why** [waɪ] 为什么

基础短语

- warm [wɔːm] weather ['weðə] 温暖的天气
- walk [wɔːk] in the woods [wʊdz] 在林中散步
- wave [weɪv] the hand 挥手
- when [wen] and where [weə] 何时何地
- water ['wɔːtə] the wheat [wiːt] 灌溉小麦
- do what [wɒt] we wish [wɪʃ] 做我们想做的事

以句识音

1. What's [wɒts] up?
   有什么事儿吗？
2. No way [weɪ]!
   没门儿！
3. What [wɒt] do you want [wɒnt]?
   你想要什么？
4. Where [weə] there is a will [wɪl], there is a way [weɪ].
   有志者事竟成。
5. I wonder ['wʌndə] whether ['weðə] he will [wɪl] be able to work [wɜːk] it out.
   我不知道他是不是能够做出来。

6. Whatever [wɒt'evə] is worth [wɜːθ] doing at all is worth [wɜːθ] doing well [wel].
凡是值得做的事都值得好好地做。

经典绕口令（运动你的舌头）

1. What [wɒt] time does the wristwatch [rɪst'wɒtʃ] strap shop shut?
表带店何时关门？

2. Which [wɪtʃ] wristwatches [rɪst'wɒtʃɪz] are Swiss [swɪs] wristwatches [rɪst'wɒtʃɪz]?
哪些手表是瑞士制造的呢？

3. While [waɪl] we [wiː] were [wɜː] walking ['wɔːlkɪŋ], we [wiː] were [wɜː] watching ['wɒtʃɪŋ] window ['wɪndəʊ] washers ['wɒʃəz] wash [wɒʃ] Washington's ['wɒʃɪŋtənz] windows ['wɪndəʊz] with [wɪð] warm [wɔːm] washing ['wɒʃɪŋ] water ['wɔːtə].
当我们走路时，我们看着清洁窗户的人用热水清洗华盛顿的窗户。

4. Who [huː] washed [wɒʃt] Washington's ['wɒʃɪŋtənz] white [waɪt] woolen ['wʊlən] underwear ['ʌndəweə] when [wen] Washington's ['wɒʃɪŋtənz] washer ['wɒʃə] woman ['wʊmən] went [went] west [west]?
华盛顿的清洁女工逝世后，谁替他清洗白色的纯毛内裤？

5. A snow-white ['snəʊ,waɪt] swan [swɒn] swam [swæm] swiftly ['swɪftli] to catch a slowly-swimming ['sləʊli'swɪmɪŋ] snake in a lake.
湖中一只雪白的天鹅快速地游动着去追赶一条慢慢游动的蛇。

影音荟萃

一 听音乐学音标

Que Sera, Sera
顺其自然

Doris Day

When [wen] I was [wɒz] just a little girl　　当我还是个小女孩，

I asked my mother	我问妈妈:
What [wɒt] will [wɪl] I be	将来我会变成什么样子呢?
Will [wɪl] I be pretty	我是否会变得美丽?
Will [wɪl] I be rich	我是否会变得富有?
Here's what [wɒt] she said to me	她对我说:
Que sera, sera	世事不可强求,
Whatever [wɒt'evə] will [wɪl] be, will [wɪl] be	顺其自然吧。
The future's not ours to see	我们不能预见未来。
Que sera, sera	世事不可强求,
What [wɒt] will [wɪl] be, will [wɪl] be	顺其自然吧。
When [wen] I grew up and fell in love	当我长大并恋爱了,
I asked my sweetheart ['swi:thɑ:t]	我问我的心上人:
What [wɒt] lies ahead	我们将来会怎么样呢?
Will [wɪl] we have rainbows day after day	生活每天都会美好吗?
Here's what [wɒt] my sweetheart ['swi:thɑ:t]	我的爱人
said	对我说:
Que sera, sera	世事不可强求,
Whatever [wɒt'evə] will [wɪl] be, will [wɪl] be	顺其自然吧。
The future's not ours to see	我们不能预见未来。
Que sera, sera	世事不可强求,
What [wɒt] will [wɪl] be, will [wɪl] be	顺其自然吧。
Now I have children of my own	现在我有了自己的孩子,
They asked their mother	他们问我:
What [wɒt] will [wɪl] I be	将来我会变成什么样子呢?
Will [wɪl] I be handsome?	我是否会变得英俊?
Will [wɪl] I be rich?	我是否会变得富有?
I tell them tenderly	我轻声地回答:
Que sera, sera	世事不可强求,
Whatever [wɒt'evə] will [wɪl] be, will [wɪl] be	顺其自然吧。
The future's not ours to see	我们不能预见未来。
Que sera, sera	世事不可强求,
What [wɒt] will [wɪl] be, will [wɪl] be	顺其自然吧。
Que sera, sera	顺其自然吧。

歌曲评论

QUE SERA, SERA（或称*What Will be, Will be*）为《擒凶记》（*The Man Who Knew Too Much*）中多丽斯·戴所演唱的插曲。轻盈的三步舞曲，歌者温婉的嗓音，完美地演绎了主题——一切不可知，不必苛求，顺其自然。此曲传唱甚广，流行一时，曾获最佳电影插曲金像奖。

多丽斯·戴（Doris Day），美国歌手兼电影演员，二十世纪五十年代在音乐片和六十年代初在性感喜剧中的演出使她成为著名的好莱坞明星。多丽斯清新的面容、天真清纯而又性感动人的歌喉，是美国流行音乐的一个历史标志。

二 看电影学音标

电影简介：

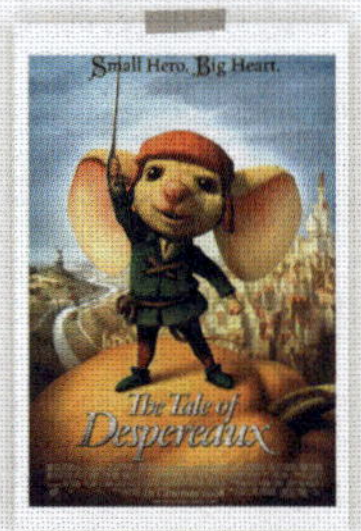

《浪漫的老鼠》（*The Tale of Despereaux*）是根据美国著名儿童文学家凯特·迪卡米罗的同名小说改编。影片讲述了一个自认是“绅士”的小老鼠的冒险故事。影片由《鼠国流浪记》（*Flushed Away*）的导演山姆·菲尔（Sam Fell）指导，延续他对老鼠题材的一贯热爱。影片由环球影业发行，上映时间为2008年12月19日。这是一部适宜小孩子观看的、具有独特魅力的经典电影。

Andre皇家厨师正在和他的神秘料理助手研究他的新汤。（节选自《浪漫的老鼠》）

—Not this much.
—Ow!
—You ruined my soup!
—I saved your soup! Those people wait [weɪt] all year, and you want [wɒnt] to give them this dishwater ['dɪʃˌwɔːtə].
—Dishwater ['dɪʃˌwɔːtə].
—Dishwater ['dɪʃˌwɔːtə].
—Dishwater ['dɪʃˌwɔːtə].
—Ow! Cut it out!

—不是这么多。
—噢!
—你毁了我的汤!
—我救了你的汤！人们等了一年，你就给他们这种洗碗水（难喝的汤）吗?
—洗碗水?
—洗碗水。
—洗碗水。
—噢，放手!

Unit 15 [l]

[l]

发音要素

[l] 是舌端齿龈边辅音。有两种发音，在元音前读清晰音[l]音，发音时舌尖及舌端紧贴上齿龈，舌前向硬腭抬起，气流从舌的旁边送出。

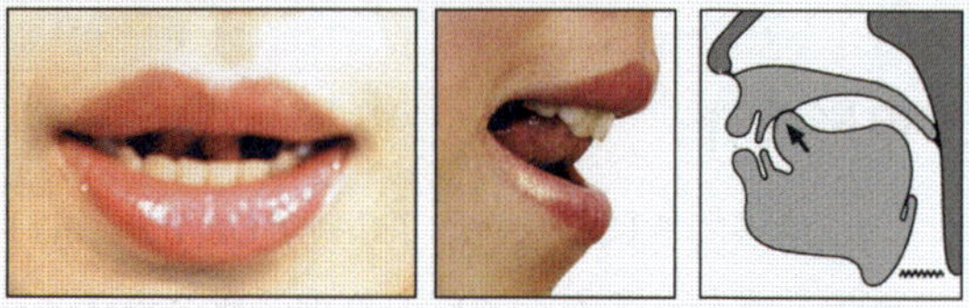

大话发音

[l] 音和汉语的“了”音相似。

汉语“生气了”中的“了”，再清楚些，就是[l]的发音。

发音代言人

lion

['laɪən] 狮子

常见发音字母及字母组合

音标	对应字母	自然发音规则	单词示例
[l]	l	字母l在词首或元音前发清晰[l]音。	**lamb** [læm] 羔羊

发音操练

[l]	
late [leɪt] 晚的	lunch [lʌntʃ] 午饭
look [lʊk] 看	luck [lʌk] 幸运
light [laɪt] 光	pill [pɪl] 药片
meal [mi:l] 饭	fool [fu:l] 傻瓜
cold [kəʊld] 冷的	milk [mɪlk] 牛奶

基础短语

- look [lʊk] like [laɪk]　看起来像
- a bottle ['bɒtl] of milk [mɪlk]　一瓶牛奶
- little ['lɪtl] by little ['lɪtl]　渐渐
- loving ['lʌvɪŋ] couples ['kʌplz]　恩爱的夫妻
- a driving license ['laɪsəns]　驾驶证
- hold [həʊld] the line [laɪn]　不挂断电话

以句识音

1. Love [lʌv] is blind [blaɪnd].
爱情是盲目的。

2. He was left [left] all [ɔ:l] alone [ə'ləʊn].
只剩他孤零零的一个人。

3. All [ɔ:l] in all [ɔ:l] it was a pleasant ['plezənt] trip.
总的说来，旅途还算愉快。

4. Like [laɪk] knows like [laɪk].
英雄识英雄。

5. All [ɔːl]'s well [wel] that ends well [wel].

结局好则一切都好。（英谚）

6. It is never too late [leɪt] to learn [lɜːn].

学习永远都不嫌晚。（英谚）

经典绕口令（运动你的舌头）

1. Very well [wel], very well [wel], very well [wel].

很好，很好，非常好。

2. Little ['lɪtl] Willie's ['wɪlɪz] wooden whistle ['wɪsl] wouldn't whistle ['wɪsl].

小威廉的木口哨吹不响。

3. Lily ['lɪli] ladles ['leɪdlz] little ['lɪtl] Letty's ['letis] lentil ['lentl] soup.

莉莉替小莱蒂盛小扁豆汤。

4. This is lovely ['lʌvli] lemon ['lemən] liniment ['lɪnɪmənt].

这是可爱的柠檬搽剂。

5. Listen ['lɪsn] to the local ['ləʊkl] yokel ['jəʊkl] yodel ['jəʊdl].

听听那个本地土包子唱的岳得尔调。

影音荟萃

一 听音乐学音标

Close to You
靠近你

Carpenters

Why do birds suddenly ['sʌdnli] appear　为什么鸟儿忽然出现

Everytime you are near?　每一次你靠近时

Just like [laɪk] me　就像我一样

They long [lɒŋ] to be close [kləʊs] to you　它们一直想靠近你

Why do stars fall [fɔ:l] down from the sky	为什么星星从夜空坠落
Everytime you walk by	每一次你走过时
Just like [laɪk] me	就像我一样
They long [lɒŋ] to be close [kləʊs] to you	它们一直想靠近你
On the day that you were born	在你出生的那一天
The angels ['eɪndʒlz] got together	天使们聚集在一起
And decided to create a dream come true	决定创造一个成真的美梦
So they sprinkled ['sprɪŋkld] moon dust in your hair of gold	所以他们于你金色的头发上洒上月尘
And starlight ['stɑ:laɪt] in your eyes of blue [blu:]	于你澈蓝的眼眸中洒上星光
That is why all [ɔ:l] the girls [gɜ:lz] in town	这就是为什么镇上所有的女孩
Follow ['fɒləʊ] you, all [ɔ:l] around	都环绕着你
Just like [laɪk] me	就像我一样
They long [lɒŋ] to be close [kləʊz] to you	她们一直想靠近你
On the day that you were born	在你出生的那一天
The angels ['eɪndʒlz] got together	天使们聚集在一起
They decided to create a dream come true	决定创造一个成真的美梦
So they sprinkled ['sprɪŋkld] moon dust in your hair of gold	所以他们于你金色的头发上洒上月尘
And starlight ['stɑ:laɪt] in your eyes of blue [blu:]	于你澈蓝的眼眸中洒上星光
That is why all [ɔ:l] the girls [gɜ:lz] in town	这就是为什么镇上所有的女孩
Follow ['fɒləʊ] you, all [ɔ:l] around	都环绕着你
Just like [laɪk] me	就像我一样
They long [lɒŋ] to be close [kləʊs] to you	她们一直想靠近你
Just like [laɪk] me	就像我一样
They long [lɒŋ] to be close [kləʊs] to you	她们一直想靠近你
Close [kləʊs] to you...	靠近你
Close [kləʊs] to you...	靠近你
Close [kləʊs] to you...	靠近你

歌曲评论

卡朋特兄妹是一对欧美兄妹组合，是20世纪70年代家喻户晓的乐队。他们共演唱500余首歌曲，几乎都是自己作词作曲，并在全世界各地开过许多演唱会。主唱：卡伦·卡朋特（1950～1983），伴唱和演奏：理查德·卡朋特（1946～）。*Close to You*是他们的成名曲之一，另一首则是*Yesterday Once More*（昨日重现）。这两首歌受到很多明星的称赞。

二 看电影学音标

电影简介：

《西雅图夜未眠》（*Sleepless in Seattle*），美国电影，又名《缘分的天空》。故事叙述一个丧偶的父亲（汤姆·汉克斯饰）和一位已订婚女记者之间，仅凭相互的声音和文字产生、发展了恋情，并终成眷属的浪漫故事。

Claire 换了个新冰箱，不过她要重新修理放冰箱的架子，这事拖了很久，一直令她头疼。（节选自《西雅图夜未眠》）

Sam: So, Claire [kleə], is there a problem?

Claire: I was tossing and turning last [lɑːst] night. You know I realized ['rɪəlaɪzd] I'm never going to fit my platters ['plætəz] in the refrigerator we ordered. When I give parties, I always ['ɔːlweɪz] put in platters ['plætəz]. So I thought I would get the Sub-Zero refrigerator instead. The only ['əʊnli] problem ['prɒbləm]...

Workmate 2,3: We have to redo all [ɔːl] the cabinets.

Sam: Pull into this wall [wɔːl].

Workmate 2: That's the bear wall [wɔːl].

山姆：克莱尔，有什么问题吗？

克莱尔：我昨天整晚翻来覆去睡不着。你知道吗，我发现大浅盘放不进我们订购的那台冰箱。我举办晚会时，总是用大浅盘装东西。所以我想换个Sub-Zero牌子的冰箱。唯一的问题就是……

工友2、3：我们要重做所有的橱柜。

山姆：得嵌进墙壁。

工友2：那是承重墙。

Unit 16 [r]

[r]

发音要素

[r]是舌尖齿龈摩擦辅音。发音时舌尖卷起，靠近上齿龈后部。舌两侧稍收拢。双唇略突出。气流通过舌尖和齿龈形成轻微摩擦。浊辅音，声带振动。

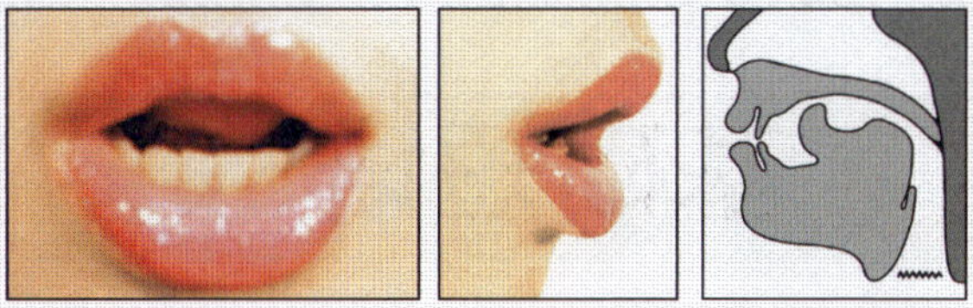

大话发音

和汉语中的“弱”音相似，但要发成平音。

口形和“弱”音一致，但要发平音，快速而短促，就是[r]的发音。

弱

发音代言人

rose

[rəʊz] 玫瑰花

常见发音字母及字母组合

音标	对应字母	自然发音规则	单词示例
[r]	r	字母r在单词中可发[r]音。	rat [ræt] 大老鼠
[r]	rr	字母组合rr可发[r]音。	marry ['mæri] 结婚

发音操练

[r]	
Mary ['meəri] 玛丽（女子名）	right [raɪt] 对的
river ['rɪvə] 河	rot [rɒt] 腐烂
read [ri:d] 读	ferry ['feri] 渡船；渡口
borrow ['bɒrəʊ] 借	sorry ['sɒri] 对不起的
worry ['wʌri] 担心	carry ['kæri] 运送

基础短语

- the driver ['draɪvə] in red[red] pants 穿着红色裤子的司机
- a rabbit['ræbɪt] near the river['rɪvə] 河边的兔子
- reading[ri:dɪŋ] and writing ['raɪtɪŋ] 读书和写作
- borrow['bɒrəʊ] a rope[rəʊp] 借一条绳子
- the reason['ri:zn] of worrying'[wʌrɪɪŋ] 担心的理由
- keep right [raɪt] and rational ['ræʃnəl] 保持公正合理

以句识音

1. It's a rare [reə] opportunity.
   这是个难得的机会。
2. The bookstore is just around [ə'raʊnd] the corner.
   书店就在拐角的地方。
3. The time has arrived [ə'raɪvd] for departure.
   出发的时间到了。
4. You are Mr. Richard ['rɪtʃəd], if I remember [rɪ'membə] right [raɪt].

如果我记得不错的话，你是理查德先生。

5. Economic recovery [rɪ'kʌvəri] is just around [ə'raʊnd] the corner.
经济复苏就在眼前。

6. All roads [rəʊdz] lead to Rome [rəʊm].
条条大路通罗马。（英谚）

经典绕口令（运动你的舌头）

1. Ruby ['ruːbi] Robby's ['rɒbis] brother ['brʌðə] bought and brought [brɔːt] her back some rubber ['rʌbə] baby-buggy bumpers.
鲁比勒比的哥哥给她买回来了一些四轮婴儿手推车的橡胶保险杠。

2. Robin ['rɒbɪn] can't bear Redbreast's ['redbrests] bad breath [breθ].
罗宾不能忍受知更鸟的难闻的气味。

3. Red [red] lorry ['lɒri], yellow lorry ['lɒri]; red [red] lorry ['lɒri], yellow lorry ['lɒri].
红的卡车、黄的卡车；红的卡车、黄的卡车。

4. Ripe [raɪp] white wheat reapers ['riːpəz] reap [riːp] ripe [raɪp] white wheat right [raɪt].
成熟的白粒小麦的收割者正确地收割成熟的白粒小麦。

5. Rita ['rɪtə] repeated [rɪ'piːtɪd] what Reardon ['rɪədən] recited [rɪ'saɪtɪd] when Reardon ['rɪədən] read [riːd] the remarks [rɪ'mɑːks].
当里尔登读评论时，丽塔重复里尔登背诵的东西。

影音荟萃

一 听音乐学音标

Crying Heart
哭泣的心

Befour

Oh I cannot stand the pain inside
Everything ['evrɪθɪŋ] my love I tried
To hold you in my arms

哦，我再不能忍受内心的痛苦
我付出一切努力，我的爱人
只为将你拥入怀中

Oh you, you're the reason ['ri:zn] of my life	哦，你，你就是我生命的意义
Will this dream my love survive	这个梦想会实现吗，我的爱人
When you hold me in your arms	当你将我拥入怀中
So if your heart will call my name	所以如果你的心呼唤着我的名字
I'l be there for you again	我会再次回到你身边
Every ['evrɪ] time I hear your crying ['kraɪɪŋ]	每一次我听见你
heart	哭泣的内心
Every ['evrɪ] time you tear apart	每一次你泪流满面
Oh you are in my heart, uhh	哦，你永远在我心中
Every ['evrɪ] time I feel your heart will go	每一次我感觉你的心将远离
Every ['evrɪ] time I miss you so	每一次我如此地思念你
'cause you are in my heart, uhh	因为你永远在我心中
Oh you, you are always on my mind	哦，你一直占据着我的思绪
Real [rɪəl] love is hard to find	真爱难寻
Please come hold me in your arms	求你回来，将我拥入怀中
I know that I'm fooling this great [greɪt] love	我知道我玩弄了这份美妙的爱情
But I cannot get enough	但我却难以满足
When you hold me in your arms	当你把我拥入怀中
So you will give my heart a chance	所以你将会给我的心一次机会
We will start a new romance [rəʊ'mæns]	我们将重新开始一场浪漫的爱情
Every ['evrɪ] time I hear your crying ['kraɪɪŋ]	每一次我听见你
heart	哭泣的内心
Every ['evrɪ] time you tear apart	每一次你泪流满面
Oh you are in my heart, uhh	哦，你永远在我心中
Every ['evrɪ] time I feel your heart will go	每一次我感觉你的心将远离
Every ['evrɪ] time I miss you so	每一次我如此地思念你
'cause you are in my heart, uhh	因为你永远在我心中
Every ['evrɪ] time I hear your crying ['kraɪɪŋ]	每一次我听见你
heart	哭泣的内心
I miss you so	我是如此思念你
Every ['evrɪ] time I hear your crying ['kraɪɪŋ]	每一次我听见你
heart	哭泣的内心
Every ['evrɪ] time you tear apart	每一次你泪流满面

Oh you are in my heart, uhh
Every ['evrɪ] time I feel your heart will go
Every ['evrɪ] time I miss you so
'cause you are in my heart, uhh

哦，你永远在我心中
每一次我感觉你的心将远离
每一次我如此地思念你
因为你永远在我心中

歌曲评论

Befour是一个来自德国的四人组合，成员分别是Alina、Manou、Dan和Angel，走的是纯流行舞曲路线，组合名字源自他们所主演的“Super RTL Channel”的“*Befour*”电视系列。他们的第一首单曲*Magic Melody*发表后就打入德国、奥地利和瑞士各大排行榜前十名。

*Crying Heart*是其第二张大碟专辑*Hand In Hand*中的一首歌曲。

二 看电影学音标

电影简介：

《神偷奶爸》（*Despicable Me*，又译《卑鄙的我》）是由克里斯·雷诺德（Chris Renaud）和皮埃尔·科芬（Pierre Coffin）导演，申科·保罗（Cinco Paul）和肯·达里奥（Ken Daurio）编剧，史蒂夫·卡瑞尔（Steve Carell）、杰森·赛格尔（Jason Segel）拉塞尔·布兰德（Russell Brand）、威尔·阿奈特(Will Arnett)、朱莉·安德鲁斯（Julie Andrews）等人主演的喜剧动画，2010年7月在美国上映。

格鲁（史蒂夫·卡瑞尔饰），这世上的恶人，正在向他的小黄人，就是格鲁的黄色小兵军团训话，描述他伟大的计划。（节选自《神偷奶爸》）

—Now, we have located a shrink [ʃrɪŋk] ray [reɪ] in a secret ['si:krɪt] lab, and once we take this shrink [ʃrɪŋk] ray [reɪ], we will have the capability to pull off the true crime [kraɪm] of the century.

—We are going to steal.

—Wait, wait! I haven't told you what it is yet.

—听着，我们已经在一所秘密实验室里，找到了一架光学微缩器。一旦搞到手，我们就有完全的能力去完成真正的世纪奇案。

—我们要去偷……

—等等，等等！我还没跟你们说是什么呢。

Unit 17 [m]

[m]

发音要素

[m]是双唇鼻辅音。发音时软腭下垂，双唇紧闭，气流从鼻腔送出。

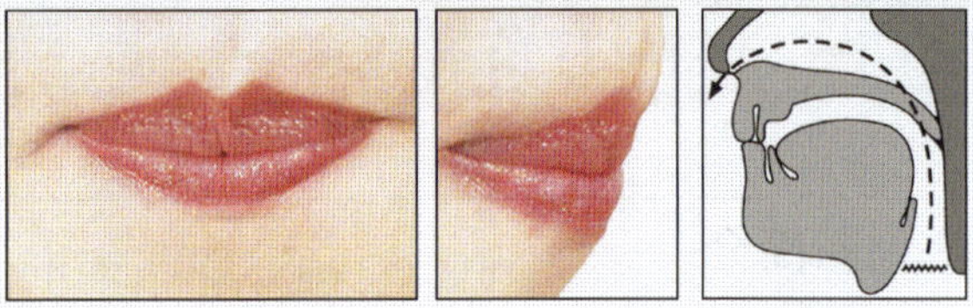

大话发音

这个音就像你闭着嘴巴念出“呣”的声音，一定不要张嘴。

闭住嘴巴发“呣”音，尤其是当[m]在词尾时，一定要养成闭住双唇的习惯。

发音代言人

mouse

[maʊs] 老鼠

常见发音字母及字母组合

音标	对应字母	自然发音规则	单词示例
[m]	m	字母m在单词中发[m]音。	**moon** [muːn] 月亮
[m]	mm	字母组合mm可发[m]音。	**swimmer** ['swɪmə] 游泳者

发音操练

[m]	
meet [miːt] 遇见	match [mætʃ] 比赛
home [həʊm] 家	time [taɪm] 时间
aim [eɪm] 目标	mistake [mɪs'teɪk] 错误
term [tɜːm] 学期	fame [feɪm] 名声
stammer ['stæmə] 口吃	hammer ['hæmə] 锤子

基础短语

- have a big name [neɪm] 名气很大
- seek fame [feɪm] and fortune 追求名利
- milk [mɪlk] the cow 给奶牛挤奶
- more [mɔː] and more [mɔː] 越来越
- a monthly ['mʌnθli] magazine [ˌmæg'ziːn] 一本月刊
- play fair games [geɪmz] in the competition [ˌkɒmpə'tɪʃn] 公平竞争

以句识音

1. She is narrow-minded ['nærəʊ'maɪndɪd].
她心胸狭窄。

2. He is a famous ['feɪməs] film [fɪlm] maker ['meɪkə].
他是个著名的电影制作人。

3. The manager ['mænɪdʒə] wants to make [meɪk] a name [neɪm].
经理想出名。

4. We play fair games [geɪmz] and compete [kəm'piːt].
我们公平竞争。

5. The more [mɔː], the merrier ['merɪə].

人越多越开心。

6. Time [taɪm] means [miːnz] money [mʌni].

时间就是金钱。

经典绕口令（运动你的舌头）

1. Jenny and Jimmy ['dʒɪmi] went to Jamaica [dʒə'meɪkə] and Germany ['dʒɜːməni] in January.

珍妮和吉米一月去了牙买加和德国。

2. My [maɪ] dame [deɪm] hath a lame [leɪm] tame [teɪm] crane. My dame [deɪm] hath a crane that is lame [leɪm].

我太太有一只跛脚的驯鹤。我太太有一只驯鹤，是跛脚。

3. Mix [mɪks], Miss [mɪs] Mix [mɪks]!

米克斯，米克斯小姐！

4. Moose [muːs] noshed on much [mʌtʃ] mush [mʌʃ].

慕思吃了很多玉米粥。

5. Swan swam [swæm] over the sea, swim [swɪm], swan swim [swɪm]! Swan swam [swæm] back again. Well swum [swʌm], swan!

天鹅游到海的另一边。游吧！天鹅游吧！天鹅游回来了！游得真好啊！天鹅！

影音荟萃

一 听音乐学音标

A Little Love

点点滴滴的爱

Fiona Fung

Greatness as you　　伟大如你

Smallest ['smɔːlɪst] as me [miː]　　渺小如我

You show me [miː] what is deep as sea	你告诉我什么如海般深沉
A little love, little kiss	柔柔的爱，浅浅的吻
A little hug, little gift	轻轻地拥抱，小小的礼物
All of little something ['sʌmθɪŋ]	这些点点滴滴
These are our memories ['memərɪz]	是我们的记忆
You make [meɪk] me [miː] cry	你逗我哭
Make [meɪk] me [miː] smile [smaɪl]	逗我笑
Make [meɪk] me [miː] feel that love is true	让我感受爱的真谛
You always stand by my [maɪ] side	你总是在我身边
I don't want to say goodbye	我不愿意说再见
You make [meɪk] me [miː] cry	你逗我哭
Make [meɪk] me [miː] smile [smaɪl]	逗我笑
Make [meɪk] me [miː] feel the joy of love	让我感受爱的奇妙
Oh kissing you	哦，吻你
Thank you for all the love	谢谢你一直以来
You always give to me [miː]	给我的爱
Oh I love you	哦，我爱你
Greatness as you	伟大如你
Smallest ['smɔːlɪst] as me [miː]	渺小如我
You show me [miː] what is deep as sea	你告诉我什么如海般深沉
A little love, little kiss	柔柔的爱，浅浅的吻
A little hug, little gift	轻轻地拥抱，小小的礼物
All of little something ['sʌmθɪŋ]	这些点点滴滴
These are our memories ['memərɪz]	是我们的记忆
You make [meɪk] me [miː] cry	你逗我哭
Make [meɪk] me [miː] smile [smaɪl]	逗我笑
Make [meɪk] me [miː] feel that love is true	让我感受爱的真谛
You always stand by my [maɪ] side	你总是在我身边
I don't want to say goodbye	我不愿意说再见
You make [meɪk] me [miː] cry	你逗我哭

Make [meɪk] me [miː] smile [smaɪl]	逗我笑
Make [meɪk] me [miː] feel the joy of love	让我感受爱的奇妙
Oh kissing you	哦，吻你
Thank you for all the love	谢谢你一直以来
You always give to me [miː]	给我的爱
Oh I love you	哦，我爱你
Yes I do	我真的爱你
I always do	我永远爱你
Make [meɪk] me [miː] cry	逗我哭
Make [meɪk] me [miː] smile [smaɪl]	逗我笑
Make [meɪk] me [miː] feel that love is true	让我感受爱的真谛
You always stand by my [maɪ] side	你总是在我身边
I don't want to say goodbye	我不愿意说再见
You make [meɪk] me [miː] cry	你逗我哭
Make [meɪk] me [miː] smile [smaɪl]	逗我笑
Make [meɪk] me [miː] feel the joy of love	让我感受爱的奇妙
Oh kissing you	哦，吻你
Thank you for all the love	谢谢你一直以来
You always give to me [miː]	给我的爱
Oh I love you	哦，我爱你
To be with you	和你在一起
Oh I love you	哦，我爱你

歌曲评论

*A Little Love*是 Fiona Fung（冯曦妤）首张个人专辑，共27首歌曲，由著名音乐人陈光荣监制，收录了Fiona Fung历年的音乐作品，包括热播作品《阳光雨》、《幸运儿》、《火星原居民》及《遥远的……》等10首单曲，demo歌曲《救生圈》等共4首耳熟能详的广告歌，《再见—警察》（电影《无间道》插曲）等13首电影插曲。*A Little Love*更专程送往日本压制，以让Fiona的歌声在最优质的环境下转化成音乐感动大家。

二 看电影学音标

电影简介：

美国情景喜剧《老友记》（*Friends*）第一季，于1994年9月22日在美国NBC首播，该季共24集，于1995年5月18日结束。平均收视率居年度第九，收视人口约1488万人。整部戏由三男三女共六位俊男美女担纲演出，不时请到明星与设计师等各界名流客串参与，播出以来一直为NBC电视网的招牌戏之一。

乔伊带钱德参加同剧组演员的派对。该演员打算搬家，建议乔伊租下他现在的房子。（节选自《老友记》）

Joey: Can you believe this place?

Chandler: I know. This is a great apart**m**ent [ə'pɑːtmənt].

Joey: I was just in the bathroo**m** ['bɑːθruːm]. There're **m**irrors ['miːrəz] on both sides of you. So when you're in there, it's like peeing with the Rockettes.

Chandler: Well, there's **m**y [maɪ] fantasy co**m**e [kʌm] true. No, seriously.

Joey: Hey, we were just saying, great apart**m**ent [ə'pɑːtmənt], man.

乔伊： 你相信这个地方吗？

钱德勒： 我知道，这个公寓很棒。

乔伊： 我刚去过浴室，两边墙上都有镜子，所以小便的时候，就好像有一排人在小便。

钱德勒： 我的梦想实现了。不，我是说真的。

乔伊： 我正在赞美你的公寓，老兄！

Unit 18 [j]

[j]

发音要素

[j]是舌前硬腭半元音。发音时舌前部向硬腭尽量抬起，舌位较低，双唇伸展成扁平状。浊辅音，声带振动。

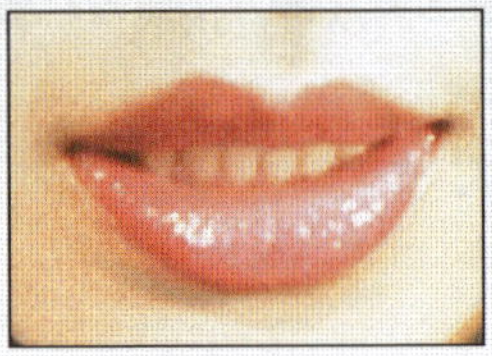

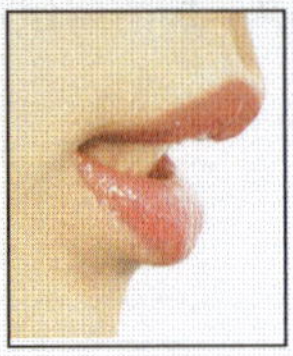

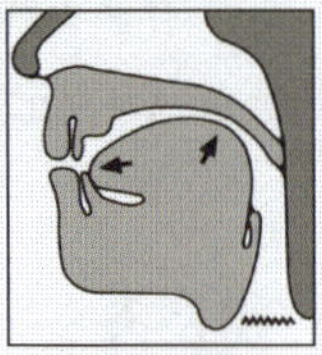

大话发音

开心时，大家喜欢发出“耶”的声音。

和表示开心的汉语“耶”的发音相似，再轻些，发音后口形迅速收回，就是[j]的发音。

耶

发音代言人

yacht

[jɒt] 快艇

常见发音字母及字母组合

音标	对应字母	自然发音规则	单词示例
[j]	y	字母y在单词中可发[j]音。	**year** [jɪə] 年

发音操练

[j]	
you [ju:] 你	**your** [jɔ:] 你的
yard [jɑ:d] 院子	**yolk** [jəʊk] 蛋黄
yawn [jɔ:n] 打哈欠	**yes** [jes] 是的
yellow ['jeləʊ] 黄色的	**young** [jʌŋ] 年轻的
yet [jet] 还	**yarn** [jɑ:n] 纱线

基础短语

- not yet [jet] 还没有
- Yale [jeɪl] University 耶鲁大学
- help yourself [jɔ:'self] 请自便
- at the back yard [jɑ:d] 在后院
- stop yawning ['jɔ:nɪŋ] 不要打哈欠
- yearning ['jɜ:nɪŋ] to have 渴望拥有

以句识音

1. Stop yawning ['jɔ:nɪŋ] in class.
上课不要打哈欠。

2. He hates you [ju:] and your [jɔ:] past.
他讨厌你也讨厌你过去干的事。

3. The young [jʌŋ] teacher is very popular with his students.
那个年轻教师很受他的学生们欢迎。

4. It's only a few hundred yards [jɑ:dz] from the supermarket.
那儿离超市只有几百码。

5. He left New York [jɔ:k] and went to study in Yale [jeɪl] University.
他离开纽约到耶鲁大学去学习。

6. You still look young [jʌŋ], year [jɪə] after year [jɪə].
这么多年过去了，你看上去依然年轻。

经典绕口令（运动你的舌头）

1. You [ju:] love the unique [ju:'ni:k] New York [jɔ:k].
你喜欢独特的纽约。

2. A young [jʌŋ] man is yawning ['jɔ:nɪŋ] in the yard [jɑ:d].
一个年轻人正在院子里打哈欠。

3. You [ju:] shouldn't always yell [jel] for your yellow ['jeləʊ] yolk [jəʊk].
你不应该总是喊叫着要你的黄蛋黄。

4. Youth [ju:θ] yearn [jɜ:n] to have a beautiful youth [ju:θ] year [jɪə] by year [jɪə].
年轻人一年年地都渴望有一个美好的青春。

5. Peasants yearn [jɜ:n] to have a good yield [ji:ld] year [jɪə] in and year [jɪə] out.
农民们一年到头想要有个好收成。

影音荟萃

一 听音乐学音标

Yes I Do

是的，我有

Rascal Flatts

Do I cry in the night	我在夜晚哭泣吗
Do I long to hold you tight	我渴望紧紧拥抱你吗
Do I wake wanting you	我醒来需要你吗？
Yes [jes] I do	是的，我有

Do I recall every day	每天，我都记得吗
How you took my breath away	你是怎样带走我的呼吸的
Do I remember loving you	我记得我爱你吗
Yes [jes] I do	是的，我有
Yes [jes] I do dream of all we had together	是的，我梦见我们在一起的所有事情
Guess it's true we lost it all forever	也许我们永远失去它了
Do I pray anyway	无论如何，我会祈祷
Yes [jes] I do	是的，我有
I don't live in the past	我不会活在过去
Wanting love that wouldn't last	想着那不能延续的爱
And I don't ache like I used to	我不会像过去一样疼
Yes [jes] I do	是的，我有
Yes [jes] I do dream of all we had together	是的，我梦见我们在一起的所有事情
Guess it's true we lost it all forever	也许我们永远失去它了
Do I pray anyway	无论如何，我会祈祷
Yes [jes] I do	是的，我有
Yes [jes] I do dream of all we had together	是的，我梦见我们在一起的所有事情
Guess it's true we lost it all forever	也许我们永远失去它了
Do I pray anyway	无论如何，我会祈祷
Yes [jes] I do	是的，我有
Do I pray	我会祈祷
Yes [jes] I do dream of all we had together	是的，我梦见我们在一起的所有事情
Yes [jes] I do — and yes I do	是的，我有——是的，我有

歌曲评论

两位表兄弟——主唱Gary Levox和贝斯手Jay Demarcus以及好朋友吉他手Joe Don Rooney三个人于1999年成立了乡村音乐三人组合“Rascal Flatts”，他们的同名首张专辑在发行后的第一周就卖出了11274张，登上了Billboard乡村音乐专辑排行榜的第14名，在Billboard专辑排行榜上名列第122。2000年以来，Rascal Flatts共卖出了四百多万张专辑，是如今不太景气的市场上的一个亮点。他们的首张同名专辑达到了白金销量，其中有四首单曲进入了排行榜前十行列。

*Yes I Do*是美国乡村音乐的新生力量Rascal Flatts的较为出色的作品之一。

二 看电影学音标

电影简介：

《幸福终点站》（*The Terminal*）是一部2004年出品的电影，由美国导演斯蒂芬·斯皮尔伯格执导，主要演员有汤姆·汉克斯、凯瑟琳·泽塔-琼斯、斯坦利·塔奇和齐·麦拜特。影片讲述主角前往美国途中家乡发生政变，政府被推翻，所持证件不被美国入境当局承认，被拒绝入境却又不能回国，被迫滞留肯尼迪国际机场期间的故事。

来自东欧国家的旅客维克多·纳沃斯基来美国完成父亲的遗愿，可是在机场检查时却遇到了麻烦。他被带到机场保安办公室接受询问。（节选自《幸福终点站》）

Policeman: What exactly are you doing in the United States, Mr. Navorski?

Navorski: Yellow ['jeləu] taxicab, please. Take me to Ramada Inn, 161, Lexington.

Policeman: Staying at the Ramada Inn?

Navorski: Keep the change.

Policeman: Do you know anyone in New York [jɔːk]?

Navorski: Yes [jes].

Policeman: Who?

Navorski: Yes [jes].

Policeman: Who?

警察：　　您到美国做什么，纳沃斯基先生？

纳沃斯基：请帮我叫出租车，去拉玛达酒店，列克星敦街161号。

警察：　　您要住在拉玛达酒店？

纳沃斯基：不用找零了。

警察：　　在纽约有熟人吗？

纳沃斯基：是的。

警察：　　谁？

纳沃斯基：是的。

Chapter 3 特殊发音现象

特殊发音现象也叫音变现象。是指在说话过程中，词与词相互影响而产生的语音变化。这种变化有音素的变化，也有声调的变化。音变既可以发生在单词内部，也可以是短语中，或者句子中。

Unit 1 连读

连读是语调中非常重要的一个组成要素。在连贯说话或朗读时，前一个词的末尾辅音和后一个词的词首元音可以连在一起读。连读的条件：相邻的两词在意义上必须密切相关，同属一个意群。连读所构成的音节一般都不重读，只需顺其自然地一带而过，不可读得太重，也不可加音。

1 “辅音+元音”型连读

在同一个意群里，如果相邻两词中的前一个词是以辅音结尾，后一个词是以元音开头，这就要将辅音与元音拼起来连读。

- Put-it-on, please.
- Not-at-all.
- Please pick-it-up.
- He will arrive in half-an-hour.

2 “r/re+元音”型连读

如果前一个词是以-r或者-re结尾，后一个词是以元音开头，这时的r或re不但要发[r]，而且还要与后面的元音拼起来连读。

- They're my father-and mother.
- I looked for-it here-and there.
- Where-are your brother-and sister?

但是，如果一个音节的前后都有字母r，即使后面的词以元音开头，也不能连读。

- The black clouds are coming nearer and nearer.（nearer与and不可连读）

3 “辅音+半元音”型连读

英语语音中的[j]和[w]是半元音，如果前一个词是以辅音结尾，后一个词是以半元音，特别是[j]开头，此时也要连读。

- Thank-you.
- Nice to meet-you.
- Did-you get there late again?

Would-you like a cup of tea?

Could-you help me, please?

4 “元音+元音”型连读

有时元音和元音碰到一起根据意群的需要也要连读。

She can't carry-it.

She wants to study-English.

I-am Chinese.

Unit 2 缩读

在日常口语发音中，不仅会把该弱读的词弱读，有时也会省略某些音，使说话和朗读更加自然流畅，达到更加光滑和柔和的效果，这种现象称作缩读。缩读是英美人习惯的发音方式，自有一套规则约束，决不能任意而为；同时缩读往往被受过教育的美国人视作不规范的英语，所以正式场合不能滥用缩读。

1. 代名词+ 助动词	
I am—I'm [aɪm]	you are—you're [jʊə]
she is—she's [ʃɪz]	it is—it's [ɪts]
we are—we're [wɪə]	they are—they're [ðeə]
that is—that's [ðæts]	there is—there's [ðeəz]
here is—here's [hɪəz]	where is—where's [weəz]
what is—what's [wɒts]	let us—let's [lets]
2. 名词+have	
I have—I've [aɪv]	you have—you've [juv]
we have—we've [wɪv]	they have—they've [ðeɪv]
3. 名词+ has	
he has—he's [hɪz]	she has—she's [ʃɪz]
it has—it's [ɪts]	

4. 名词+had	
I had—I'd [aɪd]	you had—you'd [jud]
he had—he'd [hɪd]	she had—she'd [ʃɪd]
we had—we'd [wɪd]	they had—they'd [ðeɪd]
5. 名词+ 助动词	
I will—I'll [aɪl]	you will—you'll [jul]
he will—he'll [hɪl]	she will—she'll [ʃɪl]
we will—we'll [wɪl]	they will—they'll [ðeɪl]
6. 助动词+not	
is not—isn't ['ɪznt]	are not—aren't [ɑ:nt]
was not—wasn't ['wɒznt]	were not—weren't ['wɜ:nt]
do not—don't [dəʊnt]	does not —doesn't ['dʌznt]
did not—didn't ['dɪdnt]	have not—haven't ['hævnt]
has not—hasn't ['hæznt]	had not—hadn't ['hædnt]
shall not—shan't [ʃɑ:nt]	will not—won't [wəʊnt]
cannot—can't [kɑ:nt]	could not—couldn't ['kʊdnt]
should not—shouldn't ['ʃʊdnt]	would not—wouldn't ['wʊdnt]
may not—mayn't ['meɪənt]	must not—mustn't ['mʌsnt]
need not—needn't ['ni:dnt]	

Unit 3 弱读

一般来说，句子中被强调的词为实词，包括名词、人称代词、动词、形容词和副词，这些词需要重读。与此相反，在句子中发挥辅助作用的词为虚词，包括冠词、介词、连词、物主代词和助动词等，则需要弱读。一般情况下，往往将单词中的元音弱化为[ə]。

冠词	a, an, the
介词	in, on, at, for, by, to, of, from, over, into, out, under, with, about, except, against, through等。
连词	and, but, while, so, or, since, because, as, before, after, until, till, once, though, although, then等。
物主代词	①形容词性物主代词：my, your, his, her, their, our, its
	②名词性物主代词：mine, yours, his, hers, theirs, ours, its
助动词	①be 动词：is, am, are, was, were, being, been
	②have：have, has, had, having
	③do：do, does, did
	④情态助动词：shall, will, should, would等。

Unit 4 爆破与失去爆破

1 爆破

爆破音是指发音器官在口腔中形成阻碍，然后气流冲破阻碍而发出的音。在英语中有6个爆破音，即[p], [b], [t], [d], [k]和[g]。

2 失去爆破

失去爆破，又叫不完全爆破，就是在某些情况下，在朗读句子或某些单词时，爆破音[p], [b], [t], [d], [k]和[g]不必爆破出来，就是说气流不必冲破阻碍，而只是发音器官在口腔中形成阻碍，稍作停顿后马上过渡到后面的音即只需做出发爆破音的准备，但并不发音。这种现象叫不完全爆破

失去爆破可发生在单词内部，如bla(ck)board,foo(t)ball,ke(p)t等。括号中的辅音字母对应的辅音音素[k]，[t]，[p]稍作停顿，没发出音来。

失去爆破在两个相邻单词之间出现的情况非常多。

① “爆破音+爆破音”型

6个爆破音中的任意2个相邻时，前一个爆破音会失去爆破，即由相关的发音器官做好这个发

音的姿势，稍做停顿后即发后面的爆破音。

The girl in the re(d) coat was on a bla(ck) bike just now.

The bi(g) bus from the fa(c)tory is full of people.

Wha(t) time does he get up every morning?

The ol(d) do(c)tor has a ca(t), too.

We're going to work on a farm nex(t) Tuesday.

What would you like, ho(t) tea or bla(ck) coffee?

It's a very col(d) day, but it's a goo(d) day.

You can put i(t) down in the bi(g) garden.

I bought a chea(p) book, but it's a goo(d) book.

② "爆破音+摩擦音"型

如果前面是爆破音，其后紧跟着某些摩擦音（如[f]，[v]，[s]，[z]，[ʃ]，[ʒ]，[θ]，[ð]，[w]等），那么前面那个爆破音仅有十分轻微的爆破，而后面那个摩擦音则要完全爆破。

ol(d) friends

a goo(d) view

Kee(p) silent

ge(t) through

I wen(t) there alone at nine last night.

③ 爆破音+破擦音[tʃ]，[dʒ]时，爆破音失去爆破。

This is an old pi(c)ture of a big car.

There are grea(t) changes.

It's a goo(d) job.

④ 爆破音+[m]，[n]，[l]时，爆破音也会失去爆破。

Goo(d) morning, Mr. Bell.

Goo(d) morning, dear.

Uncle Li's factory is qui(te) near to the cinema.

—Do you know his bi(ke) number?

—Sorry, I don'(t) know.

The forty-firs(t) lesson is quite difficult.

Goo(d) luck, Lin Tao.

Unit 5 清辅音的浊化

英语国际音标(IPA) 26 个辅音中，包含了6个爆破音，即：[k、g]，[p 、b]，[t 、d]，其中[k、p、t]为清辅音，[g、b、d]为浊辅音。但当清辅音[k、p、t]与清辅音[s]连拼即[sk、sp、st]时，为了发音方便而发生了“浊化”，即要读成[sg、sb、sd]。

① [s] 后面的清辅音[k、p、t]浊化

school: [k] 浊化成 [g]

stand: [t] 浊化成[d]

speak: [p]浊化成 [b]

② [s] 后面接的清辅音[tr]也要浊化

strike: [tr]浊化成[dr]

③ 在美音中：[t]在单词的中间被浊化成[d]，如：

writer—rider （writer经浊化后，发音类似rider）

latter—ladder （latter经浊化后，发音类似ladder）

美国人和加拿大人发音时为了省事，习惯清音浊化，尤其是[t]在单词的中间一定会浊化成[d]，但英国人发音不会这样，这也是英音和美音的一大区别。

Unit 6 音的同化

英语语音中的同化现象主要发生在辅音与辅音之间，是相邻音素互相影响的结果，是英语语音音变的重要组成部分，使用同化是为了达到省力的目的，使说英语更轻松、更自然、更流利。同化是指语流中相邻两个音素（主要是辅音）彼此影响，变为相同的或相似的音，有的甚至合二为一成为第三个音。相互影响的音素如果变得完全相同就是完全同化，如果没有完全相同，则是部分同化。

主要是以下三种方式：

1. 辅音[d]与[j]相邻时，被同化为[dʒ]：Would you...?
2. 辅音[t]与[j]相邻时，被同化为[tʃ]：Can’t you…?
3. 辅音[s]与[j]相邻时，被同化为[ʃ]：Miss you…

Chapter 4 语音语调

Unit 1 语音

1 音节

在音标中，一个音节包含一个元音，通常情况下，一个（或多个）辅音加一个元音构成一个音节，有时单独一个元音也可以构成一个音节。一般来说，一个单词的音节数目是由这个单词的发音元音的数目决定的，就是说，一个单词中有几个发音元音，这个单词就有几个音节。

如:

一个音节的单词:

a，I，we，me，dad，bus

两个音节的单词:

mother，father，sister，brother

三个音节的单词:

superman，butterfly，tomorrow，family

2 单词重音和次重音

重音：单音节词单独读时都重读，而不必标重音符号；两个或两个以上的音节才有重音。两个音节重音符号多数标注在第一个音节前。重音标注符号是“'”。

次重音：在含有三个或更多音节的单词中，有的除了有主重音还有次重音，次重音表示读该音节时要弱于重音节而强于其他音节。次重音标注符号是“˜”。

英语单词重音没有一成不变的规则，一般规律如下:

（1）双音节词的重音多数在第一个音节上。如：'daily, 'matter, 'clever。

（2）带a-, be-, en-, for-, im-, in-, mis-, pre-, pro-, to-, trans-, un-等这些不可分的前缀的双音节词，重音常落在第二个音节上。 如：a'bove, be'lieve, en'dure, for'get, im'portant, in'stead, mis'take, pro'vide, un'less, to'day, trans'port 。

（3）多音节词的重音多落在倒数第三个音节上。如：'satisfy, mag'nificent, i'mmediately。

（4）以-ic, -ial, -ian, -ion等后缀结尾的多音节词，重音常落在倒数第二个音节上。如：re'public, mu'sician。

（5）三个音节以上的词除了主重音外往往还带有一个次重音。次重音多落在第一个或第二个音节上。如：pro~nunci'ation, ex~ami'nation 。

除了一般规律外，还有七大特殊重音发音规律供大家参考：

（1）英语中派生词的重音和词根重音一致。派生词是指有同样词根的词。如：'act, 'active, 'actively, com'pare, com'parison。

（2）带下列后缀的词：-ary, -ery, -ory, -ism, -ist, -mony, -ment, -ary等，重音通常在第一个音节上。如：'customary, 'scientist, 'slavery, 'factory, 'realism。

（3）带下列前缀的词：a-, ab-, ac-, ad-, al-, be-, con-, de-, dis-, em-, en-, in-, mis-, re-, tans-, un-等，重音通常在第二个音节上。如：a'bout, ab'duce, ac'cede, ad'mire, be'long, con'sult, de'tect, dis'like。

（4）带下列后缀的词：-aim, -ain, -cur, -eem, -duce, -ere, -firm, -gn, -oin, -oke, -ose, -pt, -rce, -self, -ume等，重音通常在第二个音节。如：con'tain, oc'cur, sin'cere, de'sign, con'firm。

（5）带下列后缀的词：-ade, -ain, -ee, -eer, -esque, -ette, -ique, -ine, -oon等，重音通常在最后一个音节。这些词一般都是从法语中借来的词。如：emplo'yee, an'tique, maga'zine, ci'gar, volun'teer, gaso'line。

（6）带下列后缀的词：-eous, -ial, -ian, -ic, -ics, -ient, -ion, -ious, -ish, -it, -liar, -sive, -tal, -uous等，重音通常在倒数第二音节上。如：oc'casion, re'lation, as'tonish, de'posit, mu'sician。

（7）但是有些派生词，比如从名词派生出来的形容词，它的重音就得发生变化，通常是后移。如：'science, scien'tific, 'accident, acci'dental, 'democrat, demo'cratic, 'politics, po'litical。

Unit 2 语调

英语的两个基本语调是升调和降调。不同的语调可以表达说话人不同的态度和不同的隐含意思。英语中同一句话采用不同的语调会产生截然不同的语意概念。如：“Yes!”用降调表示说话者的应答，“Yes?”用升调则表示反问。语调具有强烈的感情色彩，它使语言更有表现力。下面我们来一一介绍升调、降调，以及升、降调的混合用法。

升调：升调的基本含义是：“没有结束”，“不肯定”。常见的一般疑问句用升调。它的特点是：

1. 整个句子的音调从第一个重读音节开始，从高到低，依次递降，在最后一个重读音节上语调上升。

2. 若最后一个重读音节后有非重读音节，则它们依次递升。

3. 若句子以非重读音节开始，则它们语调低平。

4. 句中的非重读音与它前面的重读音基本在同一音高，或依次降调。

快速记忆：重读音节依次递降，句末重读回升上滑。

降调：降调的基本含义是“结束”、“肯定”。常见的一般陈述句、命令祈使句和特殊疑问句都用降调。使用降调的句子有这样的特点：

1. 整个句子的音调从第一个重读音节开始，从高到低，依次递降，在最后一个重读音节上语调滑落下降。

2. 若最后一个重读音节后有非重读音节，则它们的语调低平。

3. 若句子以非重读音节开始，则它们语调低平。

4. 句子中的非重读音与它前面的重读音基本在同一音高，或略为下降。

快速记忆：重读音节依次递降，句末重读降落下滑。

英语的语调还有降升调、升降调和升降升调。降升调在英语中也比较常用。它常表示“对比”、“态度保留”、“有言外之意”。升降调常表示语气强烈、惊奇、自满得意等感情。升降升调常表示自信、欢快、洋洋得意等感情。

1 常见句式的语调

（一）陈述句的语调。陈述句表示陈述一件事时用降调。例：

1. I understand↘.
2. It's difficult↘.
3. Beijing is the capital of China↘.
4. There is a book on the desk↘.
5. They are going to have a picnic↘.
6. The balloons are flying away↘.
7. The birds are singing in the trees↘.
8. Daming is having a birthday party↘.

（二）特殊疑问句的语调。特殊疑问句一般用降调，句首的疑问词一般重读。例：

1. What's this↘?
2. What are you doing↘?
3. Who is your mother↘?

4. Who are they↘?

5. Where are you going↘?

6. Where do you live↘?

（三） 感叹句的语调

1. 感叹句表示强烈感叹时用降调。例:

What a beautiful car↘!

What a nice↘day!

Oh, dear↘!

How nice↘it is!

2. 感叹句表示惊奇时用升降调。例:

A: I bought this dress for 500 dollars↘.

B: 500↗dollars↘!

What a big ↗house↘!

How↗ cool↘!

How heavy↗the box is↘!

How tall↗the man is↘!

What a beautiful↗day today↘!

（四） 一般疑问句和答语的语调

一般疑问句用升调，它的简略回答用降调。例:

Is this your book↗?

Yes,↘it is↘.

Are you from America↗?

Yes↘, I am↘. No↘, it isn't↘.

No↘, I am not↘.

（五） 选择疑问句的语调。选择疑问句的语调主要有两种:

1. 在说话人所说的几项中选择时，前面的选择事项用升调，最后的一项用降调，中间的连接词如or用平调。例:

Shall we walk↗or go by bike↘? 我们是走着去还是骑自行车去?

Is your car blue↗, green↗, or red↘? 你的车是蓝色的、绿色的，还是红色的?

Do you go there by bus↗or by taxi↘? 你坐公共汽车去还是坐出租车去?

2. 如果还有其他选择说话人没有说出来，说话人说的几项都用升调。例:

Shall we walk↗ or go by bike↗? 我们是走着去还是骑自行车去?

Is your car blue↗, green↗, or red↗? 你的车是蓝色的、绿色的、红色的还

是……？

Do you go there by bus↗ or by taxi↗? 你坐公共汽车去、坐出租车去还是……？

Could you come Monday↗, Tuesday↗, or Wednesday↗?
你周一来，周二来，周三来还是……？

Which country would you like to go to, England↗, Canada↗, or America↗?
你想去哪个国家，英国、加拿大、美国还是……？

（六） 反意疑问句的语调

反意疑问句前一部分用降调，后一部分有两种情况：

1. 提问者对所提问问题没有把握，希望对方回答时用升调。例：

You will go to see films↘, won't↗you↗? 你是去看电影吗？

They went to the library↘, didn't↗they↗? 他们是去图书馆吗？

Daming will have a birthday party↘, won't↗he↗? 大明是要举行生日聚会吗？

He is from Canada↘, isn't↗he↗? 他是从加拿大来的吗？

2. 提问者对所提的问题有很大把握，让对方证实时用降调。例：

He is from China↘, isn't↘he↘? 他是从中国来的吧？

There are over one thousand people in the hall↘, aren't ↘there↘? 大厅里有1000多人吧？

Lily will study abroad↘, won't↘she↘? 莉莉要出国留学吧？

She is from England↘, isn't↘ she↘? 她是从英国来的吧？

（七） 祈使句的语调

1. 表示命令、语气强硬的祈使句，句末用降调。例：

Don't open the door↘! 不许开门！

Don't make any mistakes↘! 别出差错！

Don't take any chances↘! 不要心存侥幸！

Stand↘up! 站起来！

Take off your coat↘! 脱下衣服！

Close the window↘! 关上窗户！

2. 表示鼓励、态度亲切或客气的请求的祈使句，句末用升调：例如：

Don't worry about that↗. 不要担心。

Help yourself, please↗. 请自便。

Stand up, please↗. 请起立。

Give my best to your family↗. 代我向你们全家问好。

3. 表示恳切的请求，或责备或表示关心的急切警告时用降升调，第一个重读音节用降调，句末用开调。例：

Don't↘open the door↗. 不要开门。（会冷的）

Don't↘eat so much sugar↗. 不要吃那么多糖。（糖对身体不好）

Put↘your coat on↗. 把衣服穿上。（外面冷）

（八） 问候、告别、道谢与道歉时的语调

问候

1. 正常、客气的问候用降调。例:

   Good morning↘. 早上好。

   How are you↘? 你好吗?

   How do you do↘? 你好!

2. 熟人、朋友互相问候时，或表示活泼、热情时用升调。例:

   Good morning↗. 早上好。

   How are you↗? 你好吗?

告别

大部分的告别都用升调。例:

Goodbye↗.

See you later↗.

Good night↗.

道谢

1. 正常的感谢用降调。

   Thank you↘.

   Thanks a lot↘.

   Thank you very much↘.

2. 比较随和的感谢用升调。

   Thanks↗.

   Thanks a lot↗.

   Thank you very much↗.

道歉

道歉一般用升调或先降后升。

Sorry↗.

I'm↘ sorry ↗.

I do↘ feel sorry↗ for you.

I am sorry↘ I'm late↗.

2 语调进阶

语调与说话人所表达的意思、态度、感情密切相关。一个句子用不同的语调来读，就表达不同的意思。如汉语说“他开会去了。”就可以有多种语调。用降调表示陈述一件事，用升调表示疑问。英语也是如此。我们前面主要讲了常见句式的基本语调。下面我们主要介绍语调变化所表达的不同意思。

（一）陈述句

1. 陈述句表示疑问用升调。

比较：You know↘. 你知道。　You know↗? 你知道吗？

He is a doctor↘. 他是医生。　He is a doctor↗? 他是医生吗？

He has gone to London↘. 他去伦敦了。　He has gone to London↗? 他去伦敦了吗？

2. 陈述句表示安慰、鼓励和友好时用升调。

A: This is the picture of my wife↘. 这是我妻子的照片。

B: Oh, she is pretty↗. 噢，她很漂亮。

A: My English is so poor↘. 我英语不好。

B: Don't worry↗. I'll help↗ you with your English↗.

别担心。我会帮你学习英语。

3. 表示观点有所保留，态度有所怀疑或犹豫，或有言外之意，下文有转折（如but）时用降升调。

A: Do you like the house↗? 你喜欢这个房子吗？

B: It's↘new↗. (But it's small.) 挺新的。（但是小）

A: Let's go the theatre tomorrow↘. 咱们明天去看电影吧。

B: I can't go↘ tomorrow↗. (But another day will do.) 明天不行。（换一天可以）

4. 用于纠正某人的话或表示相反意见时用降升调。

A: She is ↘ a nurse↘. 她是护士。

B: A↘doctor↗. 是医生。

A: I can't finish the task↘. 我完不成这个任务。

B: You↘can↗. 你能。

（二）特殊疑问句

1. 当提问过一次问题后，因没听清或没听懂对方的回答而又提问了一次问题时，用升调：

A: When will you come back↘? 你什么时候回来？

B: In January↘. 一月

A: When will you come back↗? 你什么时候回来?

A: What's your name↘? 你叫什么名字?

B: My name is Amy↘. 我叫埃米。

A: Did you say your name was Amy↗? 你是说你叫埃米吗?

2. 重复对方的问话以得到证实的疑问句用升调:

A: When will the meeting begin↘? 会议什么时候开始?

B: When will the meeting begin↗? 会议什么时候开始?（表示你是不是问会议什么时候开始。）

3. 表示对所提问题很感兴趣的特殊疑问句常用升调。

A: I had a trip on the weekend↘. 我周末旅行了。

B: Where did you go↗? 你去哪里了?

A: I bought a car↘. 我买了一辆车。

B: What's your car↗ like? 你的车什么样?

4. 如果提问时表示温和的态度用升调。

How is your mother↗? 你妈妈还好吗?

Unit 3 句子的节奏

在实际话语中，重读和不重读的词在句中形成一强一弱（或一弱一强）、一重一轻（或一轻一重）的节奏。也就是说，英语句子中，重读与非重读音节相间出现。英语句子中的一个重读音节与其后面若干非重读音节组成一个节奏组，一句话中可以有多个节奏组。根据英语的节奏规律，话语说起来所需的时间不取决于它有多少个词、多少个音节，而是取决于它有多少个句子重音。假如句子重音之间的非重读音节数多，结果必然是说起来要快一些，含糊一些。英语句子的节奏是按重音来定时的，重音之间的间隔时间大致相等。例如:

（1）Do you think you would be able to finish it in a month?

这个句子中共有四个重读音节，这些重读音节之间所含的非重读音节数分别为：三个，一个，三个；但在话语中，人们的感觉是：重读音节出现的间隔是大致相等的。

（2）John is here now.

（3）John will be home tonight.

（4）The professor is in London this evening.

以上三个句子的音节数不同，但所含重读音节数相同，因此，在说话速度相同的情况下，完

成句子所需的时间也大致相等。再如:

(5) Jack/Mark/Joan

(6) Jack and Mark and Joan

(7) Jack and then Mark and then Joan

三个短语的重读音节都是3个，所用时间也大致相等，而听起来一句比一句快，因为非重读音节越多读得越快。重读音节的元音也会相对加快。例如:

(8) I went into the room and saw Joan.

句首非重读词“I”读得比较快，相当于空拍。“saw”和“Joan”分别为两个不包含非重读音节的节奏组，读得相对比较慢，“went into the”与“room and”为两个包含非重读音节的节奏组，读得较快，并有连读和弱读。

由此，我们可以得出以下结论:

1. 句中重读音节相继出现的地方，通常语速会慢一些，音节听起来自然也清楚一些。

2. 重读音节之间拥挤着出现的非重读音节听起来轻快而且含糊。

3. 一句话说起来所需时间长短不取决于句中的单词数或音节数，而取决于句中有多少个重读音节。

总而言之，英语的话语节奏是一种有规则的节拍。练习英语话语节奏的重点是：学会顺利地、匀称地从一个重读音节移动到下一个重读音节，特别要学会把重读音节中间夹带的非重读音节读好。在读重读词汇时，其中包含的元音要发得饱满、高亢，语速会因此而显得稍慢一些。掌握英语节奏规律可以提高话语的流利和自然程度以及听力理解的水平。

Chapter 5 英音美音

Unit 1 英音美音发音区别

通俗地来讲，美国英语外向，英国英语内向；美国英语声音外露，英国英语声音内敛；美国英语嗓门大，英国英语声音小；美国英语张扬，英国英语说话谨慎而显得绅士。美国英语里见“r”要发卷舌音，英国英语里没有卷舌音；美国英语用的是口腔“后部发声方法”，英国英语用的是口腔“深后部发声方法”；美国英语速度慢，语调爱用平拖腔，就像汉语里的一声，英国英语愿意用降调，就像汉语里的四声；美国英语因发音外露而音形对应规律明显，英国英语因发音内敛而音形对应规律被隐藏。总结一下，就是美国人的发音多数比较懒散，嘴张得没有英国人发音那样标准。

在探讨美国英语与英国英语在语音上的差异时，我们通常是将“美国普通话”（General American，简称GA）与公认的标准英语发音（Received Pronunciation，简称RP）进行比较。二者在读音上的差异主要表现在：

1. 在[s]、[f]、[θ]、[m]、[n]等辅音之前的字母a，美国英语一般读作[æ]音，而英国音则发作[ɑː]。

单词	英音	美音
pass	[pɑːs]	[pæs]
half	[hɑːf]	[hæf]
bath	[bɑːθ]	[bæθ]
ask	[ɑːsk]	[æsk]
dance	[dɑːns]	[dæns]

2. 在英国标准音中，字母r在元音前才发音，如real（真实的），而在辅音前或词尾时是不发音的。但在美语中，r在辅音前发明显的卷舌音，在词尾时亦发音。

单词	英音	美音
farm	[fɑːm]	[fɑːrm]
car	[kɑː]	[kɑːr]
large	[lɑːdʒ]	[lɑːrdʒ]

smart	[smɑ:t]	[smɑ:rt]

3. 字母e，在英式英语中读[e]，而在美语中的[ɛ]口型向两侧分得略大一些。

单词	英音	美音
bed	[bed]	[bɛd]
head	[hed]	[hɛd]
egg	[eg]	[ɛg]
red	[red]	[rɛd]

4. 在英音中很多单词中的[ɒ]音，在美音中读作[ɑ]

单词	英音	美音
god	[gɒd]	[gɑd]
box	[bɒks]	[bɑks]
pot	[pɒt]	[pɑt]
doctor	['dɒktə]	['dɑktə]

5. 当[ju:]音出现在[n]、[d]、[t]、[s]后面时，美音中可读作[ʊ]，在英音中发音不变。

单词	英音	美音
new	[nju:]	[nʊ]
duty	['dju:ti]	['dʊti]
tune	[tju:n]	[tʊn]
student	['stju:dənt]	['stʊdənt]

6. 使用相同的音标，但发音情况不同，例如：当清辅音[t]夹在两个元音之间，前一个是重读元音，后一个是轻读元音时，如writer（作家），美国人习惯将清辅音浊化，所以writer 和rider （骑马人）发音几乎相同。类似的例子还有latter（后者）与ladder（梯子）；petal（花瓣）与pedal（踏板）。

7. 在英音中，非重读音节中的元音一般弱化或消失，而美国人说话往往把非重读音节中的元音都读出来，因此美音中的音节比较清晰可辨。

单词	英音	美音

history	['hɪstri]	['hɪstəri]
victory	['vɪktri]	['vɪktəri]
secretary	['sekrətri]	['sekrəteri]

Unit 2 英音美音拼写区别

美语与英语在单词拼法上的差异主要有两种：一种是单词发生简单的变化使得个别字母不相同，另一种是美语单词较为简化。前者如enquire（英）与inquire（美），这两个单词的第一个字母不相同，都是指商品交易前，一方向对方洽询有关商品的价格、数量、交货时间及付款条件等的询价，也叫询盘；再如“车胎”英国用tyre，美国用tire；“睡衣”英语用pajamas，美语用pyjamas；“执照，特许证”英语用licence，美语用license。这类单词仅一个字母不同，发音上有的相同，有的相似。

美语的单词一般比英语单词要简单。近年来，美语越来越趋向简化，充分体现了美国人生活和工作高效快捷的现代化特性。这些较为简化的词大都源于英语，大量词汇在英语里仍然保持原貌，而进入美语后，这些单词就逐渐变得简单起来，从而使用起来较为方便。如较常见的单词colour（颜色），在美语里就拼成color，少了一个“u”字母；refrigerator（电冰箱）美语是fridge，美语比原词要简单得多。美语单词的简化现象是美语与英语在单词拼法上的差异的主要表现。现将英语中比较常见的这类单词列举如下：

英语	美语	汉语
catalogue	catalog	商品目录
woollen	woolen	羊毛
acknowledgement	acknowledgment	承认
cheque	check	支票
aeroplane	airplane，plane	飞机
honour	honor	荣誉
jewellery	jewelry	珠宝
storey	story	楼层

judgement	judgment	判断
kilogramme	kilogram	公斤
cigarette	cigaret	卷烟
programme	program	节目、程序
traveller's cheque	traveler's check	旅行支票
advertisement	ad	广告
advertising agent	ad agent	广告代理人
labour	labor	劳动

美国英语和英国英语常用不同的单词表示同一事物或概念。我们在此仅举一些典型实例供大家参考：

	美国英语	英国英语	汉语
交通类	one-way ticket	single ticket	单程票
	round trip ticket	return ticket	往返票
	subway underground	Tube(London)	地铁
	underpass	subway	地下通道
	bus	coach/bus	公共汽车
	trailer/camper/mobile home	caravan	（挂在汽车后面拖动的）活动屋
	truck	lorry	卡车
	ticket office	booking office	票房
	sidewalk	pavement	人行道
	gas/gasoline	petrol	汽油
	gas station	filling station	加油站
	windshield	windscreen	挡风玻璃

邮电类	to wire	to telegram	拍电报
	to call (up)	to ring (up)	打电话
	long distance call	trunk call	长途电话
	phone booth	phone box	公共电话亭
	zip code	post code	邮编
服装类	vest	waist coat	西服马甲
	pants	trousers	裤子
	undershirt	vest	贴身内衣
	undershorts/underwear	pants	短裤
食品类	candy	sweets	糖果
	can	tin	罐头
	potato chips	crisps	炸薯片
	French fries	chips	炸薯条
	liquor	spirits	烈酒
娱乐类	vacation	holiday	假日
	movie theatre	cinema	电影院
医疗类	shot/injection	injection/jab	皮下注射
	emergency ward	casualty department	急诊室
	operating room	operating theatre	手术室
	drugstore/pharmacy	chemist's/pharmacy	药房
	druggist	chemist	药师
	to get sick	to be taken ill	生病

其他	instructor	lecturer	讲师
	bartender	barman/barmaid	酒吧招待
	salesgirl	shop-girl/shop assistant	售货员
	fireman	stoker	司炉
	firefighter	fireman	消防员
	trash can	dustbin	垃圾箱
	sneakers	gym shoes	运动鞋
	raise	rise	增加（工资）
	to wait in line	queue up	排队